DAD'S ARMY

DAD'S ARMY

HOW FREUCHIE TOOK CRICKET BY STORM

NEIL DRYSDALE

Foreword by Sir Ian Botham

BIRLINN

This edition first published in 2008 by
Birlinn Limited
West Newington House
10 Newington Road
Edinburgh
EH9 1QS

www.birlinn.co.uk

Originally published in 2005 by
The Parrswood Press, Manchester

ISBN13: 978 1 84158 751 6
ISBN10: 1 84158 751 6

British Library Cataloguing-in-Publication Data
A catalogue record for this book is available from the British Library

Typeset by Iolaire Typesetting, Newtonmore
Printed and bound in Britain by CPI Cox & Wyman, Reading, RG1 8EX

CONTENTS

FOREWORD

The village green is one of the most precious commodities of cricket in Britain. Lifetime friendships can be forged there, children can learn about winning and losing in a healthy environment and, who knows, from time to time, individuals will move on from their local club and be blessed with the opportunity to perform in front of rapturous crowds at arenas such as Lord's or the Melbourne Cricket Ground in an Ashes Test series.

Obviously, I have benefited from this process myself, because I started my own career at Yeovil CC, and was assisted on my path to the England side by a clutch of stalwart individuals with an ingrained love for the game: unsung heroes, who never sought any financial reward for the countless hours of commitment, dedication and sheer passion which they invested in the sustenance of their club. It has been a pleasure to have known these characters and to have absorbed vital lessons from them and, if anything, Britain has greater need for these small clubs to continue their missionary work than ever before, considering how many schools have removed cricket from their PE curriculum and the number of playing fields which are vanishing in the wake of housing developments.

In 1985, I was playing for England in the Fifth Test against the Australians at the Oval, from the end of August until the start of September, and we were staying at the Westmoreland Hotel, not far from Lord's. On the Sunday evening, I strolled down to the bar with a few of my team-mates, and was surprised and intrigued to encounter a large group of kilt-wearing Scots, who were clearly in a celebratory mood. Natural curiosity persuaded me to find out who they were, and thus it was that I forged my first acquaintance with the staunch fellows of Freuchie CC, who, earlier that day, had made history by becoming the first Scottish club to win the coveted National Village Cup.

For the next couple of hours we talked, shared a few beers, swapped anecdotes and savoured our mutual enthusiasm for the game, and I was delighted to make friends with the team and, in particular, their captain, Dave Christie, who is one of that inveterate, hardy breed of cricketers for whom nothing as piffling as a thunderstorm is going to halt his Saturday's or Sunday's enjoyment. Straightaway, we established a rapport, and I could sense kindred spirits in these Fifers, who had ventured to London as underdogs, brought virtually their whole village down with them for company, and tasted victory at the sport's spiritual home, at the climax of an odyssey which had started with 639 teams. It was the stuff of dreams, and although one or two of the hotel guests tried to get my autograph that night, I told them they should be seeking out the signatures of those Scots, who had achieved something they would never forget for the rest of their lives. I meant it then and I do so now. Sport thrives on tales of the unexpected, and of champions emerging from obscurity, and Freuchie's victory was a classic illustration.

As our conversation progressed, I began to realise the scale of cricket in Scotland, and appreciate that, far from it being an English preserve, there are thousands of Caledonian players competing, week in, week out, from those at national league level through to the various regional competitions, which are as fiercely contested as anywhere else in the United Kingdom. Basically, these Freuchie men were exactly the same, only with Scottish accents, as those I had played with – and against – in Somerset, Yorkshire, Lancashire . . . wherever there is a patch of green, a bag of bats, balls and pads, and 22 individuals ready to take the field. Dave and I exchanged contact telephone numbers at the time and we pledged that, whatever else might happen, we would do our best to ensure this wouldn't be the sole occasion when Freuchie and I came together.

Since then, in the past 20 years, Scottish cricket has genuinely enhanced its reputation. The Saltires have beaten several English counties in the Totesport League and I well recall the balmy Sunday when I visited the Grange in Edinburgh, as part of the Sky commentary team, on an afternoon when a crowd of over 3,000 watched the Indian maestro, Rahul Dravid, make his début for Scotland against Hampshire. Who could possibly have believed that all these factors would have come together? But there again, who would have envisaged that Freuchie, pipers, sporrans and all, would have marched in through the Grace Gates at Lord's and triumphed after a nail-biting dénouement? We need adventures and dreams in sport, and their story is up there with the best.

I met up with Dave again and presented him with a trophy in Edinburgh last summer, but we had already bumped into each other on a number of occasions during the intervening period, as we had promised we would on that memorable evening in London. He and his team-mates joined me on a stage of one of my charity walks, which stretched from Dundee to Freuchie, and although the weather wasn't great, the hospitality and the welcome were both tremendous. The next morning, scores of children were waiting to say goodbye and it was evident that the club is at the very heart of village life, as it should be. During the last 50 years Dave Christie, a man universally known as 'Dad' by the cricketing brethren in his homeland, has been, at various times, scorer, umpire, captain, all-rounder, groundsman and president of the East of Scotland League, and whether the grass has to be cut or the clubhouse walls painted, he doesn't stand on ceremony. Instead, he goes ahead and does the job and doesn't worry if it means getting his hands dirty, and I have heard that he would sleep in the clubhouse during the summer if it were an option. Even from a distance, I know that these are the sort of rugged characters, whose unstinting efforts will ensure that cricket survives and flourishes, and the exploits of 'Dad's Army' offer proof of what can materialise when a little village embarks on a crusade and refuses to accept the possibility of defeat.

As I mentioned at the outset, Freuchie's youth development programme helps to explain why they are still recording victories in the Village Cup, and I only wish that more kids could be encouraged to taste the positive benefits of sport, and that PE were ranked as highly as any other subject by British schools. If the facilities aren't there, and there isn't a general acceptance that health and sport are inextricably linked, then, of course, what you will see is an increasing number of obese children storing up all manner of problems for themselves in the future. So we have to address this issue seriously, and do our best to find alternatives to the situation where youngsters are coming home from school every afternoon, logging on to their computers, and that is the limit of their ambition. What enjoyment is to be gained from that? These people aren't healthy. They are nerds and I am convinced that everybody involved in sport in this country has to get back to first principles and recognise the crucial nature of persuading children to participate. It doesn't matter whether they choose cricket, athletics, football, rugby, golf or swimming, the priority has to be in stressing the positives of exercise, of going out and breathing in fresh air, and feeling a warm glow inside, regardless of what standard you have reached.

Mercifully, however, at places such as Freuchie, I have learned that groups of 50, 60, 70 children are still turning up for training every Friday night and being converted to cricket by the likes of Dave Christie, Davie Cowan and his colleagues, and more power to their elbow. If the game in Scotland is to thrive, and the Saltires are to become part of a revamped international one-day structure – as I honestly believe they will – then the contribution of this Fife hamlet in raising the profile can hardly be overstated, because until 20 years ago, the general perception in England was that the Scots were into football, rugby and golf, and that was it. Which simply isn't true, of course, and hasn't been the case since Scots began playing cricket as long ago as 1785.

Ultimately, I relished hearing of Freuchie's exploits in 1985 and I hope that this book helps to rekindle the spirit of a determined group of Scots who nurtured a dream, followed in the footsteps of legends and created their own slice of history. I look forward, as a patron of Scottish cricket, to being part of further successes in the years ahead and I will be delighted to toast a dram to Freuchie when they celebrate their anniversary in 2008. Here's to them and the Saltires as they reach for the stars!

SIR IAN BOTHAM

CHAPTER ONE

SCOTLAND'S SECRET GAME

Of all the places in all the world, I should probably have appreciated that Paisley town centre was not the ideal location to ask a group of youths directions to the local cricket ground. It wasn't merely their half-empty bottles of Buckfast – that noxious brew produced by monks, apparently in order to speed up the process of meeting their Maker of those addicted to the stuff – but also the 'Hate' and 'Hate' tattoos a couple of the throng had emblazoned on their arms, which really ought to have alerted me to the possibility that I might be staring at the prospect of a right good kicking.

Eventually, after one of those frozen-in-time moments which seem to last an eternity, the most knuckle headed member of the posse piped up: 'What do you mean, the cricket ground? How the fuck would we know where it is? That's a game for poofs and fairies, for English bastards . . .' By this stage he was advancing towards me, flanked by a couple of his troglodyte mates, and it was clear that the trio weren't interested in exchanging business cards. I turned and fled, in an undignified sprawl of flailing limbs and bulging briefcase, and suddenly realised I had no idea of my bearings. Where to go, where to seek sanctuary? Help! Mercifully, a taxi loomed into view, and I flagged it down desperately, but my escape was still sufficiently fraught that one of the avenging neds caught me with his boot in my posterior as I slammed the door. 'What was all that about, you weren't trying to sell them drugs were you?' asked my saviour suspiciously. 'No, I was just asking them directions to the local cricket club,' I replied, amidst gulps and gasps.

'Aye, very good,' responded the cabbie. 'Well, if that's the case, then you would definitely have been safer trying to sell them drugs.'

This happened in the summer of 1985, so for all I know, Paisley might have been transformed into an idyllic paradise in the intervening decades. But more realistically, that incident epitomises the hostile reaction of many Scots to a sport which has been played in their backyard for much longer than football or rugby, yet continues to be viewed with mistrust and occasionally detestation by significant numbers of otherwise sane souls, who incline towards Sir Alec Douglas-Home's opinion: 'Oh God, if there be cricket in heaven, let there also be rain.'

When Freuchie's working-class warriors completed their remarkable victory in the National Village Cup competition at an incredulous Lord's 20 years ago, there ensued an outbreak of encomia and gushing tributes from the soccer brethren, who briefly interrupted their Old Firm fixation to dwell on another pursuit; but for most of these observers, Freuchie was the exception rather than the rule, a little Hampshire at the heart of Hampden Central. It didn't seem to matter that Freuchie's achievement in hoisting the trophy from under the noses of 638 rivals was the first time any Scottish contenders had achieved anything at the home of the game. No, the prejudices and stereotypes remained unchanged: cricket was a patrician pastime for public schoolboys and English émigrés and, as such, was to be viewed with loathing. It was as illogical then as it is now, but perceptions have hardly been altered, and even Dave Christie, the Freuchie skipper on that memorable Sunday in September, is at a loss to explain why the cork-and-willow business is still Scotland's secret game. 'It has been at the centre of my life for the last half a century, and I have met thousands of my countrymen who share my passion, but it's true that you have to keep explaining yourself to people from outwith the cricket community,' says Christie. 'Usually, I don't know how to respond adequately when I'm asked why I play cricket, because it's a daft question, and I've been at enough dinners to recognise when I'm being patronised. It's like being asked why two and two makes four. You know that it does, and you take it for granted, but it's difficult to explain the mathematics to somebody who doesn't want to listen. I've stopped trying to convince the sceptics, to be honest, because you can't force people to be open-minded. If soccer supporters are happy to watch 18 foreigners pick up king's ransoms to kick a ball around Celtic Park or Ibrox every week, then that's up to them.'

Christie is a pragmatist, not a defeatist, but perhaps it is time for more of us to bang the drum a little louder. Cricket has thrived in Scotland since 1785, and in the days from the foundation of Kelso in 1820, followed by Rossie Priory in 1828, Grange in 1832, Fauldhouse Victoria in 1835 and through to Penicuik, Clydesdale, Brechin, Drumpellier, Selkirk and Kilmarnock, all in the period up to 1852 – a good two decades before the Scottish Football Association was established – the game has been at the heart of hundreds of communities across Scotland, yet somehow managed to stay as elusive as Simon Cowell's charm. In and around Aberdeenshire, the Grades circuit commands widespread attention without earning a column-inch beyond the *Press and Journal*. No matter – the paper happens to be the Magic Circle of its sport, thriving on arcane customs and forging a community for thousands of part-time players and spectators, whose intensity, whether in the Doric tongue, Highland brogue or English dialect (large numbers of Southern workers packed their bats along with their thermals en route to the oil rigs in the North Sea), testifies to the culture in which Charlie Allan and his fellow-members at Methlick recently created a new cricket ground called 'Laird's'. Indeed, oblivious to the ignorance of the Central Belt, the North of Scotland League flourishes, as do the Strathmore Union, the Border League and a variety of other championships which exist separately from the Scottish national structure. Ultimately, there are more cricket clubs than their rugby equivalents amongst God's frozen people, and the notion that these organisations are exclusively the preserve of snobs and flannelled fools is absurd.

On the contrary, Andy Goram, the former Scotland goalkeeper, is exactly the kind of bristling bull in a china shop full of

porcelain vanities, whose footballing achievements, including
being part of Rangers' nine-in-a-row squad in the 1990s, mask
his insistence that cricket is actually his first love. 'Sure, I've been
in the Champions League, turned out for Scotland with 50,000
or 60,000 spectators in stadiums across the world and been in
the goalmouth at Old Trafford with a crescendo of noise
reverberating through the rafters, but honestly, these experiences
were no more enjoyable than locking horns with Allan Border,
Merv Hughes and the Australian tourists at Hamilton Crescent in
Glasgow in 1989,' recalls Goram, who has worn the whites for
such diverse cricketing teams as Lancashire Schools, Saddle-
worth, Penicuik, Uddingston and West Lothian, and whose
philosophy revolves around grasping life by the throat and
moulding it to his personal rhythm, even if some discordant
notes have occasionally marred the tune.

'Prior to coming to Scotland, I had no idea that cricket was
such a big deal, but there again, why shouldn't it be? I will never
forget the buzz around the crowd when the Aussies came to
Glasgow. I had been at a dinner with them on the Friday night,
and we had all got on like a house on fire. Anyhow, next day,
when I walked to the crease, to this huge cheer from 5000
supporters, Merv was bowling and I said hello. I imagined he
would be the same genial chap from the previous evening, and
he certainly wouldn't send down a bouncer first ball. Some hope!
Sure enough, he dropped one short, it fizzed through the air, and
nearly took my head off. Then, when I looked up, he was
standing directly in front of me. "You should have stuck to
fucking football, mate," he bellowed. "You'll soon be wishing
you were back at fucking Easter Road."

'But the thing is, I'm crazy about cricket and the money
doesn't matter, because the camaraderie and fun are so obviously
intertwined with the keen rivalry in the leagues, whether they be
in Scotland or England. I began playing when I was 12 and I have
never lost a fraction of the excitement and anticipation which
cricket generates. There's no fighting, no genuine bad blood or
anything like that. Just a bunch of lads who are nuts about the

game on the pitch, like a few beers in the clubhouse and offer it 100 per cent, whatever the standard. People should be more proud of Scottish cricket – it has a helluva lot going for it and you don't have to be a world-beater to pick up a bat or a ball.'

Ample confirmation of this stance will greet anybody who takes the trouble to visit Freuchie and survey, on the clubhouse wall, the photographs of such luminaries as Sir Ian Botham, Tom Graveney and David Gower supping ale in this Fife fastness, surrounded by a host of other, lesser-known individuals whose contribution to the club's cause over past decades can't be underestimated. It's this melding of the illustrious and the unknown, the world traveller and the bucolic local hero, which typifies the best aspects of cricket in Scotland throughout the sport's history: the former Australian captain, Kim Hughes, has amassed a stack of runs as the professional at Watsonians; both halves of the formidable West Indian opening pair, Gordon Greenidge and Desmond Haynes have plied their trade for the Scottish Cricket Union (SCU); a formidable amalgam of Test-class talent, including Rohan Kanhai, Terry Alderman, Malcolm Marshall, Bob Massie, Adam Gilchrist, Justin Langer and Rahul Dravid have lent their lustre to an adopted country and been astonished at the depth of affection which simmers and seethes beneath the surface.

And I should know. Because, even as Freuchie's combatants were battling their English rivals and the dire Caledonian weather – weekend upon weekend of implacable rain – which enveloped Scotland during 1985, I was turning out for a little-known West Lothian-based club called Atlas, whose cross-country sojourns, trials and tribulations offered both an Altman-esque tableau of vignettes and the sobering reminder that sweat and blood and commitment are no substitute for a smidgeon of talent. In basic terms, Atlas were the Little Nells of the East of Scotland club scene: poverty-stricken, burdened with facilities which would have required a coat of paint before any council would have condemned them and existing under the constant threat of imminent oblivion.

Our clubhouse, such as it was, consisted of a Spartan hut with a couple of old wooden tables. The 'toilets' were in the long grass at either side of the ground, next to the old North British Steel Group building, one of many businesses to fall victim to the Thatcher-inspired cull of traditional industries which plagued the 1980s. The pitch, a treacherous strip of pseudo-grass and dirty brown earth which often fell victim to vandalism from local gangs, might have been specifically devised as a V-sign to any effete Edinburgher who dared to sneer at Atlas's efforts to rise up the East of Scotland League. (And there were plenty cynics around who claimed our pitch contravened any number of Health and Safety regulations). And yet, despite everything – the derision of opponents and grief from the hooligans, and the tedious cries of 'Poofs, Poofs, Poofs' from passing, IQ-diminished locals – we survived on Skid Row far longer than anybody could logically have anticipated. The subscriptions were paid, the sandwiches prepared, the roller dragged out, impromptu net sessions organised, and onwards we marched, even if the ultimate destination could only ever be nowhere.

Looking back, with misty eyes, it would be easy to wax nostalgic and wallow in romantic reminiscences, but the more truthful, optimistic conclusion is that, even prior to the success of Freuchie at Lord's, cricket was in the blood of many Scots, not least due to the social intercourse and the sheer roaring-boy antics of teams in the mould of Atlas. Hailing as we did from Armadale, a grime-encrusted community where none of the local bakers would ever stock fairy cakes on the basis that no customer would risk his health by requesting them, we may have been destitute, but one or two of our personnel would subsequently go on to win the Small Clubs Cup with Fauldhouse. This, for the uninitiated, is rather similar to Exeter City holding Manchester United at Old Trafford in this year's FA Cup. The remainder of us formed a disparate mix of social backgrounds, occupations and temperaments, which is one of the greatest assets of the Scottish scene. Namely, that unlike rugby, which has withered on the vine, strangled by the perception of its middle-class status, allied to the wrecking-ball tactics of its administrators, or football, which is dominated by tribal divisions and an unhealthy fixation with the Old Firm, cricket is a truly classless activity, a vocation which has thrived in such belt-and-buckles shrines to Old Labour as Armadale and Fauldhouse, just as it has done in the affluent suburbs of Edinburgh's Stockbridge and Glasgow's Milngavie.

Nor should one ignore the heroic endeavours of a compact amateur army to maintain its obsession and preach to the unconverted with infinite patience and resolve in the face of head-shaking bafflement or downright antagonism. Now, as in 1985, at least 98 per cent of those who regularly dust down their pads at the end of April – a Micawberish clan, given the Scottish saying, roughly paraphrased as: 'Cast ne'er a cloot, till May is oot, Then wrap up agin, On June the yin' – pay for the privilege of participating in league cricket, and although the leading Scottish National Cricket League (SNCL) clubs can afford professionals, financed through private sponsorships and bar takings, these principally Caribbean, Australian and Asian recruits are paid chicken-feed compared to the string of hapless foreign mercenaries who have flocked into football and rugby. Dravid, for instance, the Indian maestro who assisted the Scottish Saltires in their maiden season against the English counties in the National Cricket League, earned around £30,000 for a string of displays which emphatically demonstrated the powers of a player who has since been officially recognised as the world's No. 1. But Dravid was unreservedly a terrific investment, when one regards the deluge of publicity and profile-raising exploits with which he became associated. Indeed, never before had the sport witnessed the kind of airport scenes which greeted his arrival in Edinburgh in 2003 to join the Saltires. Returning Gulf War veterans, Madonna and Guy Ritchie or a state visit, might routinely attract such a phalanx of photographers and pyrotechnic flash-bulb displays, but never a cricketer in a land of rabid unbelievers. In which circumstances, it was not perhaps surprising that Scottish Television's young interviewer got a little carried away

and asked breathlessly: 'What do you think of Scottish football?'
The look of puzzlement on Dravid's face was magnificent. To his
credit, he remained a model of composure and continued to
behave in that vein for the rest of the season, despite being
flooded with irrelevant requests via the column which he and
I jointly produced for the *Sunday Herald*. (I binned most of
the green-ink missives, especially the inquiries from a 'Bangla
Bisexual from Livingston', an unlikely combination which
hinted at some nefarious tabloid plotting.) But mercifully, as
one would have anticipated, the majority of those who approached Dravid were fixated on cricket and, after he and his
new wife had spent three months travelling the length and
breadth of Scotland, Rahul confessed to being a genuine convert
to Scottish cricket. 'I had not remotely envisaged I would meet
so many interested, passionate, knowledgeable people, but from
the far north to the extreme south I have walked through club
gates and the response has been amazing from seven- to seventy-
year-olds, from experienced officials to folk who have clearly
never been to a cricket ground in their lives,' he told me at the
climax of his (sun-drenched) magical mystery tour of duty.
'From what I have seen, the talent exists for Scotland to advance
on the global stage. But, in my opinion, it is just as important
that you cherish and thrive at the grassroots, where there is an
incredible enthusiasm.'

That exhortation deserves as widespread exposure as possible.
Because, whatever the achievements of Scotland's internationalists in the future, the health of the game will depend on the
second-string, part-time willow-wielders at Fauldhouse or Falkland, Murrayfield-DAFS or Methlick; the army reservists who
take the field for RAF Kinloss and RAF Lossiemouth, when
allowed to extricate themselves from the madness in Iraq; and the
combative, fiery and occasionally barmy Internet fiends who post
their messages on Rob Outram's pungently independent 'Ram-
pant Lion' website, a cricket field in a cyberspace of dreams,
nightmares, soul-searching and breast-beating which has already
received more than two million hits in as many years, including

contact from homesick expatriates in the United Arab Emirates, Chile, New Zealand and South Africa.

Tim Heald, the authorised biographer of Brian Johnston and Denis Compton, and a fellow who has written adroitly on the symbiotic relationships and inherent joie de vivre which permeate village cricket, has striven to define the quintessential ingredients of the average side and concluded: 'If something is worth doing, it's worth doing badly. It matters not who won or lost, but how you played the game. Actually, how you played the game doesn't matter that much either. It's more a question of taking part and entering into the spirit of the thing, because village cricket, in its purest form, does not aspire to supreme excellence.' Precisely. Unlike golf, with its labyrinthine regulations, stuffed-shirts of committee men and saloon-bar bores – significantly, Heald attempted an assessment of Peter Alliss's wonderland and gave up on the assignment, because, in his words: 'golf clubs were all so similar and nearly all so unpleasant!' – the vast majority of weekend cricketers couldn't care less about pitch marks, stroke averages or the intricacies of the handicap system. Show them a bat and to hell with who manufactured it!

They are simply too immersed in the raucous, full-blooded action, which commences at one or two o'clock every Saturday, the thud of leather on willow, impervious to waffle and minutiae. In a sentence, they are devotees, cut from the same cloth, but trying their damnedest in an environment where no two clubs are ever identical and idiosyncrasies abound. I suppose it boils down to one basic question – who would you choose for a dinner companion: Ian Botham or Nick Faldo? Has to be cricket, doesn't it?

Where else, for instance, would one meet such a variety of characters in the flesh and blood, let alone be standing at the other side of the wicket from them? Within the Atlas ranks there was Fred Robson, a Geordie all-rounder who taught Latin and Greek in his day job, but eschewed the 'Dulce Et Decorum Est' flummery in the middle, persuading his fielders to try and earn him wickets at third man with the nerve-shredding shriek:

'Catch it, c'mon catch it, you great fat toad!'; Peter Johnston, a keen-as-mustard, red-haired SNP adherent, who sparred with Robson about the merits of their respective nations so ferociously that rival teams must frequently have feared civil war was poised to erupt around their ears; Bill Ritchie, the lugubrious secretary/president/scorer/No. 11 batsman/umpire/newspaper contributor, whose most posthumous of deadpan deliveries frequently defused tense situations and would have put Paul Merton to shame; and Harry Cockburn, a wicket-keeper in the very loosest sense of the term, whose near-heroic refusal to put his legs together made one think he might earn a nice bonus moonlighting in a red-light district. Add to this the less-than-Fabulous Drysdale brothers, yours truly and my brother, Alistair, seven years younger, who laboured under the delusion that every innings had to be compressed into a maximum of three overs, and you have assembled a diverse group of people, who would never remotely have met in any other circumstances beyond the boundary. But we did, and somehow it all made sense.

What's more, there were Saturdays when everything clicked. The sadness lay in their infrequency. More typically, as somebody who had heeded Norman Tebbit's advice and moved to London in search of work (in the stockroom at British Home Stores: a treadmill of which we shall say no more), I acquired the habit of journeying up to Scotland on Friday nights to participate in Atlas fixtures, undaunted by the 400-mile trek, but simply dedicated to reuniting with the team, and praying for dry weather. On the first of these excursions my colleagues, realising the sacrifice I had made, asked me to open the batting, on a glorious afternoon and docile wicket, which looked awash with runs. But there were one or two drawbacks to the equation. For starters, having found myself seated, from Victoria Station to Manchester, behind a ghetto blaster-carrying West Indian whose taste in music inclined less towards Steely Dan than Bob Marley, I was absolutely knackered by the stage I walked out with Cockburn at 1.30. Secondly, I usually entered the fray at No. 6 or No. 7, and was unaccustomed to tackling the seamers, hence my delight at the innocuous full-toss, which I received first ball. Even as I chose my spot and subconsciously pencilled a four into the scorebook, I noticed my opponents hugging each other and cheering. Ah yes, it helps to strike the ball before it passes the bat, an imperative which I had omitted. On the sorry trudge back to the pavilion, I was striving to retain some modicum of dignity when I smelt a terrible odour and looked down at my feet. Hmm, what do you know, I had trodden on a steaming mass of dog turd, and had neglected to bring any alternative footwear. Naturally, everybody else that afternoon basked in sunshine and increased their averages, with Atlas reaching the giddy heights of 240, from 50 overs, and bowling out Holy Cross for 185. As for myself, I would have happily strangled the West Indian and the diarrhoea-afflicted pooch, and sung 50 choruses of 'What A Shame About Me', but for the slight problem that Donald Fagen and Walter Becker didn't get round to releasing the song until 15 years later.

However, if that fell into the category of personal misfortune, invariably the fiascos were more collective. Plenty of Scottish teams have been skittled for minuscule amounts throughout the last 180 years, and Freuchie's early history is littered with scorecards which resemble telephone numbers or an explosion in a stump factory. In fact, on their début against Kennoway, chasing 102 for 9, their line-up managed just 0–4–1–0–0–6–2–0–3–0–6, with eight extras steering them to a paltry 30 all out. But nonetheless, no matter the vagaries of surfaces or the qualities of rival attacks, there is something inherently embarrassing about being confronted with a tiny target and falling short of the mark. Especially when the details are then splashed on the front page of a local journal such as the *West Lothian Courier*, which reported, with almost gloomy relish: 'Atlas were confident they could enjoy an early finish after bowling out Trinity Academicals for 24 last Saturday. Well, they got their wish – but only because they themselves were routed for 15.' Most Scottish cricketers have suffered days where they fancied knocking off the runs quickly, and assumed the thought process: 'Ach, this is a piece of cake and even if I fail, somebody else will complete the job.' But the danger signals arrive when eight or nine players have the same addle-headed brainwave at once.

Yet, if only the hazards were confined to run chases. Down at the coalface in the minor leagues, precious few matches boast neutral umpires and the recipe for anarchy, rule-bending or downright cheating is rife. Christie has officiated at many matches, and listened to wave upon wave of absurd appeals, but the crucial factor is that he is as familiar with the laws of cricket as Richie Benaud with a microphone. Would that he could have been in charge when Atlas ventured to Cupar and Drysdale Jnr was bringing his Incredible Hulk impersonation to the party with a vengeance. Whoosh! The first delivery of an over sailed back straight over the bowler's head into the bushes. Wham! Ditto the second. Third up, a catch was offered in the deep and promptly dropped by a fellow with an unfortunate resemblance to Jabba the Hutt.

The next ball was smashed away contemptuously for another boundary, and by this point the expletives emanating from the medium-pacer had surpassed the decibel level of Concorde. The umpire at the wicket, a pallid-looking teenager with an apprehensive air, immediately decided to terminate the four-letter frenzy. Not, alas, by ordering the bowler to shut up, but by lifting his finger when the fifth delivery struck Alistair's pads, miles down the leg-side. As my disgruntled sibling walked off, muttering and moaning, he said to the official: 'That was never out, you numpty.' Whereupon, the umpire compounded the felony by blurting out: 'Well, you shouldn't have made a fool of my dad by smashing him all over the park. I have to go home with him tonight. You don't!'

In these environs, acrimony occasionally spilled over into sheer malevolence. On one such instance, at Edinburgh's Leith Links, a hitherto tepid encounter burst to life when Atlas's Bill Montgomery was clattered in the face by a ball, and even as blood was dribbling onto the crease and the semiconscious victim was rushed to hospital, the match descended into a minor

Donnybrook, with the rival captains poking each other in the stomach and a group of passing strangers entering the fray as hostilities veered towards a full-scale punch-up. By the death, Robson, a lone voice of sanity in an ocean of testosterone, was in full Kofi Annan mode, whilst I prodded around for most of our reply, in making 28 not out, oblivious to any thoughts of victory, but just for the sheer bloody-minded relish of preventing the Leith team from collecting maximum points, as the climax arrived with neither side bothering to conceal its enmity. Here was Scottish cricket at its worst and, thankfully, such lurches into hooliganism are scarce. But, in retrospect, the abiding memories of these league contests revolve around precious moments of elegance wrapped in hours of farce, based on the maxim: 'Do as I say, not as I do.'

On another Saturday, the ubiquitous Robson tore his hair out when Brian Hazzard forlornly sought to prevent Stirling from scoring a quick single, precipitating a comedic sequence worthy of Chaplin, albeit minus the grace or athleticism. Uncertain which end to throw it to, he wound up flinging it to neither, and the red sphere was speeding towards the boundary ropes before I caught up with it and hurled it back towards Cockburn, who promptly ripped the bails off without remembering to pouch the ball first. As Robson's temper seethed close to Vesuvian temperatures, Stirling's batsmen decided to advance for their, ahem, fifth, when Jim Notman, one of the few Atlas members with a decent arm, suddenly shattered the stumps from 50 metres away and completed a dismissal of which Jonty Rhodes would have been proud. It was a perfect microcosm of these contests: a testimony to the proposition that if you waited long enough, somebody would eventually remember that cricket isn't quantum physics, but a fairly basic pursuit. Yet, in the interim, we endured a terrible excess of thud and blunder.

At least, though, these were the afternoons when play was permissible. On too many instances to relate, the day developed into the Groundhog variety, with hope dashed, then raised, and deflated again as Jupiter Pluvius did his worst. Perhaps this

reliance on the weather, for those based in Blighty, explains why
so many cricketers have committed suicide and why Heather
Reid, the daughter of the prodigious Scottish bowler, Peter
Reid, who collected hundreds of wickets for Ferguslie and
Fauldhouse, has become both BBC Scotland's best-known fore-
caster and a lip-smacking fan of the game. 'I picked up the bug
when I was a wee girl, keeping the scorebook at venues across
Scotland, and I have been a dedicated follower ever since,' says
Heather. 'Even in the early days, I grew to realise the impact the
Scottish climate had on the game, and how quickly a sunny
afternoon could be transformed to a raging monsoon. Hence,
both when the cricketers were on the field, and when they were
dashing for sanctuary and searching for makeshift covers, I was
hooked. Some might describe Scottish cricket as a triumph of
hope over experience, but our people are tough cookies. They
never go off for a few spots of rain and I recall games where the
clouds were as black as the ace of spades, but the boys carried on
regardless. They had pencilled in the afternoon for duty and
nothing as insignificant as a howling gale was going to interrupt
them from their fun.'

As it transpired, given the ravages wrought by the elements in
1985, the majority of Scots had no option but to become wearily
inured to the rhythm of the rain, clattering off the far pavilions
amid scenes straight from *The Perfect Storm*. Dave Christie and his
confrères had virtually grown fins by the hour of their coronation
in London, but at least Freuchie were tenaciously determined
that, come high water or hurricane, hailstones or haar, nothing
would repel their victory charge. Atlas, by contrast, were all too
capable of drizzling to defeat in a splurge of frenzied flicks, fresh-
air swipes and futile flourishes. After one particularly gruesome
spectacle of wilful self-destruction by 3 p.m., there was the sight
in the Boroughmuir bar of Robson compiling a masterly 50-plus
break on the snooker table and Cockburn polishing off *The Times*
crossword in ten minutes, whilst I fired in a sequence of 140s and
180s on the dart-board. Across the hall, meanwhile, my brother
was performing a decent Fats Waller impersonation on the piano,

and Hamish McIntyre was beating all and sundry at Trivial Pursuit. Eventually Bill Ritchie, who had sat with pursed lips throughout the earlier debacle, could stand it no longer. 'You know,' he said to his opposite number, 'there is an awful lot of talent in the squad at Atlas . . . now if only some of these bastards could play cricket!'

That self-deprecating mindset has developed into a reflex action within Scottish circles, even amongst those who have progressed to the highest level. Mike Denness, who began his career at Ayr as the prelude to an auspicious career at Kent, must be one of the few captains in Ashes history to drop himself, in mid-series, as a consequence of struggling dreadfully with that belligerent she-cat called Lillian Thompson, Down Under, in the 1970s. His predecessor, Douglas Jardine, still one of the most widely-loathed personalities among Australian cricket aficionados, has, for the past seventy years, been portrayed as the archetypal whingeing Englishman, forever launching into grandiloquent Churchillian rhetoric and dismissing Don Bradman and his fellow-colonials with his fiendish 'Bodyline' strategy in 1933. Whereas in reality, Jardine was Scottish to his bootstraps, lived his life in the Calvinist tradition, and when he succumbed to cancer in 1958, his ashes were scattered over the top of Cross Craigs mountain in Perthshire. He was also, as I discovered from speaking to one of his daughters, the Reverend Fianach Lawry (the other children were christened Isla, Euan and Iona, which hardly suggests a residual attachment to the Home Counties), a painfully shy, reticent figure, who never recovered from the stigma attached to his name, despite spearheading a triumphant victory in Australia.

'This idea that he would deliberately set out to hurt and injure players on the other side was anathema to him, and my father was badly affected by the criticism which was flung in his direction,' said Fianach, who was ordained as a priest in the Scottish Episcopal Church in 1994 and has listened with incredulity to Jardine's memory being tainted by misconceptions, half-truths and once-young men embellishing their memories into anecdotage. 'He has been vilified for his tactics, and for supposedly being arrogant and cocksure, when the reality was that my dad was a nervous person; he bit his fingernails like mad and, because he wasn't a great conversationalist, he wasn't able to respond to the barrage of personal abuse which wrecked his career.

'It's sad that his name has been linked with one of the most infamous campaigns in sporting history. Back in the thirties he was made the scapegoat, as was his leading bowler, Harold Larwood, and my father never really recovered from the backlash which followed that tour. It's ironic that nowadays he would be regarded as a hero by his compatriots, but of course, my family has been affected by the fashion in which he has been mis-represented. [The most glaring example was an Australian mini-series, in which Jardine was depicted as some demonic yah-yah, part-Bertie Wooster, part-Mr Hyde.] You have to understand this about my father: yes, he had high standards, but he was never mean or petty and he considered himself a Scot, first and foremost, and although he held a tremendous regard for the ability of the run machine, Bradman, he knew that you will never win anything by sitting back and admiring your oppo-nents. He simply acted in his side's best interests, and the picture which has been painted of father is completely unrecognisable to me, and I am amazed the facts have been so distorted for so long.'

It must be significant that there is a common strand between these references to Denness, Jardine and Dave Christie: a re-luctance to acknowledge that they have strutted on the big stage and revelled in the spotlight. Because, despite his bullishness at close quarters, his have-bat-will-travel mentality and readiness to pitch into 100 different chores at Freuchie, the amiable Christie appears almost abashed at the deluge of publicity and adulation which followed his club's unprecedented Village Cup win. 'The best lesson I ever learned was from Bob Tully, who skippered the side for a long time, and he always reminded us that whatever we might do on the pitch on Saturday or Sunday, we would be back at work on Monday, painting the walls outside the toilets or laying down manure on the fields,' says Christie. 'It taught us that we should never get big-headed and think we were more important than we really were. When I was a youngster and had just made it into the First XI, we were toiling one Sunday, so he asked me to have a bowl. I took four or five wickets and I walked off feeling very pleased with myself. But when I got to the dressing room he came over, put his hand on my shoulder, and said: "Well done. I thought that rubbish would take wickets today." That might sound harsh, but it brought me back to earth and I kept my feet on the ground thereafter. I didn't bowl for a few weeks after that, but I had picked up a valuable lesson. If you do your best, nobody can blame you. But if you shoot your mouth off, nobody will respect you.'

All this ego-puncturing is doubtless admirable in breeding grounded human beings, but maybe it helps to explain why many of Scotland's cricketers are a saturnine breed, prepared for the worst, regardless of the circumstances. The shafts of humour tend to be dark as the clouds in November, but while one can smile at the lawyerly interest in the sport – at Clydesdale CC in Glasgow, one of the perimeter boards at Titwood, sponsored by Murray Macari of Beltrami & Co, proclaims: 'If you're in, we'll get you out' – it is worth accentuating the many positive initiatives orchestrated by the white-flannel fraternity. Indeed, wherever one ventures, it is evident that cricket is the only sport in Scotland to have successfully pursued a racial integration policy, and one merely has to cast a casual eye over the players' names in the scorecards published in any serious newspaper to acknowledge the ethnic influence of far-sighted Pied Pipers such as Mike Stanger at Clydesdale, David Barr at Ferguslie and Clarence Parfitt further north in Arbroath, all of whose Stakhanovite exertions, the majority on an unpaid basis, have acted as the spur and catalyst for a revolution in aspirations and ambitions over the last decade.

'It isn't rocket science, there is a big Asian community in the west of Scotland, and the kids are mad keen on cricket, so why not bring them into the fold as early as possible?' says Stanger, who has brought a new openness to the Scottish governing body,

Cricket Scotland, where once their dealings with the public and media hinted that they would prefer to be ex-directory or cite the Official Secrets Act rather than let their acolytes know what was happening. 'Within the current under-21 ranks there are a number of outstanding Scottish Asians, including the captain, Kasim Farid, and talented individuals such Zeeshan Bashir, Omer Hussain, Qasim Sheikh and Rajeev Routray, and there are others coming up behind at age-group level, so we have to keep the momentum going. Sometimes, Scotland is a pretty negative country and there is a tendency to ignore good news and concentrate on doom and gloom.' But we have now gained one-day international status from the ICC and it shows how far we have come that England brought their full side up here in August 2008.

Obviously, not everything in Scottish cricket is as rosy. But with Asian involvement in football and rugby a distant prospect, one shouldn't dwell on the obstacles to potential future involvement in the Test environment. It might be the case that the majority of Scots are temperamentally unsuited to the rigours of the five-day game, and it's true that attendances at domestic club matches usually number less than Sinatra lovers at a Jamie Cullum concert. But let those without brains cast the first stone at the energy, enterprise and ebullience habitually shown by Christie and his comrades.

After all, in 1985, less than a month before the trip to London, Atlas arrived at the Fifers' Public Park and received a crash course in the Freuchie Coarse Cricket School. After half an hour we were 15 for 1, with Cockburn replicating his trademark impersonation of Chris Tavaré on Valium. An hour later, we had surged ahead to 60 for 3, with Robson pacing anxiously on the boundary ropes, wondering when the realisation might dawn amongst the 'arses at the crease' (Drysdale and McIntyre) that we weren't performing in a timeless Test. Finally, Freuchie introduced what can only be described as a pity bowler, in an aid to transform the tempo, and I duly helped myself to 20 in an over filled with lollipops. In an instant, the atmosphere changed and a brief recess occurred. Or to express it more accurately, a contingent of the home team approached me with the warning: 'Don't treat the old lad with contempt, or you'll get your baws kicked in later! Okay? We're here to have fun, not take the piss. Got it?' I had. And I deserved every word of caution.

As Christie maintains, there would be nothing worth preserving in Scottish cricket if a small élite controlled and dominated the proceedings every week. His personnel may have garnered condescension from sections of the English press in 1985, with Mike Selvey summing up the mood: 'The men of Freuchie were clearly intent on enjoying the occasion. An additional qualification for their team appears to be cirrhosis of the liver, and they brought with them a lone piper – a blessing: it could have been massed pipes. The Queen Mother is woken every day by the skirl and our sympathies must lie with her.' Yet he was magnanimous enough to note that amid the caricatures of village cricket, the dirt-encrusted boots, painter's trousers, beer guts and encroaching signs of arthritis: 'Freuchie's out-cricket was superb, they fielded as if their very lives depended on it, and ultimately that contributed hugely to a thrilling victory over a side who were perhaps better equipped, but had less fire or anything else in their bellies.'

In anybody's language, it was a triumph to savour and has ensured the club's name will eternally be associated with a positive achievement. For Freuchie, a small community with a throbbing, vibrant pulse, whose citizens are as steeped in cricket as Kingussie in shinty or Melrose in rugby, the ramifications will never be forgotten.

CHAPTER TWO

THE WHITE HEATHER CLUB

There are two distinct types of committees in this world. The first confuses meticulousness with pedantry, never reaches a decision where working parties can be convened, spends hours recording minutes of infinite tedium, and generally resembles Frank Pickle and his parish delegates from *The Vicar of Dibley* driving Dawn French into paroxysms of despair. The second comprises those clubs and officials whose annual general meeting agenda is discussed and rubber-stamped quickly, quietly, efficiently, on the basis that if it ain't broke, don't fix it, and now where the hell's the bar?

Perhaps unsurprisingly, the men and women who have presided over Freuchie CC since 1908 very much belong in the latter category. From their verdant base in the lea of the Lomond Hills, generations of families have passed through the gates between the village primary school and the cricket club, and instinctively made the connection between the two organisations, not by being pushed unwillingly into the sport, but as a consequence of the sheer inherent enthusiasm of those who have preferred actions over words, and would rather encourage a child than preach to him/her. It may not sound a massive difference, but believe me, whereas certain other Scottish cricket institutions apparently operate on the basis, 'Sssh, don't tell anybody we're here, and we can ignore the proles', Freuchie's approach was socially inclusive before the phrase was hijacked by politicians, and characterised by an almost cussed determination to focus on pitched affairs and practice evenings at the expense of po-faced platitudes from jobsworths. Indeed, the Fifers, who flickered into existence considerably later than many Scottish clubs, including the likes of Kelso and Rossie Priory, whose derivation dates back to the 1820s, have never been enthusiastic about attending dry-as-dust assemblies staffed by apparatchiks listing who ordered what from whom for the purpose of blah, and Freuchie had barely been established before the minutes started to dry up between April 1910 and an undated occasion late in 1912 at which it was grudgingly agreed 'there should be at least three Committee meetings in the season'. Maybe that's one of the compelling reasons that attracted me to their methodology from the moment I first walked into the club in the early 1980s: namely, that there is no sleight of hand or Machiavellian chicanery lurking beneath the surface with these people, no pompous standing on ceremony, or indulgence in ritual for tradition's sake, and, best of all, no attempt from the senior figures, the likes of Dave Christie and Harry Barclay and Allan Wilkie, to conceal their visceral passion for cricket and all its foibles beneath a veneer of bureaucracy.

I have, in front of me, the Freuchie CC Minute Book covering the period from 1908 to 1925, and it is a slim volume, closer to a novella than *War and Peace*. The first entry is typically terse and blissfully free of the cod Latin legalese which infests so many of these documents. Dated Monday, 17 April, it merely acknowledges: 'At the meeting of the above committee, it was decided that, if the bats were forthcoming, the secretary should cycle to Ladybank and arrange a match. The secretary was instructed to write to Joe Anderson to purchase a ball about 5/- or 5/6d. This was all the business.'

As historical mementoes go, it hardly ranks in the same category as the Gettysburg Address or the Magna Carta and, curiously, the minute was unsigned and there remains no indication that any match ever occurred, not least because Ladybank was only founded officially in the spring of 1909. Yet although this was a slightly unsatisfactory beginning to their story, Freuchie had, by that stage, decided that it made no sense for so many of their players to pedal to neighbouring Falkland, two miles away, when they had all the basic commodities they required for cricket in their own community. 'Let's hold the show right here', was their verdict, from which small footsteps a concert was arranged, which raised £2 19s. 3d. (ticket prices were, expensively for the time, set at 1s. 6d. for adults and half price for children), but whilst the Fifers were gradually cranking into gear, they could scarcely be accused of rushing into action. 'We knew that things were a bit slow to start with, but you have to remember that there was a lot of informal, social cricket in those days, and workers didn't have the leisure time they enjoy nowadays, so there was never going to be a case of the team playing 20 games a season, especially given the cost of equipment and scorebooks and other gear,' says Dave Christie, the hero of our tale, who has covered every neuk, recess and corner of the Kingdom of Fife during the last 60 years, and will not hear a word against his beloved Freuchie (which means 'white heather' in Gaelic). 'Falkland were a strong side and I would reckon that several of our local lads thought to themselves they might as well stay in their own village and get a side up and running, but you know what these matters are like. They had day jobs to worry about, money was scarce, most of the youngsters either worked in the mines or on the farms and they would be knackered at the end of their shift. And cricket isn't like football, where the match only lasts 90 minutes. So, while it might seem that Freuchie were slow to get their act together, this was another time, another place. The only thing that mattered was that, regardless of the delay, they *did* get started.'

The proof arrived with the team's maiden foray against Kennoway's Second XI, on 3 July 1909, wherein, chasing 102 for 9, the debutants were skittled for only 30, with enough ducks to satisfy the Disney Corporation, and a top score of eight from that thoroughbred Scot, Eck Strass. It was a sobering reminder of the travails confronted by any fledgling club, but Freuchie's players possibly imagined things could only get better. Sadly, they didn't, as borne out by their next fixture, away to Strathmiglo on 28 August, which saw Andrew Staig's collective disintegrate like an igloo on Mercury, whilst pursuing their

opponents' seemingly modest tally of 95. Staig contributed
nothing to the cause, a fate shared by Archibald Henderson,
William Fenton, John Biggs, Bob Dall, Alex Spence, Jimmy Jack
Jnr, and Bill Pratt, and although Eck once more came to the
rescue with a contribution of 9, which advanced the final score
to 17, the new boys' confidence had taken a battering, and they
packed away their kit for the winter.

Unsurprisingly, however, these were determined, robust,
tenacious individuals, men who would not shirk a challenge,
nor resort to sulks and petted lips. The recent, excellent BBC
series, *The Lost World of Mitchell and Kenyon*, brought many of our
ancestors to life, with an eerie, subterranean beauty, as if
awakening the dead from the slumbers, and I felt a similar shiver
up my spine whilst scanning the black-and-white photographs of
those early Freuchie pioneers. There they are: the 1910 team,
and Staig stands haughtily (or is it anxiously?), with his hands in
his pockets, as slim as a whippet, and yet as olde-worlde as the
majority of his colleagues. Next to him is Willie Low, aged
around 30-something, coming on 55, and as we swivel across the
picture, there are frowns, grimaces, glowers, expressions of
solemn indifference, but absolutely nothing in the slightest
indicative of joy or pleasure. Even the Reverend J.M. Richardson, seated at the front, looks as if he is carrying the burdens of a
wicked world on his shoulders, and Jim Leishman, the only
person in the assembly with a cricket bat in his hands, is
reminiscent of James Finlayson, the downtrodden patsy in many
of the Laurel and Hardy films, with his extravagant moustache,
bedraggled hair, spindly knees and slightly glaikit stare. It hardly
requires an Einstein-sized IQ to conclude that the surprising
thing wasn't that these fellows struggled at their cricket, but that
they possessed the strength and resolve to play at all.

Yet credit to them, if their maiden summer had been cala-
mitous, Freuchie's whiskery brigade demonstrated that they
were fast learners during the following year's enlarged campaign.
On 23 May, they ventured to Springfield to tackle the Fife &
Kinross Asylum (yes, yes, I know it sounds like something out of

The Simpsons), and praise be, they won their first-ever match, totalling 70 to their rivals' 42, with Staig hitting 27 and Jimmy Low 11. Bolstered by that success, the following Saturday brought the first recorded home match when Freuchie entertained Kennoway, and were undone again, by 78 to 38 runs, yet although several of these scorecards hint at a collapse on a truly House of Usher scale, there were signs already of a persistence within this club and, a week later, they sensed the sweet smell of victory at home, defeating Ladybank by 53 to 48. Obviously, these results were tiny steps towards establishing a competitive streak on the pitch, but the seeds had been planted and 1910 yielded further wins over Leslie, Ladybank and Ceres (although the latter turned up with only eight players) and a draw at home against Wallace's of Perth, one of the many works teams to crop up in the chronicles.

Thereafter, it was remarkable how swiftly the club's profile rose within their region, and during the seasons in the build-up to the First World War – at which point cricket was suspended until 1919 – Freuchie arranged matches with a bewildering assortment of teams, featuring, amongst others, Panmure, Kinlock, Auchtermuchty, Dunnikier, Cupar, Roineach Mhor, Markinch and Victoria 2nd. As the fixture schedule mounted, there was also the emergence of a number of notable players, including the prolific batsman, David Duncan, and Edwin Croall, whose captaincy of Freuchie inspired them to new standards, and provided a fitting template for the circumstances under which these trailblazers operated, basically adhering to Norman Tebbit's infamous advice : 'On your bike!' Originally employed in the linen trade in Brechin, Croall travelled to Kennoway for a mining job, and subsequently joined Dixon's paper mill in Markinch, prior to settling down in Freuchie in 1913, where he developed into a revered and influential personality in the club's history, a sinewy pace bowler, who accounted for innumerable batsmen, as the years passed, and whose stature rose along with the hamlet he had made home.

Sadly, predictably, there were several casualties in the 1914–18 conflict, lads who left Freuchie and never returned, sacrificed on foreign fields as pawns in a chess match; yet given the ravages that were inflicted on many communities, one of the surprising aspects of the scorecards when the cricket resumed was how many of the names remained the same. Croall re-emerged with his talent undimmed after the Great War – and his side's achievements began to earn honourable mentions in the *Glasgow Herald*, on account of a series of fine displays from the skipper, in tandem with Duncan, who struck an unbeaten century away at Kirkcaldy, while Croall excelled with 6 for 9 against Dunnikier, as their playing numbers significantly increased, sparking the creation of a Second XI in 1920, and confirming one of the cornerstones of Freuchie's success.

Namely, continuity: the acceptance that nothing lasts forever, and that without proper attention being paid to youth development, any organisation will inevitably wither on the vine and slither into obsolescence. 'That has definitely been a feature of our club since we came into being, and it probably accounts for the fact that although the linen mills and the collieries and manufacturing industries have disappeared, there is still this tradition where fathers pass the torch on to their sons and the latter on to theirs,' as Allan Wilkie, the Freuchie secretary, has said since before the 1985 triumph. 'It patently helped us that the school was next to the ground, and it was therefore as natural as breathing for youngsters to be drawn to the cricket field every summer, but we have always done our utmost to ensure that, whatever might be happening at the moment, we are also laying the foundations for ten, twenty years down the line, catching the kids young and moulding them early. Edwin Croall was one of the first characters to stamp his impression on the club, and others have followed that example ever since.'

Fife, at this stage, was positively awash with cricket teams, many of whom have faded into the ether, and on various evenings in midsummer, judging from the truncated newspaper reports of the period, it's possible to envisage that there wasn't a blade of grass without a match in progress. So, too, as the 1920s progressed, Freuchie's penchant for travelling outwith their parochial confines accelerated, and their fixtures proliferated. They regularly embarked on the ferry across the River Forth for meetings with the 'Edinburgh Indians' and St Katherine's in the capital and, oblivious to the absence of a formalised league structure such as existed in the west and north of Scotland, the likes of Croall, newly-appointed captain, Jack Lindsay, Johnny Dalrymple, Jimmy Jack Snr, and the ever-reliable David Duncan, achieved a series of famous victories, not least in the ritually hard-fought local Derby at Falkland in1923, where the visitors skittled their rivals for 24, with Croall taking 5 wickets in an innings with 6 ducks. (Talk about reeling in the years and wheels turning round and round!) Off the greensward, meanwhile, Freuchie's clubhouse was upgraded to accommodate such luxuries as running water, and by the end of 1924, early caution had been replaced by bullish self-confidence, as evinced in the AGM's remarks from the president: 'We had inflicted defeat twice on all our neighbours, which proved FCC to be district champions.' Admittedly, this was a tenuous claim, but there was no arguing with the strides which had been taken in 16 years.

Nor was the success any fluke of geography or a consequence of significant investment from an Andrew Carnegie or Paul Getty-esque benefactor with the wealth of Croesus. Instead, bolstered by a string of prescient characters, blessed with the vision to recognise the necessity of nurturing youth, Freuchie opened their doors to all, including females, which at this stage was as progressive as it was rare in Scottish sporting circles (and they still aren't permitted into many Scottish golfing institutions). In the 1920s juniors of either sex were actively encouraged by the club, and whereas membership fees for adults were 1/6d, the so-called 'apprentices' only had to shell out a shilling. By November 1921, the women were growing increasingly orga-nised and the minutes contain details of a Freuchie committee club meeting, attended by 'Mrs William Grant, Mrs Peter Nelson, Mrs James Mackie and the Misses Rymer, Cochran, Leishman, Inglis, Jack, Campbell and Duncan'. Shortly afterwards, several of these enterprising souls launched themselves into competitive action, pitting themselves against their male counterparts, who were handicapped by having to bowl under-arm and bat left-handed. Indeed, the 1926 match resulted in a win for the 'Ladies' (as they were called, although the term nowadays sounds both condescending and more applicable to toilets than sentient people) and the triumphant side were photographed, in all their glory, for the Fife Almanac. Unfortunately, life has since proved a grind, a situation scarcely helped by the dearth of women's teams in Scotland, and exacerbated by the tendency of many Glaswegians and Edinburghers to ignore anything outside the Central Belt, but in the 1990s the wives and girlfriends of many of the senior team were still chipping away at the obstacles, and what do we find? A. Christie, Aileen of that ilk, as captain, in the company of various Birrells, Gourlays, Irvines and the same names which crop up, in the male ranks, decade after decade.

This is a hallmark of the club and, from the 1930s onwards, Freuchie thrived on the efforts of several redoubtable figures, chaps who may have been theoretically playing friendlies, but who still demanded a formidable work ethic from their charges. Jimmy Jack Snr, a gruff Dundonian, was the prototype of these patriarchal, Hearst-like presences, who cast a massive spell over Freuchie, from the time he arrived as their first president – by which stage he was 43 – and stayed in the position for 20 years, whilst amassing a barrel-load of runs, umpiring, cutting the grass and doing anything else which required hard graft, until his death in 1953 at the grand old age of 88. Jack Lindsay was another in his mould, a Bathgate-born linen factory manager, who joined the Black Watch on leaving school, rose to the rank of captain and was decorated with a Military Cross in the First World War. After that experience, cricket must have seemed a delicious trifle, and Lindsay rapidly established himself as a free-scoring batsman and perspicacious First XI skipper, whilst also turning out for Fifeshire, as the prelude to becoming Freuchie's honorary pre-sident in 1935. By all accounts, he didn't suffer fools gladly – who but a fool does? – but his longstanding connection with the predecessors of Dad's Army ended rather sadly, when he disassociated himself from the club in 1963 after a social event was staged in the Newton of Falkland Village Hall rather than the Lumsden Memorial Hall. A petty conclusion to an otherwise lustrous career.

While these resilient men were leading Freuchie, there was never any threat of the club developing into a clique or a vanity project. Yes, they loved their cricket, treasured the chance to meet and frequently beat bigger, ostensibly better opponents, and fought for their organisation's best interests; but the community remained at the epicentre of their thoughts and the likes of Jimmy Jack Snr weren't so foolish as to imagine that cricket was a matter of life and death. It wasn't, and although they had decisions to make and constitutions to observe, their administrative dealings remained blissfully concise and free of gobbledygook. Thus we discover that in 1935, 'It was put before the meeting whether the club should continue its membership with the Scottish Cricket Union and the meeting decided to drop out of the Union.' That's all there is: no protracted debate or bureaucratic creation of subcommittees to discuss the matter further and drag it into the middle of next century. Similar boldness was evident when Freuchie agreed to join the proposed midweek Fife League in 1937, and they were crowned as champions of the East Section for the next two years, but another global conflict was poised to rage forth and, as Hitler prepared for his onslaught on Britain, the minutes hint at the looming war.

'A communication was read from the secretary of the Fife Cricket League, asking the club's views regarding his suggestion that Freuchie and Dunfermline A hold the League Cup for six months apiece as it was unlikely the deciding match could be arranged,' records the meeting of 10 June 1940. 'The secretary also intimated that the local Food Controller had refused a supply of sugar for teas.' By October: 'The painting of the pavilion was discussed and it was agreed that this should be done as soon as possible, the colour to be green all over. It was also agreed that the windows be covered with wire netting for their protection.' By this juncture, there are shades of Private Pike and Captain Mainwaring of *Dad's Army* in some of these accounts, but the cricket had ceased and the more senior office-bearers clearly felt they had to fill their hours, amid the blackouts, with anything that might relieve the tension. 'In connection with the grazing of the park, the secretary reported a mild complaint from the tenant, re the use of the field by the Football Club. The secretary was appointed to interview the Football officials on this matter,' was recorded in November 1941. Whereupon, five months later, in a dreadfully convoluted entry, one can immediately detect the lurking tensions among the respective parties, reminiscent of the parochial bickering which simmered between Mainwaring's Home Guard and Hodges' ARP Wardens in the classic comedy series:

At a meeting held in the Pavilion between the committee, Mr Cowan Bryce, representing the Boys Club, and Mr David Christie, representing Our Boys Football Club, it was agreed to give the use of the pavilion to both clubs.

The Boys Club to have priority on Tuesdays and Thursdays and the Football Club on Wednesdays and Saturdays. Each club to have sole use of one dressing room and joint use of the tea room and all other facilities.

The Football Club to pay 1/- per week and the Boys Club to cut the grass on the pitch as rent, such rent being inclusive of all gas and water charges.

The Football Club to try and limit football to Wednesdays and Saturdays.

This statement was read to and agreed upon by all those present.

Well, thank heaven for small mercies, whilst the future of the free world was at stake! But, fortunately, such lapses into Pooterish debate are isolated. Indeed, there is a different mood to the next significant convention at Freuchie, on 9 July 1945, when a large attendance congregated in the pavilion and some kind of normal service returned: 'In welcoming the large numbers present, Mr John Dryden explained that the meeting had been called to ascertain if there was a desire for the club to resume its playing activities. Mr James Jack, Snr, apologised for his enforced absence and wished the club every success in their efforts to get play re-started. Mr Jack recalled that after the last war, the team was one of the best in Fife and called on the younger members to make it the same again. Therefore, it was agreed to get going as soon as possible.' Mr Jack had no earthly reason to apologise to anybody. He was 81, a widower, whose country had just endured six years of hellish, momentous conflagration. But here he was, flying the flag and summoning a call to arms for Freuchie, which provoked an immediate response.

'I was only 12 at the time, but I was already hooked on cricket, and there were plenty of us who flocked through the club gates to answer Jimmy Jack's plea, and it was as if the influence of those senior figures was laying down the gauntlet to the youngsters, and spelling out the question: could we help, could we build on what had already been achieved, and lay the foundations for a bright future?' says Dave Christie, one of the new breed of unashamed enthusiasts on whom Jack was counting. 'I have looked back into the archives and there was a tremendous amount of work carried out in the next ten years to create a fresh development structure, which would bring positive results. Nobody made a big fuss, the stalwarts just beavered away, but they were formidable lads.'

Just as Enid Blyton had her Famous Five, and the *Bunty* had the Four Marys, so the Fifers boasted their three Bobs, rugged individualists, who, in diverse fashions, re-established the Freuchie conveyor belt of talent. There was Bob Nicoll, a local reporter with DC Thomson and the *Fife Free Press*, who didn't actually play cricket but immersed himself in a string of other roles: treasurer, secretary, umpire, life member, preaching the sporting gospel to the brethren and sorority of the Falkland Old

Peoples' Welfare Committee: and Bob Keith, a miner until the General Strike of 1926, who moved into Freuchie with his employers in the water treatment plant of Tullis Russell, and became an invaluable all-rounder until the age of 64. As an opening batsman for a quarter of a century, he carried his bat on a dozen occasions, took a career total of 1650 wickets, and feasted in such prodigious afternoons' work as his personal demolition of Dunfermline Carnegie in 1934, where he hit 36, pouched 4 catches and snapped up 6 for 16. The last of the triumvirate was Bob Tully, a Stakhanovite captain, whose relish for hard labour and philosophy that the tea lady was as important as the skipper in the Freuchie scheme was adopted and followed by a callow Dave Christie. 'Many were the Saturdays when you would find Bob up at six in the morning, cutting the grass, going for a run and persuading a mate to go to net practice, and all before breakfast. He had graduated to our Second XI at the age of 12, and my God, he worked like a Trojan and expected others to do the same. You could get away with not being a superstar, but if he suspected you of being lazy, he ripped into you and didn't let you go,' says Christie. 'Many of the teenagers looked up to him and that was only natural, because he had a charisma about him, and whether opening the bat for the Firsts, keeping wicket or skippering, he poured his heart and soul into Freuchie and it was a pleasure to be around him. I recall that he retired from the game in 1957, and that it was very much against his father's wishes, but he probably thought he was holding back one of the youngsters and he wasn't one for overstaying his welcome. So he became honorary president and some of us were in awe of him.'

Whether in Freuchie, Falkland, Cupar or a stream of other smallish communities, cricket was thriving, regardless of the occasional grimness of the settings or the Spartan nature of the amenities. David Taylor, a policeman, who turned out for Burntisland in the 1950s, recalls that although his shift patterns often interrupted his playing schedule, Fife was rife with friendly teams, social sides and works ensembles, the majority of whom regarded a spot of rain as Tiger Woods does a 12-inch putt.

'There were no limited-overs games in these days, but instead, you had one team batting, if they were able to, until the tea interval, and the other replied until an agreed time, and if no result was reached within that period, an extension of around 15 minutes could be added, by mutual consent,' says Taylor, who returned from National Service in 1957, to discover a vibrant cork-and-willow milieu in his homeland. 'All we wanted to do was play, no matter where or when. In Kirkcaldy, there was a club attached to the Nairn's Linoleum Company, and they had a proper sports field and pavilion in Victoria Road, next to the company head office. The only slight drawback was that the ground was quite small and no sixes could be scored even if the ball cleared the boundary by a country mile. [Sadly, this pleasant pitch is now a housing scheme, but in the 1950s and 1960s there was plenty of green space.]

'We were all as keen as mustard and the rest of Fife was clearly similarly affected. After Burntisland moved to Toll Park [away from the Links, on the sea-front, where their tussles were frequently halted by curious/inebriated tourists], our secretary was contacted by a 'posh' club based in Edinburgh, looking for a match at our ground, but they said they would only send their seconds as 'it would make for a more even game'. Well, our secretary wrote back, confirming a date, but craftily never mentioned which of our sides would be playing them. Anyway, a team was selected, comprising our Second XI captain and one or two others, and then filled with members of the Firsts. On the day of the fixture, the team sheet in the pavilion was marked 'Burntisland 2nds', and our Second XI scorebook was also placed conspicuously in the box. Then we massacred them. The full details were published in the local papers and they departed with their tails between their legs. We never heard from them again.'

Similar stories of native cunning and guile are commonplace in Scottish cricket, but most clubs have instinctively appreciated that slaughter is rarely enjoyable, either for the victims or the perpetrators. Andrew Grant, another apostle of Freuchie, epitomised these ideals with an avoidance of a win-at-all-costs mentality and if the opposition were struggling or compelled to send in a youngster to bat, he would replace the likes of Bob Keith with one of his own rookies. This may seem nothing more than good old-fashioned sportsmanship, but the game in Scotland is littered with abject mismatches: experiences which could have been specifically designed to repel the vanquished from cricket for the rest of their lives. One such debacle happened at Shawholm in 1919 when the Western District of Scotland took on the Australian Imperial Forces and, as historian David W. Potter recalls: 'In two days, the Aussies accumulated 733 for 6, and then dismissed the Scots for 85 and 88, thus winning by an innings and 560 runs. Adding insult to injury, Wisden tells us that the visitors reached 638 at the end of the first day, then confirms: "They scored at a terrific pace on the opening afternoon, because it was nearly two in the afternoon before the match commenced."' Quite why this bunch of Australians batted on after passing 600 is a mystery, but only stats freaks with sadistic streaks could possibly have derived any satisfaction from pummelling rivals into the dust to that degree.

'I have never understood the appeal of embarrassing opponents, particularly in what are supposed to be friendlies, and it does nothing for youngsters to spend the whole afternoon chasing the ball to different parts of the long grass. With regards to Freuchie, if you glance at our results over the years, most of our games have been fairly close, and there certainly aren't too many hammerings in the archives, where either ourselves or the other team went away feeling disenchanted with cricket,' says Dave Christie. 'Where is the benefit in humbling players who are trying their best? I am not claiming for an instant that we didn't play hard – in the big matches, the Derbies against Falkland and the Village Cup encounters, for instance, we played *very* hard when it was required – but, for the most part, I have stuck to the idea that if both sides don't take something away from the day, it feels a bit unsatisfactory. Occasionally that approach cost us dear, and we ended up losing, because we didn't go for the jugular.

But, for heaven's sake, when all is said and done, we're only talking about the outcome of a cricket match.'

In the midst of Bill Haley and the Comets and Elvis Presley sparking the birth of rock 'n' roll and a quartet from Liverpool joining forces with Brian Epstein, Freuchie's own band of youngsters, including a couple who would feature in the march to Lord's, began creating merry havoc of their own on the Scottish circuit. There was the extraordinary afternoon when Burntisland arrived at the club with a dozen recruits and asked whether they could play 12-a-side, whereupon teenager Terry Trewartha grabbed all 11 wickets in a fiery spell, whilst Dave Christie toiled away at the other end. The latter subsequently came close to equalling his colleague, with a haul of 10 for 4 against Townhill, and the seeds were gradually being sown for future glories. Occasionally, even their most resilient customers would be confounded by the elements: although 1959 was a resplendent summer, one in which Freuchie completed all 23 of their scheduled fixtures – the highlight being John Christie's spell of 9 for 15 (all of them bowled) against Dunfermline, which earned special mention from president, John Tully, at the AGM – the following season was a dismal wash-out with the First and Seconds losing 19 matches to the weather, despite a litany of late-night sessions with the sluice pumps and mops. Such are the vagaries of life for the Scottish cricketer, optimistic on Friday, kit packed and whites cleaned, only to awaken on Saturday to the depressing rhythm of the rain.

Mercifully, however, these Fifers weren't made of porcelain and both players and spectators revelled in the crunch matches of every year's campaign, the Derby meetings with Falkland, a fixture which some have compared to the Old Firm's rivalry, but only if one ignores the spate of violence which erupts across the west of Scotland every time the footballing adversaries square up, allied to the insidious sectarianism which lurks amongst even those who would classify themselves as civilised, reasonably intelligent people. Anybody inclined to concur with Robin Williams' assessment of cricket as 'baseball on Valium' should mingle with the crowd at Freuchie during a tussle with Falkland and they will encounter a raucous, seething mass of partisan bias, the tension as taut as piano wire and the audience's nerves constantly on edge. These afternoons aren't for the faint-hearted and woe betide the umpire who denies the hosts a palpable lbw decision or misses a snick to the keeper. David W. Potter, the historian, should know – he has officiated at both these matches and Village Cup contests and willingly confesses that they tax the mind far more than the average Scottish game. 'It's remarkable that these two sides should have developed as they have done, but being so close to one another, there was definitely an edge, and the spectators used to get really worked up on the boundary edge, despite the fact the players invariably knew one another. You had to concentrate 100 per cent and not allow yourself to be influenced by the shouts and screams from the sidelines, but whilst there was a bit of extra pressure, especially whenever the contests moved towards a thrilling climax, these matches were enjoyable because you had two sides who were rivals, but they still respected each other,' says Potter. 'Of course, there was a bit of sledging and growling and muttering from the bowlers when a decision didn't go in their favour, but they got on with it, and both clubs have a real cricketing ethos. They aren't just lads who are waiting for the football or rugby season to begin again, and I always relished umpiring at these Derbies. Yes, you could cut the atmosphere with a knife, but neither side has anybody who I would describe as an out-and-out cheat – which certainly isn't the case with some of the Glasgow and Edinburgh teams – and although they flung the odd insult around in the heat of the moment, they would always meet in the bar later on good terms and share a drink and a joke together.'

Nonetheless, despite the slew of thrills and effervescence which pervaded these affairs, some of the rising Freuchie stars were beginning to press for something more than just a diet of friendlies. In 1963, a meeting was organised at Kirkcaldy to consider forming a Fife League, as was the norm in other parts of the country, but although the Christie militia agreed to join, prior to withdrawing at the end of 1964 they were frustrated by the dearth of top-class action and sought alternatives, without much initial success.

'Some of our old opponents went defunct [many of the works teams simply disappeared as soon as the firms closed or changed ownership] and we had reached a situation where we genuinely needed a fresh challenge, and for the next 15 years we looked at increasing our ambitions. We applied to join the Perthshire League, but were rejected, then the same thing happened with the Strathmore Union and eventually we were successful in being granted entry to the East League, but that didn't happen until 1980, so it was just as well really that the Village Cup competition came along, because suddenly we had a platform and a tournament which suited us down to the ground, and once it was up and running, there was a noticeable change in our attitude,' says Christie, whose life was transformed by the brainchild of the *Cricketer* magazine. 'Perhaps we should have been aspiring to a higher standard earlier, but it is always easy to be wise after the event, and we all savoured the matches against the likes of Fakland, Kirkcaldy and Cupar. But, yes, by 1970 there was a growing feeling that we had to search for a bigger stage.'

One also detects a heightened urgency in the minutes, and a general meeting on 3 May 1971 marks the onset of a brand new chapter in the Fifers' progress. 'It was decided by the committee that entry into the National Village Cup knock-out competition for 1972 should be made and that the entry fee of £2.50 be submitted,' records the chairman, Tom Trewartha, whose members were also grappling with the creation of a new clubhouse to replace the wooden hut, which was slipping into obsolescence. 'We have decided to contact the Secretary of State for Scotland to try and establish who controls the ground on which we play cricket . . . [two months later] the Secretary of State could in no way help with information as to who controlled the ground . . . [but, by the following January] sketch plans from Mr Alan Robertson were passed around and approved. It was stated that the cost of the shell of the building had been estimated at £1350 to £5000 for materials and brickwork and it was agreed to seek grant aid towards a cost of £3500.'

There ensued protracted discussions about the feasibility of the cricket and bowling clubs amalgamating [before being thrown out by twenty votes to four] and, around this period, it was evident that some individuals believed one particular family was amassing an undue influence at Freuchie. 'Mr Tom Trewartha opened the meeting [the 1972 AGM] and went on to state that he felt unjustified comment had been made regarding the feelings of himself and his sons towards the club. He wished to make it clear none of them had any desire to control, only to contribute to, Freuchie. In addition, he expressed particular concern over the methods of team selection, feeling that it was wrong that both captain and vice-captain were involved. Non-playing members should be more involved and we should seek somebody to travel with the Second XI for away fixtures to make comment on individual performances at selection committee meetings. Finally, he stated that the First XI captain [Bobby Bond] had been subjected to a great deal of criticism from players and emphasised strongly that when a captain is elected, he should be given the firm support of ALL members during his term as captain.' It sounds similar to an episode from *Family at War* and one would hardly guess that Bond's team had enjoyed a terrific summer, losing only seven of their thirty-two fixtures. Yet, after this unexpected tirade, he was, perhaps understandably, replaced as skipper by Bob Christie and normal service resumed, with Freuchie's new clubhouse development coming to fruition, assisted considerably by Alan Robertson, who prepared all the drawings, arranged for planning permission and building warrants, and was subsequently rewarded with life membership.

It merely remained for the Fifers to translate their passion for the Village Cup into victories. But in retrospect, Dave Christie regards the 1970s as the defining decade in his cherished organisation's history. 'When you cast your gaze back at the 1976 team, the season we became Scottish regional champions for the first time, you can't help but notice the flowering of the talent which would later bring us success. There is Niven McNaughton, and George Wilson, and Pete Hepplewhite and Terry Trewartha, and yours truly standing at the back with a frown on my face, but that doesn't reflect what was going on inside my head,' says Christie. 'On the contrary, I was thinking to myself: We have the potential, the commitment, and the enthusiasm to do our community proud. And that has always been one of the cornerstones of my philosophy: that we are here not simply to do ourselves proud, but to make Freuchie folk feel proud as well.'

The subtext was clear that although other Scottish organisations might recruit high-profile overseas players, Christie's team would rely on their own progeny even if the policy occasionally returned to haunt them. In 1980, the Fifers entertained Watsonians and seemed to have victory wrapped up when they dismissed their Edinburgh opponents for just 79. However, their pursuit was hampered somewhat by the presence in the visiting ranks of one Terry Alderman, the Australian fast bowler who, 12 months later, would be heavily involved in the famous Botham-dominated Ashes series, and was named Wisden's Cricketer of the Year in 1982. Without working up too much sweat, the illustrious paceman ripped into Freuchie's batsmen and finished with figures of 6 for 6 as the hosts slumped to defeat by 21 runs. 'He had me caught behind, and I will never forget the ease with which he clicked into the groove and started wreaking havoc, despite the fact he wasn't at full speed. We had seen nothing like it before, but, to his credit, Terry played very fair with us, pitching the ball up throughout his spell, so that there was never any real danger, although the wicket was a bit bumpy,' recalls Christie.

'I suppose it was a reality check for us, but there again, we felt privileged to be on the same field as the likes of Alderman and it wasn't the first time we had suffered at the hands of an Australian. Another Test player, Andrew Hilditch, came down to tackle us with Forfarshire, and scored a masterly 110. These boys are way out of our class, but it's good to be put in your place occasionally. It just shows how much you have got to learn and if these professionals can improve standards in Scotland, that's fair enough.'

A trifling matter of 17 years before a British premier-in-waiting spelled out his priorities as 'Education, education, education', Freuchie had sent out the message that they would battle on in the business of self-improvement. As we will discover, that infinite capacity for taking pains was to reap spectacular rewards for the White Heather Club.

CHAPTER 3

THE DADDY OF THEM ALL

It's just after New Year 2005 in Freuchie, and as Dave Christie strolls down from the cricket club for a lunchtime snack at the Lomond Hills Hotel, there ensues what has developed into a normal routine for this svelte sexagenarian. 'Hi Dave, compliments of the season to you,' cries an elderly woman across the road from the church. A council lorry passes and the driver peeps his horn. At which, Christie offers a wave, almost visibly embarrassed by the fashion in which, wherever he ventures in his beloved domain, he is the lord and master of all he surveys. 'How are you doing, Dad?' yells Niven McNaughton, one of the merry band who stormed the citadels at Lord's, albeit from the sanctuary of the toilets, as the match progressed towards its dramatic climax.

'I'm fine, Niven, just doing away as normal. What you see is what you get.'

Never was a description more truly applicable than in the case of this fellow, Christie, who has lifted a trophy at cricket's spiritual home, lent his name to an entire housing development, jested at more functions than Dorothy Parker, and been pursued for autographs across Fife, whilst he has striven to combine his job as painter and decorator with the 1001 chores which are regularly required to steer Freuchie CC towards a secure future, without dwelling dewy-eyed on a halcyon day in London 20 years ago.

That, of course, is as unfeasible, in the circumstances, as the idea of Christie moving away from Freuchie. He tried it once, after marrying June, his wife of 46 years, but couldn't bear to live in Markinch – all of two and a half miles away. Since when, his hair may have turned a smidgeon greyer and the lines on his forehead are slightly more pronounced, but in every other respect 'Dad' is wearing remarkably well.

The sobriquet originated when David's son, Brian, had earned his spurs in the Freuchie Firsts. In the changing-rooms, the youngster would inquire of his father and it was 'Dad' this and 'Dad' that, to the extent that the other team-members copied his example. 'I was happy about it, because it helped increase the bonds which we had forged within the side and we genuinely were a family, so what was the harm in a bit of mickey-taking?' says Christie. 'Mind, it was a bit different when my grandson, Graeme, started playing for the Seconds, and all the guys began calling me 'Grandad'. To me, that was too reminiscent of Clive Dunn and old chaps sitting in rocking chairs with their cardigans on. But hey, I look back and think to myself: "Blimey, where has all the time gone?"'

Well might he ask. But Christie, a spry, wiry 68-year-old has neither the ego nor the inclination to waste breath indulging in *recherche du temps perdu*. Instead, replete with the insouciant pride of a true sporting nonpareil, allied to the down-to-earth demeanour which saw him laughing at his Village Cup charges being labelled the 'Mean Machine' (the bowlers) and 'The Animals' (David Cowan and Stewart 'Jasper' Irvine – the nickname originated from his blazing red hair), he habitually rolls back the clock and speaks languorously of his addiction to cricket without forgetting to focus on the next generation of wannabe Lord's larrikins.

'There are always the questions: Why Freuchie? Why has the game taken root here with such a vengeance that football is an activity the cricketers play to keep fit during the winter, rather than the other way around? But, basically, I turn these inquiries full circle and respond: "Why ever not?" I was born here in 1936 and brought up here, and the gate out of the primary school led to the Public Park and if the weather was fine, we were taught in the open air, and the kids grew up surrounded by people practising in the nets, or rolling the pitch, or cutting the wicket,'

says Christie. 'Well, it was no huge mystery why so many of us
became involved with the cricket club and from the age of five
or six, I would have one eye on my maths and English books and
another on the cricket.

'At the outset, I just watched, because there was no junior
team – this was during the Second World War, remember – but
from the age of 12 onwards, I started to keep the scorebook for
the Second XI and I would pack my whites and patiently await
my chance. One day, we travelled up to Newburgh, and we
were a man short, and I was hooked forever in the space of a
couple of hours. I was No. 11; I didn't bat, all I did was fill in the
details in the book and field, and I even fell in a cowpat when I
was chasing after a ball, and stank for the rest of the afternoon.
But, who cared, I returned home that night with the feeling that
it was the best game in the world. My parents weren't particularly interested in cricket, but they were glad to encourage us and
it must have worked, to some extent. Three of us, myself and my
brothers, Bob and John, have captained Freuchie, as has my son,
Brian, so you can't exactly describe it as a passing fad.'

This was another time, another place, when only the gentry
possessed televisions and phones were a rarity, and Christie filled
his hours either by reading comic books, if the weather was *really*
foul, or practising for hours on end, oblivious to what was
happening outwith his own private heaven. Every Monday,
Tuesday and Thursday he sprinted along to the ground where,
under the tutelage of Bob Keith, Freuchie's seasoned opening
batsman and bowler, he and a string of other lads would strive to
prise a sixpence from under their mentor's nose. Scottish football
may have unearthed its tanner-ba' players, men in the mould of
Jimmy Johnstone and Jim Baxter, but here was the cricketing
equivalent and, while Christie was an amateur, with no desire to
leave his environs in search of bigger rewards, he was unstintingly
inured to hard graft.

'Old Bob was a canny soul – he knew that the boys might get
bored if the game ever turned into a grind, so he used to put a
sixpence on the middle stump and tell us it was ours if we could

get him out,' recalls Christie. 'Well, we tried our hearts out all night, because the money was worth having in those days, but Bob would stand, quite purposefully, in front of the stumps with his pads and it was virtually impossible to hit the wicket. What we learned later was that he was driving home to us the message that cricket required discipline and commitment as well as enthusiasm, and, whilst one of us might eventually win the tanner, he was damned sure he was going to make the task as difficult as possible for us. No matter, we slogged our guts out in the process, and if we returned home tired, our parents were happy. It meant we weren't up all night, yakking about sport and wondering how much pocket money we would need to buy a bat.

'With hindsight, it was Bob Keith and Bob Tully who started me on the road to becoming a cricketer. The former was as tough as old boots; he hated losing his wicket, whatever the circumstances, and we were brought up with the philosophy that we weren't merely playing for ourselves, but also our community, and when you are living in a small village that counts for more than in the cities, where you can vanish into the night if the result has gone against you, and nobody knows your name. Tully was the First XI captain and, my God, he was hard as hell. If you turned up late, he bawled you out, if your whites were dirty, he rammed home the message that they had better be the colour of snow the following week, and if you dropped a catch . . . let's just say there wasn't a whole lot of "Bad luck, old boy" in his vocabulary. But if you persevered and demonstrated the right amount of application, both the Bobs acknowledged the fact. Neither of them was big on speech-making, but we would have trodden on hot coals for them and there are hundreds, if not thousands, of cricketers in this area, who owe those lads a huge debt.'

By 1954 Christie's dedication and sheer reverence for the game had allowed him to advance to the Firsts, but even then he was the resident last man in, meriting a place solely on his athletic, never-say-die fielding, which would later become a feature of all the Freuchie teams he captained. Weeks passed, months elapsed, and as he travelled with the team Christie was gradually introduced to the more outlandish arenas for cricket in the Kingdom of Fife, from the beach at Elie, where matches are still staged in the middle of summer, as long as the tide permits – under the watchful gaze of Richard Philip, the infinitely enthusiastic host of the Ship Inn – to the slightly surreal experience of competing in Burntisland, a popular holiday destination in the period prior to mass air travel to Europe and cut-price package tours to Benidorm and the Greek islands.

'I guess that it was a wee bit strange; you would be standing on the links at the sea-front, trying to hold your concentration, whilst women in prams walked over the pitch, or Glasgow visitors strolled up to you and asked for an explanation of the rules in the middle of a match,' says Christie, whose sanguine description of these interruptions suggests he would have played in a blackout had somebody supplied him with a miner's lamp. 'Sometimes a lad who had enjoyed a touch too much hospitality in the Burntisland taverns would wander erratically onto the field, and, occasionally, there might be one or two spectators shouting abuse at us, but that was never a very smart move – after all, there were 22 of us, we had cricket bats and we knew how to use them if there was any danger of an altercation developing into something worse. But all that was important was the fact we had a match, a pitch, opponents to lock horns with, and the opportunity to share a beer after the battle was finished. That is one of the beautiful things about cricket – it has a rhythm, a continuity and a pattern all of its own, and it moves at its own pace. And there is always the chance to rub shoulders and have a drink with the person whose head you have been aiming to knock off for the previous three hours.'

Unsurprisingly, Christie has always found leaving his roots a wrench. Having completed his apprenticeship as a painter and decorator with J. & W. Forrester of Markinch, one of the recurring themes espoused by him and his colleagues is a collective attachment to Freuchie, irrespective of whether it meant relinquishing ambitions of international recognition. Down the generations, from Bob Keith in the post-war years through to Scott Gourlay's decision to remain, limpet-like, within shouting distance of the Fife hamlet, even though he might have collected 50 Scotland caps had he joined one of the leading Edinburgh or Glasgow teams, Christie and his kin have relished the role of parochial champions. In which light, one can empathise with the disorientation felt by 'Dad' when he was conscripted by the army for National Service in 1957. One might as well ask George W. Bush to excel on the stand-up comedy circuit or beseech Gordon Ramsay for calmness following a salmonella outbreak in his kitchen as inquire whether Christie was comfortable, either on a posting in Germany for a year, or while stationed at Windsor Castle. But, in keeping with this pragmatic character, he bit his lip, counted down the months and, exuding the same patience he had exhibited on the Freuchie periphery in the prelude to Bob Tully eventually flinging him the ball in a First XI match against Dunnikier focused on the single thing guaranteed to banish the tristesse and speed up the process of heading home.

'I played cricket, didn't I? Loads of it. As soon as the military chaps had discovered that I was mad keen on the game – and I never stopped dropping hints and reminding them of the fact – they fixed me up with a place in the Scots Guards Battalion team and we participated in a league in Kent, tackling a string of the clubs along the south coast,' says Christie. 'Most of the lads involved were officers, and I was one of the few NCOs in the ranks, but I made the best of the job and, for the first time in my career, I was able to show the English that Scots could play a bit, which was always a motivating factor for me, either then, or when Freuchie were participating in the Village Cup.

'In the 1950s, the general attitude down there was that cricket and Scotland went together like whisky and wine. The majority of the soldiers knew that cricket happened in the North, but their condescending remarks made it clear that they thought we were useless at it. In all my time at Windsor Castle, I only met one other Scot – a laddie called McCubbin from Glasgow, and I lost touch with him – but I have to admit that I was always delighted to grab a catch or take a wicket or hit a few runs if it was an Englishman on the receiving end. Not for any nasty reasons, you understand, but to prove my belief that there is absolutely no reason why Scots should not be as good at cricket as the English if we put our minds to it. Let's face it, we are the same shape, we both love our football and our rugby, and we are as competitive as hell when it comes to knocking seven bells out of each other in sport. So why exclude cricket from the equation?'

In 2008, this opinion has been reinforced by the clutch of Scots – amongst them Dougie Brown, Gavin Hamilton and John Blain – who have succeeded in making an impression on the English county circuit, while Craig Wright and Ryan Watson's Saltires have enjoyed a decent sequence of victories over their professional rivals. Yet, 40 years ago, there was no question of achieving victories over these sides, let alone pushing Pakistan to the point of near-defeat in 2004, as the precursor to beating another Test country, Bangladesh, at Raeburn Place. Instead, Christie and his Freuchie personnel were involved in an endless sequence of friendly games, the majority of them contested on uncovered surfaces, which perhaps explains why the annals are littered with recitations of teams crashing to humiliating totals in conditions where crash helmets and chain mail would hardly have ensured their safety.

As Christie is honest enough to admit, he thrived on these paddy-fields masquerading as cricket pitches. One afternoon, whilst performing against Townhill, he found his rhythm quickly and, for the next half hour wreaked havoc on his opponents. One wicket fell, then two, three, four, and so the carnage continued, until the bowler had dismissed the entire team – for just four runs. 'It was one of these experiences where everything works in your favour: the ball was swinging all over the place, it was a green, nasty surface, and I landed the ball in the right spot. You never imagine that you will grab all ten wickets, especially considering that bowling was our strong suit, and there were plenty of guys in the teams who were desperate for a piece of the action, but you have to grab these occasions by the scruff of the neck, because there were other afternoons where I beat the bat 20 times and didn't get a single nick, and matches where catches were spilled, or the batsmen had the run of the luck and you were left tearing out your hair. I have never really checked on whether that analysis is the best ever recorded – I was concerned about the team, not myself – but it's true that I was pretty chuffed at the death. I am not kidding myself though, the pitches definitely suited the bowlers most of the time and that's why the newspapers were packed with results where one side made 58 or 65 and the other team couldn't chase down the target. It was a bit different at some of the big clubs in the cities, where they could afford covers and employed full-time ground staff with their schools, but frequently, in Fife and further north in Scotland, some of these pitches were stinkers and you have to remember this was in the days before we had helmets.'

Certainly, Ross County's cricketers will have cause to rue that fact as they recollect the grisly events of their North of Scotland League game against Elgin in May 1964, where the hosts batted first and amassed a reasonable, if not apparently earth-shattering total of 145 for 5, prior to the proceedings taking a dramatic twist to rival anything from the fevered brow of M. Night Shyamalan. Granted, Elgin's pace attack, in the shape of postal worker Bernard Woolfson from Norwich, and Forestry Commission employee, Dave Murray, were both experienced campaigners and perfectly in tune with their surroundings, but neither could have predicted the rout which would subsequently unfold. Up strode Woolfson for his first ball. 0 for 1. In rushed the seamer again and clean bowled the No. 3. Normality resumed for the remainder of the over, but Murray then delivered a wicket maiden, and three further wickets fell to his opening partner as Ross County's innings disintegrated in an ecstasy of fumbling incompetence and shattered stumps. Murray, by this stage realising that something special might be in the air, only required one more over to finish the match, grabbing another trio of

victims and, given that the hapless visitors had arrived a man short
(perhaps he had experienced a premonition), they were kaput
without breaking their duck.

One observer, Andrew Ward, who later chronicled this
debacle in *Cricket's Strangest Matches*, wrote:

> Ross County deserved praise for their sportsmanship. Most of
> their away fixtures involved travelling between 100 and 200
> miles. The home team were glad their opponents had turned
> up, so they could play cricket, let alone beat the longstanding
> record for low scoring. In 1896, Kinross had mustered just one
> against Auchtermuchty, while Arbroath United had totalled
> two against Aberdeenshire in 1868. But Ross County had
> gone as low as it was possible to go.

Christie and his club have been the architects of many similar
demolitions, but although Freuchie's squad had become well
known across Fife and the east of Scotland by the start of the
1970s, they were itching to test their mettle at a higher level.
Hence the jubilation around the Public Park as the members
learned of the formation of the National Village Cup competition, one of those concepts which immediately strikes one as
being so stunningly, marvellously effective it was remarkable that
nobody had dreamt of it before. The basic premise of the
tournament revolves around bringing together the best village
sides from Scotland and Wales and uniting them in battle with
their English counterparts, who obviously represent the vast
majority of the entrants. 'The idea and organisation came from
Ben Brocklehurst of the *Cricketer* magazine, and Freuchie and 16
other Scottish villages [defined as having a population of less than
2000] joined over 600 English and Welsh ones to form the
largest adult cricket competition in the world,' says Allan Wilkie,
the meticulous Freuchie secretary. 'The sponsor for the first six
years was John Haig, whose home was only four miles from us,
but despite the extra spirit his [whisky] company's involvement
gave us, we didn't enjoy much early success in the competition:

in 1974, Terry Trewartha threw a cricket ball over 100 yards to earn the reputation of being the village player who could throw the ball farthest, but as for the team's displays, there was a steep learning curve which had to be negotiated.'

Indeed, these early forays scarcely suggested that Freuchie would eventually be acclaimed as champions of Scotland, let alone Britain. In 1972 they lost to St Boswells in the Tartan section, a reverse repeated at the hands of Ellon, Crathie and Falkland in the next three seasons. 'It was a real eye-opener, but the lads recognised they had to get off their arses and sharpen up their act in every department. At the very outset, one or two of them had actually gone around telling the Freuchie folk: "Och aye, we'll get to Lord's, no problem, just watch us." Sheer bloody presumptiousness!' says Christie, whose sojourn in England during his period of National Service had taught him the scale of the challenge.

'Finally, in 1976, we won the Scottish group, by triumphing over Falkland at home in front of a fervent, incredibly vocal crowd, with the cars parked up at the boundary edge, and that was a sign that we were improving and getting to grips with the opposition. We had a team which had all grown up together and we knew our strengths and weaknesses, and although we didn't live in each other's pockets there was this powerful *esprit de corps* developing between the lads, which increased as the seasons passed by. Terry [Trewartha] became head coach, and he was the best man in the job we have ever had, so the results from 1980 onwards testified to how we were bridging the gap between ourselves and the English teams. It was hellish tough, mind you, and the rivalry in Scotland was pretty intense. In fact, if I'm being honest, I thought that Meigle might win the whole competition before we did, and I wasn't getting any younger by the time we entered the 1980s. We had endured a torrid patch in the Village Cup, and between 1977 and 1981, I know that I was growing seriously frustrated at the disappointments. I was 44 by then and you might have seen the banners emblazoned with the slogan 'Remember Bannockburn'. Well, a few folk in and around the clubhouse were beginning to joke: "No, we don't, but why not ask Dave Christie – he fought in it." Funny, eh! The curious thing is that I still felt as fresh as a daisy when I woke up every Saturday.'

Freuchie, at this juncture in their history, had elected to go for broke. No more internecine warfare within Fife for them, or reliance on deteriorating facilities. First, they joined the Ryden East League, which presented them with regular jaunts to Edinburgh and beyond. Secondly, they carried out extensive improvements to their ground and clubhouse and, under Trewartha's tutelage, individuals such as Dave Cowan began to attract the attention of the international selectors. Overall, this was the onset of a new professionalism in Scotland, albeit without cash payments to the locals, and Cowan was soon associated with his country's early, faltering footsteps over the minefield of tough-as-teak English counties in the limited-overs Benson & Hedges Cup. The question, now, was whether these adjustments would spark an upturn in Freuchie's fortunes.

'I suppose that we could have lost heart, given our early tussles with the English village sides, because there were no easy pickings against these boys. All that "Bally good shot, old man" and cosy cream teas at the interval was a million miles removed from the atmosphere at these places and there was no doubt that the prize of playing at the home of cricket was a massive incentive for every single side in the competition. In 1981, for instance, we were away to Sessay, near Thirsk, and they absolutely pulverised us, putting on 171 for the first wicket, and never remotely letting us into the game. At the climax, once we had trudged off the pitch, we all just sat there in the dressing-room, bedraggled, knackered and demoralised. You could have heard a pin drop. I recall somebody spluttering out: "God Almighty, if that's what we have to beat to get to St John's Wood, then we might as well pack it in, because we'll never manage it." There wasn't a dissenting voice until we had all climbed onto the bus, and I simply spelled out the message to the boys: "Look, lads, we lost today and we deserved to lose. They were much better than us. But nobody ever reckoned that this would be a piece of cake. We just have to go home tonight, knuckle down, practise longer and apply ourselves more to the task. If we don't, we had better accept that we will go nowhere in this competition. But listen boys, I don't think any of us are quitters and the key factor from this debacle is that we absorb the lessons from what Sessay did to us and ensure there is no repeat." Half an hour later we were singing together and our spirits were rising.

'In short, we were in it for the long haul, and although we lost to Meigle the next year, it was in 1983 we genuinely showed that we could win the Village Cup. In the Scottish final we had to travel to Kintore and we beat them comfortably. Then – and this was a major breakthrough for us – we went to Lindal Moor in round 6 [where Christie opened the batting and struck an unbeaten 70], then Kirkley in round 7, and were emphatic winners on both occasions, which demonstrated we could be successful on English soil. I had never really doubted we could climb up the ladder, and by this stage it was a simple job to be the captain of Freuchie. In fact, any of the other guys could have done it, because we were such a well-oiled machine. We had been a loyal band of brothers for four or five years, the same small squad of 12 or 13 players, and, as a consequence, whenever we took the field I never had to tell any of them: "Go there, or there." They knew what was what, we had an incredible bond, and if I decided to change the bowling, they all moved accordingly. Maybe they looked up to me because I was some kind of elder statesman, and they all paid extra attention to me because of my seniority, but there was a rising conviction that we didn't need to be afraid of anybody.

'Granted, we were beaten by Sessay – again – on their own patch in the quarter-finals that summer, but the margin was just 29 runs in this instance and it was obvious that we had cleared a significant psychological hurdle. I think the English teams started to recognise it as well, and there were fewer of the cheap jokes and 'Daft Jock' references flying around. But there again, it was a pretty good time for Scottish sport in general. Aberdeen had just beaten Real Madrid to lift the European Cup-Winners' Cup [Dundee United would subsequently reach the 1987 UEFA Cup final, signalling life outwith the Old Firm vortex], and Scotland, under Jim Aitken, won rugby's Grand Slam in 1984. So there was this confidence amongst the Freuchie boys that we were contenders and we were 100 per cent prepared to burst a gut to make sure cricket also came to the party.'

Harking back to the pictures of Christie from that vintage, there is a notable resemblance to Stewart Granger and even now, in his late sixties, he remains a handsome character. Other players may have been ripe for sledging – the cricketing term for verbal intimidation – but the Freuchie captain lacks the essential ingredients for the insults to start flying, not being bald, or fat, or ugly. The Australians, predictably, are the global masters of this nefarious craft, and once, when Ian Botham marched out to the wicket, the boisterous, moustachioed Rodney Marsh greeted him with the one-liner: 'Hello Beefy, how are your wife and my kids?' On another instance Shane Warne, not exactly Twiggy himself, was trying to tempt Sri Lankan batsman, Arjuna Rana-tunga, out of his crease, and asked wicket-keeper Ian Healy for advice. 'Put a Mars Bar on a good length and that should do the trick.' However, one of the Aussies' favourite sons, Glenn McGrath, fell victim to a terrific riposte from Zimbabwean batsman Eddo Brandes, when he screamed at his opponent: 'Why are you so fat?' Totally unfazed, the chicken farmer fired back: 'Because every time I fuck your wife, she gives me a chocolate biscuit.'

All this is designed to demonstrate that John Major, the former prime minister whose arrival at Test matches invariably preci-pitated a dire England collapse, could hardly have been more addle-headed in his doomed efforts to steer the country back to a time when maiden aunts cycled to church on Sunday evenings, whilst cricketers swapped pleasantries on the village green and supped tankards of warm ale in the tavern afterwards. No doubt there still exist doe-eyed ingénues who believe that the summer game is an ocean of tranquillity and civilised behaviour – these people probably also dwell under the misapprehension that Major and Edwina Currie spent hours discussing the price of eggs – but Christie has seen enough and heard enough to appreciate that cricket can be as much a haven for unabashed bampottery as Ayrshire Junior Football and as packed with X-certificate cursing as an average episode of 'Deadwood'.

'It's nonsense to pretend there aren't places I never want to visit again. One of the worst was Bardsey, north of Scarborough, where the atmosphere was horrible all through the match [in 1995], and we were just glad to reach the bus and get the hell out of there as quickly as we could,' recalls Christie with a sad shake of his head. 'You expect banter and a few slanging matches to erupt when the tension starts to crank up, but this was something else; it was naked hostility, and I had to instruct the lads to ignore all the flak and abuse, because we wouldn't have stood an earthly if a fight had broken out. Their supporters were frightening, and it was as if they had been bearing a grudge since the previous summer, but they beat us at Freuchie in the quarter-final, so I don't know what their problem was. Eventually, I had to move one of the fielders, Blair Forrester, a Second XI regular who had been drafted into the Firsts at the eleventh hour, because the spectators never stopped screaming abuse at him, when he was standing down at the boundary. He is bald and a little rotund, and he was taking dog's abuse – there was effing and ceeing and the works – and finally Dave Cowan, who had plenty of experience at national level, walked over to Blair and said: "Right, I'll take your place."

'Well, Dave was wearing a pair of spotted pants under his whites, so you can envisage that the idiots in the crowd latched on to that and one guy in particular began shouting "You nancy boy" and "You spotty-panted poof" and worse. Until, at the end of the over, Dave marched straight over to the boundary fence and eyed this guy up and down, before saying forcefully: "Do you know where I got these pants? I took them off your wife last night." The boy was fuming, but Davie is a tough nut, and although I was a wee bit worried that we might have a repeat of *Braveheart* on our hands, he stood his ground, stared the Englishman out, and there was a brief lull before the expletives resumed.

'The other nightmarish visit was to Kington, right on the Welsh border, which is just a godforsaken spot where we fought out a semi-final battle and lost the game in 1993. The circumstances there were rather different from those at Bardsey, because a group of lads had gone away to play football and by the time they returned to the cricket ground they had been at the beer and lager and were clearly seven or eight sheets to the wind. There had been a pretty poisonous atmosphere even before they inflamed the situation, but things got ridiculous as the day wore on. The Kington officials were forced to send for extra police, and I honestly feared that we were going to get our heads kicked in. Our young boys were sitting at the front of the boundary, and they were shaking and shivering, the more so when the football clan started coming up and pouring pints of beer – or I assume it was beer! – over their heads. Fortunately, they were booted out of the competition shortly afterwards, not that it did Freuchie much good, because they weren't a village, they were a town, and it was ludicrous they were involved in the tournament. I mean, they had 18 pubs. Eighteen, for heaven's sake! Whereas here, we have one hotel, one pub, a village store, and that is about your lot. But, of course, many of these places are being transformed by housing developments, as people look to escape from the cities. It means that the whole environment of these communities is changing, and I suppose that is progress, but some of the sides in the Village Cup are so desperate to book their passage to Lord's they seem prepared to do anything to gain an advantage, whether fielding ringers or disguising their real populations. It is clearly a concern for the tournament, but Freuchie hasn't changed significantly in the last two decades.'

That much is indisputable. As Christie continued his conversation, Niven McNaughton sauntered into the Lomond Hills Hotel, shortly to be joined by Andy Crichton. Then, in a blink, the company was swelled by the presence of Stewart Irvine. It was a triumvirate of the 1985 heroes, whose tributes to their skipper were as effusive as Halle Berry on Oscar night and far more sincere. 'This man here would sleep in the clubhouse if June would let him,' said McNaughton, as Christie turned a vivid shade of red. 'If he tries to convince you that anybody could have captained Freuchie in the 1980s, don't listen to him for an instant! The fact is that Dad has poured his heart and soul into a hundred different tasks, and he instilled in us the idea that we could be the kings of Britain. There is hardly any role at this club which he hasn't performed throughout the last 50-odd years [one noticed a momentary wince from the man himself], and not a single person in Freuchie who wouldn't raise a glass to toast his contribution to the village.'

For his part, Crichton offered a scarcely mentioned facet of the admirable Christie: 'He makes everybody who comes to the village feel welcome, even if he winds up with a sore head the next morning. After Lords he was awarded a gallon bottle of whisky which he held onto, assuring his team mates that it would make a good door-stop for his hotel door. On another occasion, whilst on tour in the north of England, he allegedly lost his false teeth after a drinking spree and he had to crawl on his hands and knees to the bedroom – it was a minor miracle that he didn't crash on somebody else's room at 4 a.m. We have entertained Ian Botham at the club and the pair of them clicked immediately: they had a million stories and they wanted to spend all night sharing them.'

These testimonies exemplify the qualities which Christie has brought to Scottish cricket and explain why Stewart Irvine branded him 'simply unique'. Even the Scottish Cricket Union, with whom he has not always agreed, holds the man in lofty regard. 'Dave still played and captained regularly until the mid-1990s, and during his stint as leader, Freuchie had a deserved reputation amongst opponents and umpires as being hard, competitive, but totally fair and sportsmanlike,' says their official, umpire and bibliophile, David W. Potter. 'Dave has never had any time for tantrums or any sort of loutish behaviour, and his captaincy and leadership skills were not unlike those of Mike Brearley, but his greatest contribution to Freuchie and Fife cricket lies in his encouragement and development of youth, something which has yielded a rich harvest of talent and is continuing to do so. His painter and decorator's vehicle has often been used for transporting youngsters, even at the very young softball level, and the affection in which he is held (not least in neighbouring Falkland) speaks volumes for him, not merely as a cricketing stalwart but as a human being who has helped countless others.

'There have been matches which I have umpired in, where he has defused powder-keg situations or gone over to more volatile Freuchie characters and instructed them to button their lips. He is also scrupulously fair and has instilled that trait in his players. I recall one game where the wicket-keeper, Alan Duncan, appeared to have run out an opponent, and the batsman was disconsolately on a slow trudge back to the pavilion when Alan called him back, explaining that he had dislodged the bails with his pads. In another tussle, Dave seemed to have taken a clean catch at silly mid-on, and I was ready to give the verdict in his favour, but he simply smiled at me and remarked: "I don't think there was any bat on that, so I am not appealing." None of this should give those who don't know Dave the impression that he is soft. What he *is* is a gentleman and I don't believe you will meet any opponent who would disagree with that estimation.'

Christie's life, whether working with Brown's of Leslie, or Scott and Simpson of Markinch, has been resolutely unglamorous away from the cricket square. But, as he retorts, how many other amateur cricketers have been blessed with the chance to hoist a trophy at Lord's or bask in the company of Botham, Tom Graveney, David Gower, Graham Gooch, John Edrich, Terry Alderman and too many others to relate? 'I like to speak my mind, and I am under no illusions that one of the reasons why I have enjoyed success with Freuchie is because I never had the brains to think about doing anything else,' he says, laughing in the self-deprecating manner which epitomises this blithe man.

'No disrespect to anybody, but we don't have a lot of folk moving here, so we have to rely on our own people, who are a wee bit dottled or thick, and they have to restrict their ambitions to labouring or plumbing or painting. That's just the way it is.

'All right, Terry Trewartha was a teacher and Alan Duncan a social worker, so I exclude them from the previous comments, but I don't think you could find a more working-class team if you scoured the length and breadth of Scotland. What counts is that there is a rare passion for cricket and for constantly bringing players through the system, because I want the club to be here long after I am gone. Yes, 1985 was a fantastic achievement, but it would be nice to do it again in 2015 or 2025. Just to prove that it wasn't a fluke.'

Only a mean-spirited ingrate would begrudge Christie his pleasure in the miracle that is Freuchie CC. When he isn't painting the clubhouse, or marking the pitch, or hoisting the flag to half-mast when a member dies, he is working with the kids and nurturing the next generation of Fifers in his mould. The suspicion persists that when Dad ultimately departs to the pavilion in the sky, he will be an incredibly tough act to follow.

CHAPTER 4

LOOK COO'S TALKING!

It's seven on a grim January night in Edinburgh and a group of Scotland's leading performers are practising with single-minded intensity at the National Cricket Academy within the confines of Mary Erskine's School. Craig Wright, the indefatigable (if that word hasn't been hijacked, ad infinitum, by George Galloway) Saltires captain, is both working on his own action and nurturing a collection of his country's Wannabe Willises and Waqars in the art of fast bowling. One of these is Dale Cowan, a member of the under-13 squad, whose father, David, sits upstairs and revels in the flowering of his offspring. Just another product from the conveyor belt of Freuchie cricketers, whose passion has been passed down from generation to generation for close on a century.

While the session continued I caught up with the proud father and soon discovered that the 'Coo', as he is universally known in Scottish circles, had memories aplenty of his involvement, not just with the Village Cup-winning side of 1985, but of myriad other occasions when he represented his international team with distinction. There was the occasion when a bunch of bedraggled players arrived at their Northampton hotel, well after midnight, at the climax of a protracted, obstacle-littered bus journey from Glasgow. A few hours later these same stalwarts were tackling, and mastering, the English county in a B&H Cup encounter, which featured a typically rambunctious display from the ever-willing Cowan, who captured three wickets in a parsimonious spell as the Scots emerged victorious by just two runs to record their first-ever away win against county opponents. 'It was a terrific showing from our lads, because these were the kind of tight matches where the more streetwise professionals usually prevailed as the tension kicked in at the end,' recollects Neil Leitch, one of the scorers at the Northants contest, who still has an autographed scoreboard on the wall of his study. 'David came on at a critical stage and bowled really well, keeping the runs down and making regular breakthroughs in his spell [3 for 36 from 11 overs]. The success was genuinely unexpected, especially because Northants at that time had personnel of the calibre of West Indian maestro Curtly Ambrose, Wayne Larkins, Geoff Cook, Rob Bailey and David Capel, but we were always in contention, we deserved to edge them out, and they admitted that afterwards.'

Granted, such triumphs were few and far between. Lancashire were bested at a sodden North Inch in Perth in 1986, but usually these tussles unfolded with all the ghastly predictability of a teenage revolutionary metamorphosing into a middle-aged Blairite. Mercifully though, amid the debris of the SCU's finest collapsing to 150 all out, chasing 300, while being simultaneously outclassed and patronised by their rivals, robust characters in Cowan's mould have regularly proved capable of transcending the mundane, thinking outside the circle, or being plain barmy, in the face of adversity.

How else does one explain the devil-may-care approach which saw Cowan discard his helmet when confronted by Pakistani merchant of menace, Wasim Akram, at that stage plying his trade with Lancashire? 'It was the first time I had ever worn one of those contraptions and it felt awkward and uncomfortable, so I said to myself: To hell with this, I have a bat in my hand and I can always duck if the ball is veering towards my head,' relates Cowan. 'I was out in the middle at that point with Omar Henry [the South African-born naturalised Scot who subsequently became the first non-white to play Test cricket for the Proteas in the post-apartheid era] and Omar demanded a mid-wicket chat with me when he saw me flinging off my helmet. "What on earth are you doing man, this is Wasim Akram you are dealing with here", he told me. To which I replied: "I don't care who it is, that thing is making me sweat and chafing at my neck, so I will take my chance without it." Next ball, I smashed him through the cover area for three runs and, although it maybe sounds like a minor triumph, I felt completely relaxed with myself.

'Don't get me wrong; I wasn't being arrogant or big-headed, but you have to understand that ever since I was at primary school and started playing cricket in Freuchie – my father, Archie, was an all-rounder in their First XI in the 1970s – I developed this confidence and trust in my own abilities. I always reckoned that you shouldn't be afraid of anybody or you would freeze, and Dave Christie hammered home the message that I would get hurt occasionally, but it was simply an occupational hazard. When I was 11, Niven McNaughton was bowling to me in the nets and one delivery reared up and cracked me in the face and smashed my lip. I suppose I was a wee bit shocked, but Dave was calm as you like, he walked me down to the changing rooms, bathed my injury, cleaned up the blood and said quietly: "Right, Davie, this is the first time you've been hit in the mug, but I can assure you that it won't be the last. Now, let's get back out there and start playing again." And I did. I guess I may have been concussed, but they breed them tough in Freuchie and we had the philosophy that nothing would get us down.'

By 1985, the Fifers had demonstrated sufficient consistency during their Village Cup peregrinations to be quietly optimistic of advancing to a September assignation at Lord's, but before they could even entertain such fancy notions they had to dispose of their Scottish opponents. A grand tally of 639 teams had entered the competition, but the Freuchie members were fully aware that, whilst they were favourites in their homeland, brash talk was as cheap and irrelevant as a second-hand Bay City Rollers' LP. Instead, in a message which would be rammed home repeatedly by Christie, it was up to 'The Animals', in the guise of Cowan and Stewart 'Jasper' Irvine and the 'Mean Machine' (their relentlessly disciplined bowling attack) to mask over the top order's occasional predilection for folding like a Jiffy bag. All that could be guaranteed was that Dad's Army would field and catch as if their lives depended on it, and that, if it rained, they would take to water with the efficiency of Ian Thorpe.

There were no problems in the early stages, except a few portents that the weather that Scottish summer would frequently descend to the kind of bleak, all-encompassing squalls and implacable torrents which must have persuaded Roman soldiers, despatched to guard the Antonine Wall, that they had been inadvertently diverted to Hell. After receiving a bye in the first round, Freuchie travelled through incessant driving rain en route to the Ayrshire hamlet of Dunlop (the birthplace of the 2002 Olympic curling champion, Rhona Martin) and, barring a slide or two on the road, the experience was largely trouble-free for everybody, except the secretary, Allan Wilkie, who seemed to shoulder the blame for every piffling inconvenience with the eternal patience of a modern-day Job.

'During the journey my sanity was questioned and my life threatened, and the elements were terrible, but eventually I did manage to rendezvous correctly with my opposite number, and got everybody supplied with a bar lunch. This was in the good old days, when I could fit the team and supporters into a single coach and not even cause enough interest to merit a police escort,' says Wilkie. 'Once we had reached our destination we won fairly comfortably in cold, damp, miserable conditions, which weren't exactly conducive to T-shirts and Bermuda shorts. Dave Christie lost the toss, and we only mustered 142 in our 40 overs, with decent contributions from George Wilson (42), and Fraser Irvine and Terry Trewartha (who mustered 25 apiece). But we dismissed them for just 69, all our bowlers discovered their rhythm, and they never seriously looked as if they would get anywhere near their objective. So, all in all, it was a decent workout, even if the conditions set the tone for the rest of the summer.'

As Cowan relates, there was nothing namby-pamby about these combatants, no recourse to light-meters, nor pleading appeals to the umpires. On the contrary, Scotland's cricketing fraternity are a magnificently steely band, and I remember one jet-black Saturday when Atlas met Haddington in a downpour which stretched on throughout the afternoon. After an hour, several of us in the field were wearing parkas or Mackintoshes, and there was only one logical conclusion. 'Bugger it!' said Bill Ritchie. 'We have to sort this out. Let's go and get some brollies for the chaps.' Anybody passing the ground for the rest of the proceedings would have been mystified as to the rationality of the participants, and the flu cases were stacking up as the evening dawned, whilst catching was rendered difficult for those carrying umbrellas in one hand, but we persevered to the death. Call it as you will, but when summers are as wet as they tend to be in Scotland, nothing as trifling as a blizzard or monsoon is going to spoil our pleasure.

'Aye, that's right, I've gone home after some games and squeezed pools of water out of my whites, but we stuck to the task and the Village Cup was full of instances where teams remained on the field when the weather was absolutely atrocious,' says Cowan. 'The alternative option of a bowl-out, which is similar to a penalty shoot-out in football, never appealed to us, and the other sides felt exactly the same. It's a hell of a way to be eliminated, especially if you've travelled hundreds of miles to fulfil a game, so if there was any prospect of playing on, Dave Christie and his counterpart invariably came to some sort of arrangement whereby we would stay on the field and get the business done, no matter the conditions or the fact that we were all on the edge of darkness.'

Freuchie's next assignment, another away trip to the picturesque domain of Rossie Priory, was amazing only in that the sun blazed down on the combatants, which seemed to dazzle the visiting openers into premature surrender. At 0 for 2, other teams might have been a tad worried, but the Fifers kept their composure, Andy Crichton steadied matters with a composed 55, from 96 balls, and, in tandem with Cowan (46 from 26 deliveries), the visitors eventually reached 163, which was more than ample. The Priory men, lending service to one of Scotland's

oldest cricketing institutions, had been bolstered by Alan Oud-
ney's six-wicket spell, but they never had a prayer during their
reply, being routed for 88, with Freuchie's spinners, Peter
Hepplewhite and Andy Crichton, inducing their foes into a
series of increasingly desperate swipes.

If that was a clinical victory, Freuchie's Scottish semi-final was
a shortlived affair to rival any of Robbie Williams' many flings in
the public gaze. Tackling Breadalbane at Aberfeldy, the Mean
Machine were at their most Scrooge-like, restricting the opposition to a paltry 73 for 7, and, oblivious to the blanket of rain
which gradually enveloped the ground throughout their innings,
George Wilson nudged and nurdled his path to an unbeaten 35
and his team completed an emphatic seven-wicket success without any trouble. One last hurdle remained to be negotiated, in
the shape of Meigle, who were no slouches, but significantly,
Freuchie enjoyed home advantage, and for anyone who has ever
stepped into their auditorium on match days and encountered
the cacophony of biased but knowledgeable support from the
locals, that was no minor consideration.

'You can't over-estimate the influence our supporters had in
lifting us up and spelling out the message that we were playing
for the whole village, not merely ourselves,' says Cowan. 'If you
wanted a space on the boundary to watch the game from your
car, you had to park it on Friday night and, by the start of the
action on the Sunday, the scene resembled a drive-in movie.
There would be 1500, 1600 spectators at these Village Cup
fixtures, and, considering that was more than the entire population of Freuchie, we gradually realised that our exploits were
capturing people's imaginations. They would come from Newburgh, from Cupar, Falkland and Kirkcaldy, in fact the whole of
Fife, and the buzz around the arena was ear-piercing. One old
lad, Dave Peebles, was a particular fan of mine and, amid the
commotion, I could always hear his comments. "Chin up, Davie,
you can get this boy out" if I had just been struck for a boundary,
or "You've got him on the ropes now, Davie," if I had beaten
the batsman twice in a row. He knew his cricket, he never missed

a match, and his approach was a million miles removed from England's Barmy Army, because he kept his own counsel and didn't disturb anybody else with inane chants and raucous songs. But nonetheless, you knew from looking at him that he cared, that it mattered to him deeply. And that spurred you on to greater effort, doing your best to make sure he went home happy at the finish. Perhaps that's one of the major differences between the city clubs and a place like Freuchie: the Glasgow and Edinburgh players usually worked in big offices, where they were anonymous and their interest in cricket could remain a private matter. As for me, well, the chances were that if I played a daft shot on the Sunday, I would be fixing somebody's roof the next morning, and they would be ready to ask: "What *were* you up to yesterday?" '

Cowan may have had nowhere to hide, but he was in the midst of making a significant decision that would affect the rest of his life. By 1985 he was 21, and had exhibited sufficient talent in football to earn trials with Rangers and Dundee United before being offered a contract at Raith Rovers, the Kirkcaldy-based organisation, whose name has grown synonymous with the famous Colemanball '. . . And they'll be dancing in the streets of Raith tonight'. Almost a decade later, these redoubtable warriors would carve out their own niche in Scottish sporting lore by beating Celtic, after a penalty shoot-out, in the League Cup final, thus qualifying for Europe and drawing the exalted Bayern Munich, against whom they scored in the German team's Olympic stadium before slipping to honourable defeat. Yet, although Cowan turned out in their colours for two seasons, under manager Gordon Wallace, the pressures of combining the twin pastimes ensured he had rapidly to choose one or the other. It was no longer a viable option to contemplate emulating the example of Scott Symon, the former Rangers manager, who represented Scotland at both cricket and football, and although Andy Goram followed in his footsteps in 1989, the fact that he was fined by Hibernian boss Alex Miller for appearing against Allan Border's Australians testified to how the soccer calendar was engulfing everything in its wake. The situation has, of course, worsened ever since, to the extent that the summer shut-down appears to consist of a long weekend in June, as the prelude to Sky TV replacing the Giant Tonka Lorry-Driving Challenge from Basingstoke with some spurious World Masters Challenge, concocted solely to pad out the hours and swell the already bloated coffers of the Arsenals and Cheseas of this world.

Hence Cowan's plumping for Freuchie, despite his realisation that there would be less money, a far lower profile and nagging thoughts of what might have been. 'I didn't mind skipping the fame bit, because I can't believe what footballers have to endure, with photographers hanging around outside their houses and tabloid journalists raking through their rubbish bins,' says Cowan. 'I guess I do have a wee bit of regret, but that's only natural in the circumstances, isn't it? I was in the same Scottish Juveniles side as Robert Fleck and Gordon Durie, I met up with Paul Sturrock and Jim McLean during my fortnight at Dundee United, and I was at Rangers when the late Davie Cooper was in his prime. But it's not as if I have missed out entirely on football, when you consider that I have played for Arbroath, for Brechin, and been involved with the Junior scene at Dundonald, and I have made many friends in both sports these past 20 years.

'Andy [Goram], for instance, is a great mate to this day. I remember going to Malahide in Ireland with him in 1991, as part of the Scottish cricket team, and we worked hard and played hard. He was on the verge of joining Rangers at that stage and I travelled to Ibrox with him for his medical and told him: "God, if they take a urine sample, it will come out as straight gin." But he was brilliant company and a lot of the Rangers boys, including Ally McCoist and Mark Hateley, used to pop along to Scotland's matches in Glasgow, and it was clear that if some folk believed cricket was a joke, they certainly didn't.

'Yet, ultimately, the nettle had to be grasped and whatever else I might be, I have never been afraid of sticking to my principles. I had the opportunity of a new contract at Raith, but Freuchie were going strong in the league and the Village Cup, and I was

gaining more international call-ups, so there was no delaying the
inevitable. I arranged a meeting with Gordon Wallace, thanked
him for his faith in me, but informed him that I was making
cricket my No. 1 priority and that ruled out a full-time soccer
career.

'He seemed surprised, but he was a decent fellow. I wouldn't
have wanted to have got on the wrong side of Gordon, but most
of these managers were fine with the cricket. I heard horror
stories about Jim McLean at Tannadice, but he knew the
situation with Freuchie and the bottom line is that I might have
been a reasonable bet as a centre-half in the Scottish League, but
there was – and is – something special about cricket and the
rapport and team spirit which Dave Christie generated. I suppose
that those people who only care about cash, material goods and
bank balances won't understand why I acted as I did, but hang on
a minute: we had a Village Cup to win and that was a pretty big
deal.'

The preparations for meeting Meigle entailed the usual
triumph of meticulous labour and all hands to the pumps.
Despite the team's having been christened 'Dads' Army', there
were no pompous officials presiding over disorganised chaos,
doom-laden Scots and arthritic corporals in this particular regiment. On the contrary, whether in the Stakhanovite work ethic
of Dave Christie's players, under the gaze of their phlegmatic
coach, Terry Trewartha, or the perfectionism of Allan Wilkie
and the rest of the officials behind the scenes, Freuchie's collective ethos provides a stirring antidote to some of the sozzled
blazerati who infest rugby and football in Scotland, dwelling
under the sorry delusion that sport owes them a living, a regular
supply of free tickets for internationals and a limitless drinks bill.

None of which is designed to suggest that Cowan and his
confrères were always paragons of early-to-bed temperance. 'On
one of the Village Cup days, Colin Hepplewhite and I had been
to a party the night before, and you know, when you are really
enjoying yourself, when the music is loud and the banter is
flying, and time seems to disappear . . . well, we realised, to our

horror, on our way home that it was half past eight on Sunday morning,' says Cowan, eyes glinting with mischief at the recollection. 'We walked together down towards the cricket ground and, because we were feeling a wee bit shattered, we decided to have a lie-down on the grass. Next thing, we were dozing off when, suddenly, Dave Christie strolled through the gates, and perked up when he spotted us. "Ah, good on you, lads, I didnae know if anybody would be bothered to set their alarms and come down and help me get the wicket ready." Colin and I both looked at one another and thought: "Jesus, we can't let him know that we haven't been to our beds at all. He'll go through us like a dose of diarrhoea." So we grinned and started mucking in with him and we collected a few brownie points, even though we were knackered.

'In a sense, mind you, that was one of the terrific aspects of playing for Freuchie. That we trusted each other, whatever we might have been doing on Fridays or Saturdays, to get our act together once we stepped onto the pitch. Even when we reached Lord's, the routine didn't change; we shared a few drinks on the evening before the final, and invited the Rowledge captain, Alan Prior, for a friendly beer. Anyway, we were both staying at the Westmoreland Hotel, near Lord's, so Alan duly popped downstairs and met up with Dave Christie at the reception, and you could detect the slight air of bafflement in his expression, before he blurted out: "It's good to see that your supporters are having a good time. I take it that your players, like ours, are safely tucked up in bed." David, cool as you please, simply replied: "No, Alan, these *are* my players, they are just relaxing for a couple of hours." It must have looked funny right enough – we were playing headers with balloons and singing and having a laugh. But so what! We were young, we were pretty fit and we weren't worrying ourselves about special diets and video analyses and all that palaver. To be honest, I sometimes think there's an excess of that in modern sport, where you discuss everything to death, and recruit mass ranks of psychologists and motivational gurus and nutritional experts, and all you do in the process is screw up the

heads of a lot of people. It's like messing with a golfer's swing or
changing a bowler's action. Sandy Lyle had one of the most
beautiful rhythmic swings in the game and look what happened
to him when he started tinkering with it in search of some
mythical improvement. The same goes for Steve Harmison, on
the recent trip to South Africa. The fact is that some people
would love to make sport an exact science. It never will be and
that is one of the reasons why so many of us are in love with it.'

There was certainly nothing sophisticated about The Animals,
Cowan and Irvine, whose double act was nearer to Reeves and
Mortimer than Peter Cook and Dudley Moore. But in their
gloriously idiosyncratic fashion, they terrorised attacks the length
and breadth of Britain by evoking the spirit of the barracking
spectator who once derided the hapless Arthur Mailey with the
observation: "Hey buddy, you've got him in two minds – he
doesn't know whether to hit you for four or six." It might be
true that their tactics were more ideally suited to the tip-and-run,
here-today-gone-tomorrow milieu of the 40-overs format than
they would have been in a longer version of the game, but
whenever critics strive to depict village cricket as a haven for
knock-kneed, wheezy old has-beens or never-will-bes, they
should heed the example of somebody such as Cowan, whose
wickets, on Scotland duty, include Tests stars of the calibre of
Michael Atherton, Chris Broad, Allan Lamb, David Capel and
Robert Bailey. Not bad for an amateur whose day job with Fife
Council in building maintenance is the exact antithesis of his
cricketing incarnation as a devastating wrecking ball with a
willow in his hand.

It was just as well for Freuchie that he and Irvine were on hand
to help rescue their side from another parlous position at a
packed auditorium on a day which ebbed and flowed and
reverberated to triumphalist chants from the hosts and occasional
lapses into stunned silence. Dave Christie's sequence of lost tosses
continued, as the precursor to a hesitant start from his men, and,
despite a belligerent knock of 28 from Fraser Irvine, Stewart's
younger brother, their initial attempts at acceleration precipitated

a collapse to 50 for 4 in the 25th over. 'I can't give you an explanation, beyond a desire to keep everybody interested, but Freuchie have suffered for a long time from this affliction, whereby they revel in shooting themselves in the foot, digging themselves into holes, and making life a thoroughly treacherous business,' says Cowan, who was consistency personified, at least in comparison to some of his team-mates. 'Dave Christie swears that's why he's so grey in the hair these days – it was the amount of worrying and fretting that we put the poor fellow through – and it can't really be denied that if we had the choice of winning comfortably by five wickets with three overs to spare, or by the skin of our teeth in the last over, we seemed to conjure up the latter scenarios with almost wilful regularity.

'Mercifully, however, we usually had the resilience to escape from these situations, and the Meigle match was an ideal case in point. After scrabbling around in edging to 50, we finally started to clout their bowlers into the gaps in the field, and by the end of our innings we had reached 175, with 125 coming off the last 15 overs. It wasn't my best performance by a country mile – I amassed 17 from 9 deliveries, then got myself out just when I was beginning to find my rhythm, but Stewart carried on with a trademark demonstration of his powerful striking, whacking 40-odd [46 from 34 balls] and George Crichton batted sensibly [for 34] to make sure that we reached a decent score. We knew at the tea interval that we had gained a reprieve, but we also realised that there was plenty of unfinished business. Dave said to us: "Right, lads, we have to catch and chase anything which comes in our direction." Then, in the first over of their reply, George Wilson dropped Willie Scott off Niven McNaughton, and the tension noticeably heightened. You could feel it in the air, and our supporters were a wee bit too quiet for comfort. Mind you, when Meigle had advanced to 83 for 0 from 20 overs, you couldn't blame them!'

Under the mask the captain's heart might have been racing, but characteristically Dad switched his bowlers around, brought in his fielders, introduced his spinners and virtually dared the visitors to dominate the psychological battle, not with singles, but by taking the aerial route. The consequence was exactly as he had desired and, befitting the often spectacular transformations which permeate village cricket, Meigle's previous serenity disappeared in a flurry of clattered stumps and shattered dreams. In consecutive overs, Andy Crichton and Pete Hepplewhite had Scott and Ralph Laing – their side's pivotal duo – stumped by Mark Wilkie [Allan's brother, just to enhance the family ties which bonded Freuchie together] for 35 and 37 and the balance shifted dramatically during the next half hour, as their hopes went up in smoke. Andy Crichton claimed another brace of victims, Brian Christie chipped in with two scalps, and on every occasion that Meigle strove to extricate themselves from the shackles, they discovered the quality of their adversaries' throwing in the most painful manner, with a hat-trick of run outs completing a 40-run success for the Fifers. By the climax, a few of the home faithful, who had committed the supreme sacrifice of pledging to purchase a beer whenever their heroes made a breakthrough, were on the verge of entering the Twilight Zone, but the hangovers could wait a while. There was a party to organise.

It may not have been an entirely convincing victory, but this encounter embodied many of the virtues of the whole Village Cup philosophy. Much had happened since Ben Brocklehurst, the publisher of the old *Cricketer* magazine, launched his innovative tournament, identifying suitable hamlets by using his AA directory, but the more some things changed, the more they stayed etched in tablets of stone. Meigle's rapid demise, for instance, merely reflected the reality that the majority of village sides are dependent on three or four stalwarts, accompanied by a collection of futility players: men with no special gift for batting or bowling, whose pinnacle of achievement probably extends no further than struggling into their whites again every April, but who are nevertheless addicted to the sport and blessed with an unquenchable enthusiasm.

Freuchie were better than this, of course. Quite apart from boasting a stingy collective of bowlers – 'We would rather give

away money than runs,' ran Andy Crichton's mantra – it helped
to be skippered by somebody with Christie's pedigree and
intelligence, even if he would prefer the plaudits to be doled
out elsewhere. 'It wasn't my doing, but the feeling was growing
by 1985 that we had assembled an impressive team, and that we
didn't need to fear anybody if we played to our strengths,' he
says, impassively. 'At the conclusion of the Meigle game, we had
achieved the only thing that mattered and we were through to
the English section, but there were areas we knew we had to
improve. That was one of the best traits about that bunch of lads:
they never grew complacent, they always toiled away on practice
nights, and weren't scared of the unglamorous chores. And,
naturally, it was a godsend to have somebody like Davie Cowan
in the ranks, as keen as mustard, reaching for the sky and
dreaming of playing for Scotland as well as his birthplace.'

In no other environment would The Animals have found
their métier to such pronounced effect. Indeed, as the competition progressed, they formed an almost symbiotic relationship,
and pity the poor paceman who strayed short against either of
these left-handers, whose sole mission was to disrupt, unnerve
and demoralise the man 22 yards away. 'There was nothing
sophisticated or genteel about our methods, but cricket's not
rocket science, is it, and you can either seize the initiative by the
scruff of the neck or allow the opposition to dictate the tempo,'
says Irvine, a bluff, no-nonsense larrikin, who looks as if he could
be Paul Scholes' father. 'Davie and I had no difficulty deciding
what strategy we would adopt, and whilst sometimes it came off
and other times it didn't, we both loved batting, and serving up
some entertainment, and if that meant bringing a bit of agri-
culture to the party, what's the problem? The scoreboard ticks
along quicker if you're moving in boundaries, and the Freuchie
set-up, where we would aim to consolidate and lay down a
platform in the opening hour, meant we usually had to get our
skates on. Don't forget, either, we only had 40 overs in the
Village Cup tournament, and we had to make them count. The
trick was to have a platform to blast away in the last 10.'

For Cowan, the partnership offered him an opportunity to flex his muscles and dish out punishment with the relish of Wackford Squeers. He was, first and foremost, a bowler, whose stints on Scotland duty saw him appearing down the order at No. 9 or No. 10, but when lent a sniff of the average village fare, his glee was unconfined. 'I had no illusions, I never reckoned myself to be a Brian Lara or Sachin Tendulkar, and when I turned out in the same Scottish team as Gordon Greenidge, it was a revelation and a privilege to be in the company of a true batting great,' recalls Cowan. 'With Freuchie, however, both Stewart and myself shared an uncomplicated notion. Namely, that if we could manage to knock the bowlers off their stride, surprise them by chancing our arm, and refuse to let them settle, the odds were that they would lose either their discipline or their line – or both – and, if that transpired, we had won half the battle. As you might expect, there were some weekends where we came a cropper, and we would be sitting there in the pavilion in mid-afternoon, cursing in unison and wishing that we had taken a few balls to size up our rivals before trying to despatch them into the Lomond Hills, but cricket, especially at our level, shouldn't be a grind, and, luckily, the chances were, most Saturdays and Sundays, that one of us would succeed and we would make somebody else squirm.

'I was fortunate in that I had a good eye and I recall one league match against Stenhousemuir, where I scored 176 not out from 76 balls. It was mayhem, and the ball was flying to every part of the ground, and the atmosphere was electric. I had gone to the wicket with Freuchie searching for some quick runs, following a century opening stand, and we wound up at 340 for 1, which left their guys looking pretty deflated. The first four scoring shots were all 4s, and they had this Australian professional who persisted in trying to bounce me and intimidate me, which was a wee bit daft, because I just kept bashing him over the fence and he was going nuts when it might have been smarter to pitch it up. My century arrived from 54 deliveries and, although I'm not overly obsessed with individual records, hitting another 76 in the next 22 balls felt bloody good and the adrenaline was really flowing. When I walked off at the end, Stewart said: "Typical of the Coo. We ask him to raise the momentum and he goes totally berserk and lets the rest of us sit around on the sidelines, twiddling our thumbs and itching for a bat . . ." I can't remember whether we actually won that game, but you have to savour these occasions and capitalise on them. They aren't too common in the grand scheme.'

Two decades on from Freuchie's visit to Lord's, Cowan remains an engagingly ebullient boy, replete with stories of Bacchanalian excess, and of forays abroad with Scotland, which didn't always conform to the dour-as-I.M. Jolly regimen of Duncan Fletcher and Nasser Hussain, those Brothers Grimm of the cricketing fraternity. Instead, whilst some internationalists, even several from unheralded Scottish backgrounds, have inclined towards shying away from their roots, and drawing a veil over the communities from which they originated, Cowan's centre of gravity is and will forever be Freuchie.

'Wherever I venture, I'm always thinking about home and when I will be back in Fife. That's just the way I am, and why not, considering my passion for the place? But that doesn't mean I'm averse to travelling abroad, or that I'm some cricketing equivalent of Dennis Bergkamp [the veteran Dutch footballer with a fear of flying],' he insists. 'There was one trip to the ICC Trophy in 1997 in Kuala Lumpur, where Jim Love, who was the SCU's national coach, asked me and Ian Beven to check out the potential of Hong Kong and Bermuda, both of whom we were scheduled to meet later in the competition. We were supposed to be taking notes and analysing their strengths and weaknesses, but it was scorching, we were melting, and Bev said to me: "You fancy a pint?" I said yes, and we spent the next couple of hours exchanging libations while the match was progressing in the background, and we hadn't written a thing and, whoosh, the match was over. What do you do in these circumstances? Return to the coach and explain that you had been inadvertently delayed by an appointment with your landlord? What we did was find the scorebook, scribble down the details on a couple of sheets of paper, and pretend we were au fait with the teams. It sort of worked, but when Bev had to make a speech to the Scotland players, telling them about the teams, I had to sneak away because I was splitting my sides. He had hardly seen a ball bowled in the whole game.'

It would be simplistic to depict Cowan as a peripatetic wanderer with parochial yearnings. Down the years, his CV has become littered with sojourns away from his beloved birthplace, whether on the less-than-magical mystery tours of Scotland duty to English suburbia and the tedium of hotel check-in appointments in faceless locations, or further afield, locking horns with West Indians and Indians and anybody who is content to switch the conversation to cricket. Ultimately, one can detect a slight twinge of tristesse in his footballing reminiscences, which is hardly surprising, given that even the lowly part-timers of East Stirlingshire, slogging their guts out on £10 a week at the rear of the Scottish Third Division, are still paid more than the majority of Craig Wright's Saltires. Yet, if it is undeniable that nobody with a Tartan twang ever entered cricket in pursuit of the wealth of Croesus, Cowan has experienced his own brand of riches, and although many of the villages which used to participate in the national Cup have recently fallen prey to the whims of developers and/or fiscally-challenged councils across Blighty's rural belt, Freuchie hasn't been affected by this malaise to a similar degree.

'A few more houses have been built since 1985, and there is the estate which bears Dad's name – Christiegait – but this community hasn't been destroyed by the bulldozers or converted into some dormitory town, straight from *The Stepford Wives*, and life around the cricket club is pretty much the same as when I was growing up,' says Cowan, whose employment with Fife Council, on myriad roofs, surveying a multitude of vistas, has equipped him to beat the drum for Mark Twain's argument in favour of preserving playing fields: 'The trouble with green space is they're not making it any more.'

'Just as it was then, so it is nowadays; we have a group of talented youngsters emerging at the club and every Friday night, there will be 50, 60, 70 kids, some of them as young as five, waiting impatiently with their gear for a chance to bat or bowl. Sometimes, if you're feeling a wee bit arthritic, there's no better antidote than to venture along to the ground and watch these youngsters bursting with raw energy, and it galvanises you.

'If I have learned anything, it's that children haven't suddenly become apathetic or chained to their computers. If you put in the effort to encourage them, they will be converted to sport, but you have to instil the enthusiasm in them and that requires commitment. At the moment, I'm doing a bit of football coaching with the former Motherwell player, Steve Kirk, at Kennoway, and helping out with the Freuchie juniors as much as I can. I want Dale to have the opportunities that I did, and there is no reason why he can't. This is an exciting time to be involved in Scottish cricket, and who knows how far we can go in this sport? Let's face it, when I was at the start of my career, who had heard of Sri Lanka? Or Bangladesh? Who would possibly have dreamed that Kenya would reach the semi-finals of the World Cup in 2003? I guess that I'm an optimist by nature, but I look around me here at the National Cricket Academy and I am excited and proud that I have played some small part in putting cricket on the map.'

That is one of the pleasures of meeting these individuals. That modesty is their middle name and they are still slightly abashed to be the subject of attention. It offers a nice contrast to those over-hyped prima donnas from football and rugby (and the James Bond films) who dwell under the misapprehension that Scotland owes them a living.

CHAPTER 5

TERRY'S ALL GOLD

'The beatings will continue until employee morale improves.' So read the staff notice on the wall of the Whey Pat Tavern in St Andrews, the home of golf, English students who can't get into Oxford and Cambridge, and Terry Trewartha, the man who coached Freuchie to National Village Cup glory in 1985. A sprightly 55-year-old who has been teaching physical education for a quarter of a century, he might not agree with the sentiment expressed on the pub sign, but equally, Trewartha has as little use for kid gloves as George Foreman. Whether ramming home the message to youngsters during his day job, as Head of PE at Madras College, that sport and health are inextricably linked, or teaching Freuchie's emerging stars two decades ago that runs needlessly conceded are like unfriendly ghosts – they will come back to haunt you – he is steeped in cricket and rugby minutiae and harbours trenchant views on everything under the sun.

Our meeting occurred on 7 February, two days after Scotland's rugby team had been narrowly, undeservedly, defeated by abject French opponents in Paris at the start of the 2005 Six Nations Championship, and Trewartha's hackles began to rise the instant I let him digest an interview with Gordon Strachan, the former Aberdeen and Manchester United footballer and ex-manager of Coventry City and Southampton. 'I have said it before and I have found myself being hammered for it, but the truth that is we are not very good at team sports in Scotland,' alleged the little red-haired firebrand, whose disputatious nature makes the notion of rational debate resemble playing squash with a dish of scrambled eggs. '*Cricket has always been rotten*, rugby's not very good, football's not very good, anything healthy we don't seem to be good at. On the other hand, we are all right at pub games, like darts and snooker. And we are great at heart attacks. In fact, we are world leaders when it comes to heart attacks.'

The italics are mine, but Strachan's words, which otherwise raised a valid observation, were all too typical of the endemic prejudice harboured against cricket by many Scots, and Trewartha's riposte was as rapid as it was sharp. 'It's incredibly unfair to bracket cricket in the same category as football and rugby,' he said, his eyes blazing. 'The last two pastimes involve professional sportsmen who, especially in soccer, are earning thousands of pounds a week, whereas 99.999 per cent of Scotland's cricketers are amateurs who pay for the privilege of picking up a bat or ball, who travel hours across the country to get to matches, and who have all kinds of circumstances against them: the weather, the cost of nets and covers, the ignorance of those who still believe the sport stops at the River Tweed, and the demands of keeping spouses or girlfriends or children happy when you are away every weekend during the summer. [Or, as Denis Norden expressed it: 'October is a funny month. It's when you remember that your wife left you in May.] Frankly, I think it's absurd to try and argue that the thousands of people who love the game should be tarred with the same brush as the national football and rugby teams. If anything, the cricket fraternity has actually punched above its weight.' Precisely!

As you may already have gathered, Trewartha doesn't suffer stuff and nonsense lightly. He was similarly cussed and un-compromising 20 or 30 years ago, either sniping away as an elusive scrum-half at Kirkcaldy RFC, or revelling in the role of rumbustious all-rounder with Freuchie, prior to moving into coaching at both organisations, and his entire life has revolved around nurturing, promoting and encouraging talent. His sur-name might suggest Cornish origins, and he has grown wearily accustomed to being described as 'English' in the press, parti-cularly during the Village Cup conquest, but he was born in Dundee, moved with his parents to Freuchie at the age of four, and bridles at the suggestion that he is some kind of interloper. 'It can be a bit irritating, constantly reading about how you were the only non-Scot in the side, but there again, I have heard people say that Alan Duncan [the Fifers' wicket-keeper] is an impostor, because he was born in Glenrothes, so I guess there will always be those who don't regard me as being pure Freuchie flesh and blood,' said Trewartha, displaying the sort of mystified countenance one associates with Frasier Crane after his latest inamorata has dumped him. 'My father hailed from Lancashire, and I really can't recall a time when I wasn't involved with the cricketers in Freuchie, because I was keeping the scorebook for the Second XI when I was eight, and playing for the youth team from 11 or 12 onwards. It was just taken for granted that if you went to school in the village, you would want to drift over to the clubhouse and that taught me an important lesson. Namely, that there's no reason why kids won't develop an interest in sport if you capture their attention early enough.

'In that respect, I suppose it was unbelievable how many cricketers were produced by Freuchie in the 1960s and '70s. Precious few didn't catch the bug, and it was like a giant conveyor belt of children rushing out of the classroom and straight onto the pitch. Dave Christie always seemed to be in and around the club, and if he wasn't actually playing, he would be cutting the grass, or painting the square, or doing something which the rest of us would have considered pretty tedious. But that was just his approach to the game and it filtered through the whole system. Every night in the summer, it would be him or Bob Keith or Bob Tully and if you showed any enthusiasm, they would fling you the ball, and most of us were fixated. Why not? Cricket in Scotland has nothing to be embarrassed about and there are more players per head of population in Aberdeenshire than there are in Yorkshire, so if we're a minority, we're a very large minority.'

Trewartha's restless spirit has steered him in a variety of directions – he moved from Freuchie to Fifeshire as a teenager, and subsequently joined detested local rivals Falkland ('Which was akin to a criminal offence', he remarks, not wholly in jest),

whilst guiding Kirkcaldy into rugby's Premier League in 2000 –
but the litany of achievements on his curriculum vitae brook no
discussion as to the quality of his coaching and motivational skills.
By the mid-1970s he had become a regular part of Dad's Army,
and irrespective of Freuchie's struggle to make an impression
during their fledgling assignations in the Village Cup tournament, the nucleus of a formidable squad was patiently,
methodically being assembled. A dramatic transformation had
materialised by 1985 from the team beaten by Etherley nine years
earlier, in which light it was fitting that the Scots drew the same
opponents on the first leg of their quest for qualification to
Lord's.

'It was like a different world, because in the 1970s the Scottish
club which progressed to the national section would invariably
be eliminated straight away, and there was a lack of conviction
that we could take on the English sides, let alone beat them,' says
Trewartha, who, bolstered by Christie's blessing, decided to
focus on two key areas which he was convinced would boost
Freuchie's aspirations. 'Getting the fielding up to scratch was
crucial, and we genuinely put the lads through their paces and
reminded them that there was no excuse for dropping catches or
not throwing accurately. It might sound elementary, but too
many sides just want to bat and bowl when they hold their
practice sessions, whereas we always made sure there were just
three bowling and one batting at any one time – the rest were
focusing solely on fielding and we must have devoted hours
every week to that discipline. We had guys in the team, like
Stewart Irvine, whose hands would be red raw after we had
hurled the ball 100 times at him and he had pouched 99 of them,
and I guess it was similar to how David Beckham kept practising
free kicks in the pouring rain in Manchester until he had
mastered the art. I wouldn't go so far as to say that Jasper never
spilled a catch, but if he did, then I can't remember it. And that
was all down to work, work, work. You just don't acquire that
expertise by accident.

'The second priority was tightening up the bowling and

striving to ensure we restricted opponents to under 150 from their 40 overs, which wasn't easy at the start, but eventually started to come to fruition. There was no great secret to it: we had fathomed that many of the village teams had two or three batsmen who could genuinely bat and maybe one or two others who were big hitters and, in these circumstances, we knew we needed five front-line bowlers, with a sixth in reserve, and no part-timers needed apply. We witnessed the phenomenon, time and time again, of sides who had a couple of good bowlers but had only bits-and-pieces cricketers for back-up, and all you had to do was wait for the first pair to finish their spells, then you could bash the rest all over the park. At Freuchie we resolved that we would never fall into that trap, which helps to explain why the Mean Machine gradually became one of the stingiest miserly attacks in the competition. Perhaps we didn't have any out-and-out whistling dervishes, but they knew their role, they were happy with the system, and generally, they were hard to over-come.'

The batting, it has to be admitted, was never of comparable standard. Many Scots, confronted with the sight of David Steele or Chris Tavaré, Graham Thorpe or Mark Richardson, would agree with Lord Mancroft's assertion: 'Cricket is a game which the British, not being a spiritual people, had to invent in order to have some concept of eternity.' But there was scant danger of the Fife line-up overstaying their welcome, and even during their victory procession to Lord's their progress was regularly imperilled by their top order apparently vying with each other to see who could dash to the showers the quickest. Dave Christie won the toss in the meeting with Etherley and inserted the Englishmen, whereupon Davie Cowan snapped up two wickets in the match's opening three deliveries and the Bishop Auckland side were unable to stem the tide for the rest of their innings, as they succumbed to a meagre 93 all out, with Cowan taking four for 17 and Brian Christie three for 30, on a pitch which suited the medium-pacers.

It should have been a straightforward pursuit, but the word

'cakewalk' clearly wasn't in the Freuchie dictionary. On the contrary, they seemed determined not merely to flirt with danger, but invite it upstairs for a shag, and the next hour proved a sorry tale of wanton self-implosion. Mark Wilkie exited for two, Fraser Irvine mustered one less, Dave Christie was caught by Paul Watson off the bowling of Harry Allen for five, and the large band of home supporters could hardly credit what they were beholding as Andy Crichton and George Wilson both departed without troubling the scorer. At 21 for 5, a trip to Lord's seemed as remote as the Outer Hebrides, but fortunately Cowan and Trewartha steadied matters and demonstrated that they weren't playing in a minefield.

'We had been in these situations before, and the match was very much back in the melting pot, but we recognised there were loads of overs left and we had the suspicion that their change bowlers wouldn't be as effective – heaven knows, we had to believe that was the case – so I told Davie: "Right, we have to get our head down here and graft, let's have nothing fancy, nothing extravagant,"' declares Trewartha. 'It wasn't our natural game, given that we both liked to be aggressive and give the ball a thump, but there was no option and, mercifully, the remainder of the attack wasn't in the same league, so our task grew more comfortable as we occupied the crease. Davie finished with an unbeaten 44 and I finished with 31 not out, so by the death it sounded like a relatively simple triumph. But, if they had possessed one more bowler with the ability of Watson and Allen, we would have faced a genuinely testing examination of our credentials.'

That tussle was a microcosm of the virtues and vices in Freuchie's armoury, yet, in their defence, the club's deficiencies were transcended by their camaraderie and collective resilience in the midst of adversity. Better still, although Dave Christie had issued an edict proclaiming that his foot-soldiers shouldn't mention either of the 'L' words, Lord's or London, Trewartha had noticed the glint in the eyes and spring in the step of his charges. It would, he surmised, require a bloody good side to undermine their ambitions and sap their confidence, especially if the linchpin, Cowan, kept fit and healthy.

All these qualities were sorely examined in the next round of the tournament when Cleator, from Cumbria, came calling to Fife on an afternoon straight from the worst excesses of *The Day after Tomorrow*. Heavy rain had enveloped the Kingdom for the previous 24 hours, and it was a tribute to the ebullience of the participants that they elected to continue playing through conditions which were more suited to Ellen MacArthur and her seafaring odysseys than cricket on the village green. 'You can imagine what Michael Vaughan or Graham Smith would have done in these kind of circumstances. They would have stayed in their dressing-rooms until the umpires had checked their light meters and abandoned the game,' says Cowan, whose philosophy is based on the theory that if Freuchie had marched off the field every time the heavens opened, they would have fulfilled around three fixtures every season. 'Fair enough, if you're in a Test setting and it's your livelihood, and you happen to see Steve Harmison or Shaun Pollock sprinting towards you in the midst of a blackout, it might cause you to order some brown trousers. But Cleator were in the same boat as us (almost literally!). There was a serious incentive for them to disregard the weather, because nobody wanted a shoot-out at the end. So, we all pulled together and adopted an attitude that the show must go on. Yes, it might have been a wee bit hairy, and you had to be careful to avoid drowning when you dived for the ball. But it was the same for both of us and we had worked our backsides off on the Saturday night clearing rain from the outfield.'

Amidst the mud and glaur, with Freuchie being invited to bat, there was a horrible sense of déjà vu as the hosts slumped to 5 for 3 in the space of the first 30 fraught deliveries, with Fraser Irvine, Alan Duncan and George Wilson back in the pavilion. 'We were in trouble, no doubt about it, and when we went off for 13 minutes, with the rain pelting down, it seemed for a wee spell as if the day was going to be a total wash-out,' says Dave Christie, who had surveyed another miserable collapse, despite changing the batting order. 'It was a nervous time for the lads, and I knew that the forecast for the rest of the day wasn't brilliant, but I met up with the boys from Cleator and they were as desperate as us for the match to continue and be settled properly, not artificially. So that was it, the die was cast and rather than throw in the towel, we bit the bullet and marched back to the fray. Seventy-five overs were subsequently played in lashing rain in front of several hundred fans, who couldn't tear themselves away although they were soaked to the skin.'

The ensuing contest was as engrossing as any of Freuchie's challenges, complete with a magnificent display of derring-do from the ubiquitous Cowan, who ignored the elements and launched into a cavalier demolition of the Cleator bowlers when the action resumed. Never one for sophisticated kidology or mealy-mouthed gestures, the left-hander held his patience until his side were 14 for 3 after 10 overs, at which point he grabbed the game by the collar and remoulded it through the sheer force of his personality. The next ten overs yielded 48 runs, the ten after that 65, as Cowan illuminated the darkness and cheered up the shivering masses on the sidelines with a series of imperious drives, pulls and hooks which allowed Freuchie to recover rapidly from their abysmal opening. The onslaught lasted a mere 80 balls – and it shouldn't be forgotten he had been a paradigm of studied stoicism at the outset – but by the time Cowan was eventually caught on the mid-wicket boundary, his swinging in the rain had amassed 94, including six 4s and six 6s, during a stand of 132 with Andy Crichton, the steadying hand at the other end.

'They made us work hard at the beginning, but if the ball was in the zone, I was going to give it a good smack and the longer the innings progressed, the more I felt in control,' says Cowan. 'You shouldn't underestimate Andy's contribution, because he had walked to the wicket in a crisis, dropped anchor, pushed hard for the singles and allowed me plenty of the strike, and that established the platform, from where I could let rip. I was a wee bit annoyed when I got out, not because I missed out on a hundred, but because I was seeing the ball as big as a melon, but

Andy kept the momentum going and carried his bat for 57, and although we lost a few wickets in the final overs, 180 wasn't bad. It wasn't great either, but at least we had given ourselves a chance in the second half and we knew that we had the target on the board and that our bowlers weren't drenched.'

Much of that testified to the fortitude of the younger Crichton, a mechanical fitter whose contribution to the Freuchie cause might have been overshadowed by some of the more voluble characters around him, but whose limpet-like refusal to surrender his wicket, once he had settled into the groove, was clearly a genetic phenomenon, given the manner in which his brother, George, repeated the routine as the tournament continued. Most good sides boast these taciturn individuals – the inscrutable fellows who push a single here, prod a couple in the deep there, or divert the ball down the legside for the occasional boundary, all performed with such classic understatement you think they have scored 5 or 6, then glance at the scoreboard and notice they have 25 or 30 to their name. It's a cherished attribute for the storm-tossed village side, inclined to horrid collapses, and yet Crichton could hardly be more modest about his qualities.

'It's horses for courses, isn't it? I couldn't have gone out and tried to clatter sixes all over the field, but I knew where my stumps were, and it normally didn't take very long to fathom if Davie Cowan was ready to light the blue touch paper and, by God, when that happened, he was a fearsome adversary at Village Cup level,' says Chrichton. 'Once he had his eye in, all he was concerned about was peppering the boundary and yet he wasn't just a slogger. In the Cleator match, for instance, he was fairly introspective at the outset – Freuchie were in a hole and the English opening bowlers were no mugs. But, gradually, Davie found his range, and, if you were standing at the other end, you could just sit back and admire the power and strength with which he struck a cricket ball. In an hour, he had transformed the nature of the game and dragged us back into contention. After he was out, I kept my head down and returned to keeping the board ticking along. Maybe it wasn't showy and there were rarely

pyrotechnics when I was at the crease, but Davie and I were the
only two Freuchie batsmen who hit 50s in the competition in
1985; we thrived from having different people in the mix and we
can't all be flashy showmen. I was soaked by the conclusion of
our innings, but Dave Christie gave me a quiet pat on the
back. He appreciated that, in our different ways, we had built a
platform.'

Back on dry land, Trewartha also remained quietly confident
that the Scots would prevail, yet nobody could have surmised
how the dénouement would leave all the combatants on tenter-
hooks. Once again Cowan, maturing with every passing week,
perfected his peerless Scrooge impersonation, taking a wicket in
his first over, and recorded an analysis of 2 for 10 from his
allocation. But, unfortunately for the locals, Niven McNaughton
failed to muster any similar rhythm, found it mission impossible
to bowl uphill in the prevailing conditions, and was hastily taken
off by his captain after conceding 13 runs in his opening over.
That proved the cue for the introduction of Brian Christie, who
confirmed his burgeoning reputation with an economical spell,
but Andy Crichton's efforts at spin, amid squalls out of Force 10
from Navarone, bore all the subtlety of washing crystal in a
cement mixer, and, for once, the Mean Machine looked stran-
gely vulnerable. At the climax of the 28th over, Cleator were 115
for 3, with Jim Cummings in menacing nick, and, with the
visitors requiring 66 from 72 deliveries, the stage was poised for
one of those feverish finales at which Freuchie specialised.

'It might sound as if I am speaking with the advantage of
hindsight, but, regardless of the scoreboard, I always had the
notion we would find a saviour throughout the 1985 campaign. I
mean, all our games against the English sides were at home and
that was worth around 20 or 30 runs for starters, and apart from
their cricketing ability, there were a lot of confident characters in
our team, who never thought about the possibility of defeat.
"Hard men" may be the wrong description, but guys like Davie
Cowan and Stewart Irvine and Dave Christie knew exactly how
to get the best out of themselves, and they weren't scared of

getting their hands dirty, which was just as well in the Cleator match, because we were absolutely encrusted in mud by the finish of it,' says Trewartha. 'There was also another element which can't be disregarded, where the chance of beating the Sassenachs offered an extra incentive for the likes of The Animals and Geordie Crichton, and the truth was that the Scottish crowd backed them up. The 'Battle of Britain' nature of these fixtures definitely added fuel to the fire, especially as we began to progress in the Village Cup, and it was no longer solely about Freuchie, but a bandwagon effect took over. The same thing happens whether it's rugby's Calcutta Cup, or whenever Scotland and England are pitched against each other in football, and I reckon that half the country would be hooked to their TV screens if they showed two snails climbing up a wall and one was wearing blue and the other red and white.

'I noticed that sense of nationalism rising as our victories stacked up. I would meet people in Cupar and Kirkcaldy and other parts of Fife and they would congratulate me and say: "Aye, we popped along to Freuchie last Sunday. It was brilliant. Keep beating these English buggers." It was an eye-opener, but, for once, cricket, which until then had been distinctly low-profile in Scotland, gained an opportunity to enjoy countrywide support and there wasn't a backlash. People were genuinely thrilled at the team's success, and it was a roller-coaster ride, because the crowds kept getting bigger and bigger, the matches grew tighter and tighter, but the one constant in the equation was the rain, and as Scots, we are always likely to thrive when the skies pour down their worst on us.'

With the prospect of a highly-charged climax looming, Dave Christie turned to the one person he knew could be relied upon to listen to sage advice and remain sensible. Himself. Disinclined to retreat from the spotlight when the pressure was increasing, the veteran bowler backed his own judgment and although the bedraggled spectators could hardly bear to watch – whilst those in the comfort of their cars had switched on their lights, as the evening beckoned and the players took a necessary diversion into the Twilight Zone – his decision was partially vindicated, even if the statistics from his next three overs appear the stuff of Penn & Teller. In his first, Christie went for 12 runs, but claimed a Cleator scalp; in the second, he celebrated a double-wicket maiden; and in the third, he was pelted for 16 runs, as both sides remained neck and neck. Trewartha, meanwhile, snapped up the menacing Cummings, trapped lbw for 60, but these Englishmen were a tenacious bunch and with four of their 40 overs left they required a mere 18 runs, and Cowan and Trewartha had finished their work for the day.

It was time to go against the tide, hence the captain's recall for Niven McNaughton, who had been standing, agitated, forlorn and freezing, since his early problems. 'I was cold and wet, but then, so was everybody else inside the ground, and I jumped at the chance to get involved in the action again, because I was pretty worried that I had blown it for Freuchie at the start. It was one of these situations where you are either going to emerge as a hero or an arse and I was in my own backyard, so I was bloody determined that I wouldn't be the man who blew it for his team-mates,' says McNaughton, efficiently summarising why his club were such imposing adversaries in these Village Cup tussles. 'I found it easier to keep my length and line, coming down the slope, and only conceded four runs from my first over, and Dave Christie managed the same, but I have to admit I was getting seriously apprehensive when they scored four runs off the first five deliveries of my last over and were sitting on 175 for 7 with seven balls remaining. We all knew we couldn't hope to contain them without taking wickets and it was time for a big push. I ran up, my heart pounding, but with the adrenaline flowing and, lo and behold, clean bowled Allan McCartney for 9 and I went a wee bit berserk for a minute or so.

'That put the pressure back on Cleator – they needed a run a ball and Dave was a wily old fox in that scenario. Their tail-enders clearly hadn't been told about the Freuchie fielding, because they went for a suicidal second run and their batsman was never in with an earthly of making his ground: we were well used to throwing in wet balls! That effectively sealed their fate and the skipper wrapped matters up three balls later. But it was a damned close thing and it could have swung either way at the death. I still remember seeing a photograph of Dave thanking the supporters for braving the elements after we had beaten the Cumbrian champions, and there was a decent party in the clubhouse that night. The next morning we began to hear one or two of the locals mentioning the dread words "Next Stop Lord's", but we genuinely ignored the hype and hysteria, even if the residents in the village were obviously becoming excited, along with the media. We just focused on playing cricket, full stop, and I appreciate that the phrase "taking one match at a time" might be a cliché, but it surely constitutes a far more sensible approach than buying your postcards before you've gone on holiday.'

Freuchie's hard-earned success had allowed them to advance to the quarter-finals, but the dearth of whooping and hollering testified to the influence of Trewartha behind the scenes. As he recognised, there were weaknesses, which had to be rectified before they could contemplate a trip to London and it wasn't enough to rely on a couple of performers to keep their ambitions intact. 'Don't get me wrong, the spirit in the team was terrific and these boys had risen up the ranks together, but we knew there was no room for complacency, particularly with our next opponents [Oulton] coming from Yorkshire. I suggested that we try and organise some extra practice sessions and, credit to them, the lads were as keen as mustard on the idea, even though some of them were shattered by the time they had finished their work at the quarry or with the council,' says Trewartha, whose coaching philosophy is closer to the quiet persuasiveness of Ian McGeechan than the boot-kicking, hair-drying diatribes copyrighted by Sir Alex Ferguson.

'But that enthusiasm explains why Freuchie have had sustained success since the 1970s. Working with the youngsters, our aim was always to try and make them better players than the people who were already in the First XI and it created a structure where we managed to bring through one or two new faces every season. You need that in sport, whether it is cricket, football or rugby. Yes, you need continuity, but you also have to be cajoling the kids to be hungry and to be chasing the places of the established stars. If you don't, you inevitably wind up stagnating, and I have never overstayed my welcome anywhere, because I happen to think that too many sports clubs rely on the same small base and that if that shrinks away, you will ultimately be left with nothing.

'The Freuchie officials understood that 40, 50 years ago and they have reaped the benefits of their foresight. My three sons, Craig, Gary and Grant, all came through the youth set-up, and even while the 1985 team was being fêted across the land, we were actively developing a string of talented youngsters who would be ready to fill the boots of the 30-somethings down the line. Indeed, within the next three or four years, Scott Gourlay was earning international recognition as a teenager, Alan Duncan Jnr was making a name for himself, and if there has been one message which has come loud and clear from this village, it is that you should never, ever rest on your laurels.'

One wishes this counsel had been heeded by the SFA and SRU, both of whom have slipped into ignominy, largely as a consequence of their officials blaming the teachers' strikes of the 1980s for leaving the voluntary sports sector under-staffed: a blatant piece of buck-passing, which, as a teacher himself, Trewartha recognises in all its flummery. Nonetheless, he has first-hand knowledge of the debilitating effects of successive governments failing to invest properly in sport and confesses to worrying about the future in a land where the supply of raw talent seems to be drying up. 'I have heard that Freuchie are still attracting lots of kids to their training nights and that is really heartening, because elsewhere there appears to be a culture mushrooming in which youngsters won't turn up for practice unless they're promised a free T-shirt at the end of the evening,' says Trewartha, whose job description has been transformed in the last decade. 'I'm not really one for being pessimistic and falling into the trap of arguing things were better in my day, but cricket has to study the likes of Freuchie and use their template as a model, because it is astonishing what such a tiny place has achieved.

'On the global stage, you look at Australia and the importance they attach to sport, and keep tabs on the success they achieve, and you soon appreciate it can't be a coincidence. But in Scotland, we talk a lot, and agonise a lot, but there isn't the same political will to make hard choices and invest significantly in sport and leisure. Living in St Andrews, I know the Scottish Executive is putting a lot of cash into golf and, in my opinion, they aren't reaping a huge reward from that venture. So we have to sit down and formulate a strategy for the future, and not waste our breath lamenting the sickly state of Scottish sport.

'That is where the Freuchie story is so revealing and instructive. Their success didn't come to pass because they had millionaire investors, or players born with silver spoons in their mouths. It happened as a result of Bob Keith and Bob Tully and Dave Christie spending countless hours at the coalface, for no reward other than the satisfaction of knowing they had sparked something magical, and that is the true glory of 1985.

'After all, on the road to Lord's we weren't the most naturally-gifted collection of cricketers you will ever come across. Not by a long chalk. But, by heaven, we were competitive, we were as proud as hell of our heritage, our roots and the community which had nurtured us. There were eight or nine of the side living in the village at the time and they must have bumped into one another nearly every day of their lives. That breeds a kinship and a dedication, but it also means that everybody knows what everybody else is doing. So you have to avoid growing too insular and stuck in the same groove. The important thing about being a part of Dad's Army was that we struck the correct balance and, from a coaching perspective, I couldn't have asked for more. Yes, the lads shared a couple of beers on the nights before matches, but I trusted them, they loved their cricket too much to go gallivanting to nightclubs until four in the morning and I didn't change the routine, even when we had qualified for Lord's. Why should I? We had faith in each other and a mutual desire, so I didn't have to be some martinet, laying down orders and insisting on curfews. It worked for Freuchie.'

At the end of November 2000, Trewartha surprisingly stood down as coach of Kirkcaldy RFC, who were, at that juncture, lying fifth with 24 points in the Premier Division. He had been involved in fostering such talents at Beveridge Park as Scotland internationalist Gordon Simpson, and had been the catalyst for the Fifers scaling the heights of domestic rugby, albeit for a brief period. Since his departure he has been otherwise engaged with a mounting level of bureaucracy and educational programmes at Madras College, and Kirkcaldy have suffered relegation and struggled to maintain their standards at a time when many other clubs are withering on the vine of falling attendances, spiralling debts and apathy.

It would be easy to link Trewartha's resignation with the slump, but the man himself has other ideas. 'Basically, I needed to get my life back, because rugby had been taking over, to the extent it was occupying nine or ten months of my year. It wasn't like the old days before professionalism arrived [in 1995]. All of a sudden, there was video analysis and fitness schedules to worry about, and organising extra training sessions, and it had grown too time-consuming,' concludes Trewartha. 'It was the same in cricket, and though I used to help out with the youngsters at both Freuchie and Falkland, the school activities have to take precedence over anything else. I'm actually quite optimistic about Scottish cricket: the Saltires getting into the NCL with the English counties has been a big fillip and I've noticed lots of young folk wearing the cricket gear and that can only increase if we qualify for the next World Cup in 2007. But, personally, nothing will top 1985. It was everything I had expected, and then around 50 per cent more, from start to finish.'

The Dundonian impostor may dwell in St Andrews now. But one suspects that Terry Trewartha has never really left Freuchie.

CHAPTER 6

THE SON ALSO RISES

Alan Duncan was a busy fellow in the autumn and winter of 1984 and onwards into 1985, adding a 100-square-metre extension to his house in Freuchie. Day after day, when he wasn't plying his trade as an office sales manager, he and his wife, Ann, would spend hours transforming the appearance and specifications of their residence. Christmas passed in a whirl, and the New Year was celebrated in peremptory fashion. The couple had more pressing priorities than partying and besides, as Alan recalls, he was desperate to have the redevelopment completed in readiness for the new cricket season.

Predictably, therefore, he paid scant notice when he started feeling increasingly tired and lethargic around the middle of March, convincing himself that he was merely suffering from the debilitating effects of candle-burning at both ends. Yet Duncan's apprehension increased after he participated in a few matches the following month and was dead on his feet by their climax, overwhelmed by an exhaustion that the lithe little wicket-keeper had never experienced before. Eventually, his condition grew so distressing, after a tussle with Glenrothes, that he visited his doctor and was immediately rushed to hospital for a series of tests. It might have been the demise of his dreams of helping Freuchie to Village Cup glory, but all he was concerned about was discovering the cause of his fatigue.

At first, the medics were baffled: the scans were inconclusive and he was released a fortnight later with the vague advice to take things easy. In the next few days, he was stricken again and his anxiety mounted. What on earth was happening? 'It wasn't pleasant, to say the least, nobody seemed to have much comprehension of what was wrong, and that just added to my concern. But finally, after an incredible amount of tests, it was discovered that I only had one kidney [which was now inflamed] and for the next few days everyone was really worried,' says Duncan, with the understatement which is his trademark. 'Around this time, Freuchie had won the Scottish final against Meigle and I was starting to resign myself to the fact that I would miss out on the competition because the doctors told me I wouldn't play cricket again that season, which left me fair depressed. They gave me antibiotics and other pills, and placed me on a special diet, and strove to reassure me with the information that I had nephritis [inflammation of the kidney], but that I was certainly in no mortal danger if I behaved sensibly and paid attention to their treatment. All of which was pretty little consolation to me as I lay on the sidelines.'

In Duncan's absence, Mark Wilkie wore the keeper's gloves and was impressive in the victory over Etherley, while his team-mate watched forlornly. Yet, if there is one general characteristic which defines these Freuchie personnel, it lies in their fortitude, their ferocious determination to surmount obstacles, laugh at adversity and spit in the face of medical diagnoses. Throughout his spell in hospital, Dave Christie, Terry Trewartha and the rest of the squad rallied round their afflicted confrère and urged him, reticently, behind the nurses' backs, to force himself back into contention for the later stages of the Village Cup. It may not have been the most logical or sensible counsel, but it paid dividends. Boosted by his tablets, spurred on by Dad's Army, and motivated by an underlying feeling that 1985 was destined to be Freuchie's vintage summer, he made a significant improvement, was granted permission by his GP to begin practising once more, and in the space of a few weeks had returned to competitive action. Against the odds, and regardless of warnings to recuperate slowly, Duncan appeared in the merciless rain which greeted Cleator, ignored the elements to assist his side in reaching the quarter-finals, and has been merrily accumulating victims ever since (over 1100 at the last count), oblivious to the effects of the medication he will require for the rest of his life.

'Obviously, it was a shock to hear that I only had one kidney, but apparently, this isn't that uncommon – around three in every thousand people have the same problem and manage to lead normal existences. Ann was an absolute treasure during the illness, and the Freuchie lads . . . well, to be honest, if you have never grown up in a tiny community, it might be difficult to appreciate how close we were to each other,' says Duncan. 'Some may think that it's suffocating or believe that you wouldn't be able to go anywhere without having your privacy invaded. But when the chips are down, and when you need friends and companions to lift your spirits, you could not have asked for better support than what was offered to me by my mates at the club. They visited me every day, cajoled and encouraged me, and we had a laugh together, and although there was a period where I genuinely feared that my career was in jeopardy, they made all the difference.'

Restored to rude health, Duncan and his colleagues were agog, in the post-Cleator euphoria, for news on who their opponents would be in the quarter-finals. Yet there was to be no swift resolution to the question. Indeed, within hours of the dramatic finale at a sodden Public Park, where both teams had braved horrible conditions, the Scots were disgruntled to learn that their two potential North Yorkshire rivals, Oulton and Cropton, had postponed their match without showing the slightest inclination to start, let alone finish, the proceedings. Allan Wilkie duly contacted the tournament organisers at the *Cricketer* to register his club's dissatisfaction with the situation and was rightly scathing of the Tykes' attitude. 'Even on the Saturday, when our East League match was washed out, there were a lot of our club members out in the murk until late at night, clearing water from the outfield and doing their utmost to make sure we would be able to fulfil our Village Cup fixture, and it is irritating that all their labours were in vain,' says Wilkie. 'I always used to think that Yorkshiremen were tough customers, but this episode painted them in a poor light. For heaven's sake, if we called a halt every time the weather intervened, we would spend far more time in the pavilion than on the pitch. But we had to wait another week to face Oulton and let's just say that we were utterly determined to ram home the message that this isn't a game for wimps.'

The county of Trueman and Hutton, of Brian Close and Geoffrey Boycott and, more recently, Darren Gough and Michael Vaughan is, of course, renowned as one of the great bastions of cricketing tradition, but Freuchie's derision was by no means unique. Down the years, there has always been something intrinsically laughable about the parochialism of Yorkshire's one-eyed wonders: rather like Welsh rugby teams, one never actually beats them, merely scores more points. Michael Parkinson, who springs from their stock and recognises the traits which typify his compatriots, tells the story of one Yorkshire cricketer who began to harbour ideas above his station after receiving his maiden England cap. The trip to Lord's changed him completely but he was, at heart, a rustic buffoon who once looked out of his bedroom window and pronounced: 'The rain is terrestrial.' His team-mate looked dumbfounded. 'Surely you mean torrential?' he asked. Whereupon the new England star shrugged his shoulders. 'It's all imperial to me.'

Trueman, meanwhile, invariably resembles an embittered graduate from Curmudgeon College, forever lamenting the death of an England that never was and echoing the philosophy of the golfing doyen, Henry Cotton, who lamented: 'Can't stand those fellas who jump on the bowler when he has taken a wicket. It's like assistants at Harrods mobbing a chap when he has sold a tie.' In these buffers' spheres, Freuchie were probably regarded as jumped-up oiks with the impertinence to believe that cricket and progress are not mutually irreconcilable, that winning matters more than taking part and that their advance to Lord's was not the collapse of civilisation as we know it.

If anything, the tardiness displayed by Oulton merely cemented their doom, because although the Scots were forced to dig deep in the majority of their Village Cup matches, there were no seismic tremors after the Yorkshire side arrived, belatedly, in Fife. From the moment Dave Christie won the toss and inserted the opposition, this was an afternoon when his son, Brian, seized his opportunity to thrust himself into the spotlight, and the consequence was sporting carnage on an extravagant scale. The visitors were in contention for roughly 20 minutes, during which time their openers, Ian Hunt and Paul Faulkingham, amassed a stand of 25, but as soon as the latter had been bowled by Dave Cowan for six, the ensuing collapse was as spectacular as Junior's spell.

'We were a wee bit under the cosh in the early overs, but there are days when you feel you can do almost anything with a cricket ball, and this was one of them. I had Hunt caught behind by Alan Duncan for 22, and after that we just seemed to relax, and it was as if they had had the stuffing knocked out of them,' says Brian. 'Suddenly they were dropping like flies, I slotted into my rhythm and I was swinging it all over the place, and we were in total command. I kept waiting for somebody in their ranks to fight back, and implement a recovery, because we figured out that if they were in the quarter-finals, they must be a pretty handy team, but there was nothing in the tank. The lad, Hunt, was comfortably their top-scorer and by the climax, when I wrapped up their innings, they had only managed 73 and I had figures of 6 for 15 in 7.2 overs. These occasions where everything clicks into place don't occur very often, but when they do and the crowd are chanting their approval and the boundary edge is littered with hundreds of your fellow-villagers, it's a magical sensation. There haven't been many better days than that.'

Or, paradoxically, worse ones if you happen to recognise the scenery in *Last of the Summer Wine*. As soon as Hunt had been removed, the ensuing procession proved as swift as it was depressing for the visitors. Peter Lloyd was bowled neck and crop by Christie for four, the same tally attained by John Baddeley, before he snicked to Duncan and the Fife supporters were in their element at the mayhem being perpetrated by

Number One son. Chris Stead briefly hinted at a revival, but perished against Trewartha on 13, as the prelude to the same bowler knocking Steven Preshaw's stumps out of the ground without another run being added. In previous seasons Freuchie might have slackened their grip a little, but they had developed the executioner's mentality and Christie mopped up the tail with ruthless precision, dislodging John Fox, caught and bowled for three, and accounting for the Oulton captain, Peter Grainger and Mark Baddeley, both for ducks. In the midst of this debacle, Doug Greasley was methodically run out for four, just to emphasise the multifarious menaces in the Freuchie armoury, and it was a crestfallen bunch of Englishmen who convened for tea and shortbread.

'I still think it would have been a very different story if we had won the toss in these conditions, because the pitch was doing a bit, we had some talented bowlers of our own, and I am convinced that we would have posed them serious problems if they had gone in to bat first', says Grainger, whose recall of the match is diametrically opposed to that of his Scottish counterparts. 'Don't get me wrong, they capitalised on the conditions, and fair play to Freuchie, 1985 was the making of them, and they were a fiercely competitive bunch, but the way the coin landed had a massive bearing on the outcome.'

This isn't exactly the recollection of both Christies 20 years later, to such an extent one is tempted to inquire whether there was another confrontation with Oulton in a parallel universe. As somebody who spent a week on jury service back in 1999 and heard apparently sober, respectable witnesses proffering hopelessly contradictory testimony, to the stage where it was easy to brand them all as a pack of liars, I realise it isn't that unusual for human beings to indulge in selective amnesia or plain forgetfulness, but even so, the variations in the memories supplied by Grainger and Freuchie are quite amazing. 'Och, there's no doubt the Oulton match bucked the trend, we were in control from beginning to end, and I was as surprised as anybody, considering their reputation. The game just seemed to pass in a flash, and we hardly had to do much more than turn up and, basically, it was a stroll in the park,' says Dave Christie. 'They appeared ill at ease, they had no stomach for the fight, no passion, and whereas Cleator were clearly a well-marshalled side who you could imagine marching on to Lord's, my remembrance of Oulton is that they fell apart like a house of cards when Brian came on to bowl.

'He was an undemonstrative lad, not given to loud appeals or extravagant gestures and, perhaps because he was my boy, I always felt that Brian had to do better than the other guys, so that I couldn't be accused of showing favouritism. Maybe that was harsh on him, as if I was striving too hard to be impartial, but on his day, when the wind was in the right direction, if it was coming off the hill, with a nice gentle breeze, you could bring him on at the bottom end and pretty much wait for the wickets to fall. Against Oulton, for instance, he was thoroughly in his element, and afterwards a couple of the Yorkshire supporters told me that they hadn't seen a better exhibition of swing bowling, outwith the English county circuit, in 30-odd years of following cricket, so yes, he was masterly in that game, and they barely knew what had hit them. Frankly, we stuffed them, and while we had plenty of hard scraps in the Village Cup that year, this was the exception.'

There merely remained the task of chasing 74 for an unprecedented qualification to the semi-finals, and although torrential rain briefly interrupted the proceedings Alan Duncan and Mark Wilkie were soon walking to the middle, safe in the knowledge that their mission was nearly accomplished and that the dark clouds would be no impediment. Time, gentlemen, please, for some gentle prodding to third man, a few comfortable singles here and there, and a sedate progression to their goal, perchance? Hah! This is Freuchie, lest anybody sleepwalk into Wonderland. With the Baddeley brothers operating in tandem upon the resumption Duncan continued his inauspicious form, caught by Faulkingham for zero, off Mark, whilst John bowled Andy Crichton, with a single to his name, to reduce the Fifers to

5 for 2. 'It was a bit mortifying and embarrassing to keep returning to the pavilion without bothering the scorer, and the rest of the lads quickly spelt out what they thought of my efforts,' relates Duncan, who had suffered the same fate in the previous round (and would do so in the next). 'George Wilson ran a JCB business and he actually popped round to my house and asked me if I wanted him to dig a pond in my garden for all the ducks, which was quite funny with hindsight, but wasn't especially hilarious at the time. The sole conclusion I can reach is that I was a bit rusty after missing so many games with illness, but it was one of the defining characteristics of the down-to-earth atmosphere in Freuchie that the same boys who had showered me with sympathy and best wishes were the first to slag off my batting displays.'

Fortunately, Mark Wilkie and the aforementioned Wilson knuckled down to forging the partnership which would confound any lingering Oulton optimism. Both sensibly eschewed flamboyance and settled for a prosaic approach and it was a measure of the visitors' mounting frustrations that their sibling duo stumbled into their own version of Men Behaving Baddeley, whilst the Scots kept schtum and observed the internecine warfare with the satisfaction of winners-to-be. 'The brothers were highly-strung, tense individuals and they began arguing with each other the closer we moved towards our target, which was a sure indication that they knew defeat was inevitable,' says Duncan. 'You have to appreciate that village cricket is a testing environment, with intense rivalries, and that there will be days where things go wrong, where the conversation isn't confined to pleasantries, and where matters eventually grow heated. It's in the nature of the beast, and the Baddeleys didn't behave any worse than scores of other cricketers over the years, but it was a bit curious to watch them flinging insults around at their own players. In psychological terms, they might as well have hoisted a white flag.'

As Freuchie passed 50 there wasn't quite an abject surrender, but despite the further loss of Wilkie, caught by Faulkingham off

John Fox for 20 and Wilson, safely pouched by Greasley from Mark Baddeley for 23, the climactic scenes exemplified the mixture of insouciance and indomitability which the Fifers possessed in abundance, with Dave Cowan savouring the opportunity to polish off the match with a symbolic gesture of his team's superiority, majestically striking a six to complete the job. 'I knew we had plenty of overs at our disposal, but what the hell, if the ball was in the slot, I wasn't going to pussyfoot around, and it sent out a resounding signal to the rest of the teams in the competition: Watch out, Freuchie are on the march!' says Cowan, who finished unbeaten on 15. 'I hadn't been pleased with my bowling earlier in the day, but the encouraging thing about our side was the fashion in which different people came to the party whenever it was required. Honestly, Brian performed superbly from the moment he began his spell and it was his match, his triumph, which explains why we all rushed to congratulate him at the death. At that precise moment, I don't think we were looking too far ahead, and although lots of jubilant Freuchie spectators were parading around afterwards, chanting slogans along the lines of: "We're going to Lord's", the players were simply glad to have beaten Yorkshire opponents, because we had endured some torrid clashes with them in the past. Of course I would have been mightily disappointed if I had been involved with Oulton. That is understandable. But ultimately a six-wicket win, with tons of time remaining, is an emphatic victory in anyone's language.'

It was a heaven-sent moment for Brian Christie, whose knack for havoc-wreaking had been implemented with his normal reticence. One of the curses which pervades sport, at any level, is prima donnaism: the feeling that the world revolves around a player's every haircut, holiday, passing whim or political opinion, which helps explain why large numbers of Britons have grown so weary of the Beckhams, Henmania and the deification of Paula Radcliffe and the tracks of her tears. Even at a lower grade, whether in football, rugby or cricket, most clubs have at least one member who fancies himself as a notch above the rest, oblivious to whether the evidence is flimsy to non-existent. Yet, in Freuchie's case, whilst Dave Cowan had graduated to the ranks of professional football and Terry Trewartha would later steer Kirkcaldy RFC to the premier division of Scottish rugby, the egos were grounded on a permanent basis. It wasn't simply that Dave Christie's charges recognised that, whatever their heroics on Sunday, they would have returned to drudgery and civvies the next morning, but also the priceless ability of Scots in general, and Fifers in particular, to treat flannel with scorn and deflate swollen heads at a hundred paces. Some commentators have criticised this trait – and the likes of Sir Sean Connery and Billy Connolly habitually blame the press for spawning a cesspit of negativity and cynicism – but, personally, most of the people I have met in journalism are delighted to lavish praise and accentuate the positive when it is merited. Just don't ask us to be shiny, happy people in the same breath, as we glance over the obesity figures, or the blight of sectarianism, or the litany of other social problems afflicting Scotland.

Mercifully, Freuchie is a different matter and anybody would be proud to raise a toast to a modest, unassuming character in the mould of Brian Christie. He had grown up on a diet of cricket, just as his own sons have done, and it was with genuine, spontaneous joie de vivre than he accepted the Man of the Match award (of a cricket bat) for his feats against Oulton. 'You have a few nerves before the action starts, but once the umpire said "Play", the adrenaline would surge through my body and I was as pleased as punch to be part of the team. I guess that with my father as the captain, I might have had the extra burden of not wanting to disappoint him or let the side down, but it never felt like that when we were out on the pitch. In the dressing room, he was Dad, but in the middle, I was just desperate to do my damnedest for Freuchie and family considerations didn't enter the equation,' says Brian. 'We had all realised that we were a bit fortunate to get past Cleator and we had prepared ourselves for the games to get harder and harder, so it was difficult to absorb when Oulton capitulated in the manner they did. But, of course, it was nice to get that match out of the way and look forward to the semis.

'There was a bandwagon building up, not only in Freuchie but across the whole country, but I kept my head down and carried on as normal. Good things happen, bad things happen, that's part of life, and you have to take the rough with the smooth, but I was foreman at a structural steel company in Cowdenbeath and I realised that the Village Cup was a fantastic adventure, but it wasn't going to make me a millionaire, and that, win or lose, I would still have my friends, my neighbours and my folks around me and they were more important than any transient glory. I suppose that may sound a bit corny, but my dad had always reminded me that Freuchie was there before I was born and it will be there after I have gone. All right, let's not pretend I wasn't excited when I grabbed the six wickets – and that it didn't give me a tingle to hear the crowd going nuts on the boundary edge – but that was only one chapter in what seems like a grand fairy tale. I glance at the scorecards now, and it feels as if it was about 50 years ago, but basically, it doesn't matter whether it's the Village Cup, the Fife Cup or a friendly Second XI match, if there is the chance of playing cricket, then it still provides me with an enormous buzz.'

Unsurprisingly, as the Scots celebrated their Oulton adversaries were deflated, and the £100 cheque presented by the sponsors offered scant consolation to Peter Grainger and his colleagues. Yet, whilst their hopes had been dashed, they stayed to observe Brian Christie's ceremony, clapped him on the back in recognition of a stirring performance, and rapidly packed away their petted lips. No wonder that Professor William Barclay, the noted Scottish theologian, once commented: 'Ah, cricket, the sight of bowler and players genuinely applauding a century against them. If a Rangers soccer side stood to applaud a Celtic goal, I would know that the age of miracles had come. Cricket's greatness lies in the ability of players to honour a foe. It is the way life should be lived.'

Without wishing to become too mistily sentimental, these

words should be enshrined at the gates of Celtic Park and
Ibrox, because if the Old Firm were genuinely, truly serious
about tackling the cancer of sectarianism head-on, they would
appreciate that the malaise will never be eradicated while the
racist chants, bigoted anthems, Nazi salutes and IRA symbo-
lism in the crowd are accompanied by the sight of millionaire
players regularly losing their cool in a cauldron of hatred. No
one is pretending that any pastime holds a monopoly on
moronic behaviour, but whenever cricket has strayed into
similar controversy, whether in Dennis Lillee aiming a kick at
Javed Miandad, Vivian Richards walking into the crowd to
confront one of Yorkshire's myriad racist fans, or England's
Barmy Army causing offence with their casual, infinitely
tedious loutishness, these incidents are as isolated as they
are unusual. Nor can the Old Firm claim – though they
are world champions at straw-clutching and buck-passing –
that the majority of the trouble which follows their scabrous
tussles is fuelled more by alcohol than the religious divide.
Cricket, a sport which lasts for six or seven hours a day,
provides far greater scope for tanked-up hooligans to create
havoc, yet mercifully violence, riots and crowd trouble are as
rare from the village green to Lord's and the MCG as they are
commonplace around the Old Firm beat. Ultimately, the
bottom line is that if Rangers and Celtic accepted their
responsibilities, introduced a strict zero-tolerance policy and
encouraged their leading personnel to be belligerent, but not
bampots; competitive, but not churlish, the sectarian blight
would start to wither. That it still manifests itself with sickening violence in Glasgow and the west of Scotland five or six
times a year offers support to Barclay's views. Yet if mutual
respect is a feature of cricket (and golf and rugby), why don't
we witness the same in football? One might assume the SFA
would investigate the matter, and not simply leave the analyses
to pressure groups and politicians, but on past evidence we
shouldn't hold our breath for prescience or foresight from Park
Gardens. Better, perhaps, to return to Freuchie's ground, in

the aftermath of their Oulton demolition, while the news sank in that they were just one step away from Lord's.

As the evening shadows lengthened, Alan Duncan allowed himself a fleeting moment of contemplation as he reflected on the dramatic transformation in his fortunes. Only a month previously he had been a doleful figure, trepidatiously awaiting medical reports as his life threatened to veer down a cul-de-sac of vulnerability. He certainly had not envisaged a phoenix-style recovery and resurgence from his sick-bed to the cricket field, and now, here, he was within a maximum of 80 overs from gaining the chance to journey to the game's spiritual home. Little wonder that, whilst the clubhouse was a seething mass of frenetic commotion, Duncan resembled Bart Simpson unleashed in a fireworks factory. 'It felt pretty unbelievable and the players were suffused with a warm glow that night. Wherever you looked, Freuchie dwellers were cheering, passing on congratulations, and there was no longer any doubt that Lord's was on the tip of many people's tongues,' declares Duncan. 'I remember Dave Christie sitting with a beatific smile on his face and when I spoke to him, he simply said: "Let's enjoy tonight, we can worry about the semi-final tomorrow. I mean, look at this around you, isn't it incredible? Who would have dreamt that a wee cricket club, a wee *Scottish* cricket club, would be full of people singing their hearts out and talking about batting line-ups and what a googly is, as if these were everyday happenings in Fife. We have to do it for them." It was the right message, and when I think about that occasion, it summed up all the essential qualities of the Village Cup tournament. Sure, there were a few days where the atmosphere turned sour, but I reckon that from the moment Dave Christie first heard about the competition, he realised the effect it could have on Freuchie and he was absolutely spot-on.

'What nobody could have appreciated, or anticipated, was the wholesale fashion in which men, women and children flocked to the cause: cricket had become the pivotal feature around which our community revolved and it was bigger news than football or anything else. I'm aware that in lots of other parts of Scotland, the game commanded significant attention, but we must have been one of the few places in 1985 where, no matter whether you walked into John Bryce General Drapers, or the grocer's store, or the H.B. McCombie radio and television shop, or the Freuchie Antiques emporium, everybody could tell you about the cricketers and their victories in the Village Cup. The danger was that folk organised their London plans before we had even qualified for the final, but Dave was as good as his word. From the Monday onwards, he battened down the hatches, reminded us that we hadn't won anything yet and gave us a dose of reality. And, by that stage, we had learned who our opponents would be and that it wouldn't be easy.'

Billesdon, of Leicestershire, had secured an equally incident-packed passage to their appointment with Freuchie. The campaign commenced serenely enough with an elementary nine-wicket win at Bitteswell, followed by a 98-run success over visitors Queniborough, as the prelude to their skipper, Graham Butler, hitting 91 at Gracedieu Park in his side's eight-wicket stroll. That allowed Billesdon the luxury of a home tie against Fillongley, but they were to be stretched all the way in a classic contest which, for long periods, seemed to be inexorably slipping out of their grasp. 'We were well placed at 140 for 2 in the first game, which was abandoned because of the weather, but when we met again a week later, it was a titanic struggle,' recalls the club's chairman, Paul Miles, one of the combatants in that game. 'They batted first and rattled up 177 for 5 and we collapsed to 39 for 4 before a partnership of 65 between Andy Townley (22) and John Ford restored our hopes, but they kept winkling out our batsmen and we required 38 from the last six overs, with just two wickets remaining. I walked to the wicket and all I was interested in was giving the strike to John as much as possible, because he was one of those rugged, tough-as-teak characters, capable of forcing his way out of any scrape, and we ended up adding 31 for the 9th wicket. Even then, Fillongley had a decent chance, but John was in wonderful nick, and it was appropriate that he collected the winning runs, as we edged home by the skin of our teeth. He was unbeaten on 91 at the death, and even though they were gutted, our opponents accepted he would have deserved a hundred in the circumstances, and the afternoon was a tremendous advert for village cricket.'

In the next round, the weather again intervened – North and South, the summer of '85 brought a Dickensian landscape of saturated greenswards – but Richard Nourish's 54, allied to tight bowling from the two Johns, Elliott and Ford, produced a narrow 11-run victory over Treeton of Yorkshire, and Billesdon's aspirations were increasing. They faced another stern examination against Bramshall from Staffordshire, but their No. 9 batsman, Phil Greasley, captured headlines in both the local and national press when his Bothamesque exploits retrieved a dismal situation for his side. As he marched to the wicket in yet another rain-truncated tussle, Billesdon were 97 for 7 with 7 of their 32 overs remaining. However, in the space of 26 balls, the 'Bramshall Basher' powered his path to 53, including five sixes, which steered the visitors to 160 for 8 and, no sooner had the action resumed than he was in the wickets, taking 5 for 55, as the hosts, dominant for the lion's share of the game, were eventually frozen out by a mere eight runs.

'That took us to the quarter-finals, and, naturally, local interest was rising in our feats. Northop Hall, of North Wales, were our opponents, but surprisingly, they put up little resistance, and it was a fairly comfortable match for us,' says Miles, emphasising the similarities between his team's season and that of Freuchie. 'The game was reduced to 26 overs a side, and we managed a pretty formidable 151 for 8, with the prolific Elliott holding the innings together with 65. We imagined that they would at least have a thrash, despite losing early wickets, but Bill Armstrong was his usual tight self, picking up 4 for 25 in the process, and they finished on 98 for 7, without ever giving the impression they fancied themselves to chase down the runs. It was all fairly straightforward and routine, not that anybody was complaining after our previous brushes with defeat.

'Well, by this point, we were all starting to wonder: was this going to be the year when we entered the history books, when we put our name firmly on the map, because we had been in existence since 1872, but there hadn't remotely been this amount of publicity surrounding Billesdon before, and you know what Andy Warhol said about everybody getting their 15 minutes of fame? We had heard that Freuchie were formidable opponents, and we obviously faced a lengthy journey to Scotland, but we were no slouches ourselves, so we began the preparations and fixed up a few interviews with the media, who were becoming captivated by the news. None of us had ever been to Freuchie, but we had maps, we had compasses, and we couldn't wait to climb onto the bus and take the next step forward. It was a really exciting time for all of us.'

Back in Fife, even if the national broadsheets hadn't quite clicked into gear, the *Dundee Courier*, the *Sunday Post* and the *Fife Free Press* were beginning to expand their coverage substantially and Dave Christie's name was attracting sizeable column inches, not least because of his ability to impart geniality and toughness, pragmatism and patter in the same breath. 'I wasn't counting any chickens, because sport is full of teams who got ahead of themselves and came a mighty cropper, and the Village Cup, in particular, was a competition where the cherished prize, the opportunity to play at Lord's, was only granted to the two finalists, and we knew fine well that Billesdon would be as highly motivated as ourselves,' says Christie. 'Mind you, I had to keep reminding myself of that message, because everywhere I went, in the build-up to the semi-final, the Freuchie folk were saying: "So we'll all be going to Lord's then, Dave." Or: "Where are you planning to stay in London?" And so on and so forth. You couldn't really criticise them – it was terrific that there was so much focus on cricket – but I had locked horns with enough English sides to recognise that the Oulton experience was probably a one-off and that if we had played them again the next day, we might have found life a lot more tricky. So I had to try and calm things down and be sensible and ignore the hype, and that's where Allan Wilkie, was so valuable. He wouldn't tolerate nonsense from anybody, be it the papers, the tournament organisers or the opponents, and he made sure we did things on our own terms, which was important. Otherwise we might have been swamped.'

That level-headedness was shared by most of the Freuchie players, not least Alan Duncan, whose year had commenced so inauspiciously that he wasn't in the mood to lose sight of the bigger picture. 'We had no idea what to expect from Billesdon, and they were in the same boat as us, but given the summer we had endured, the only thing that was virtually guaranteed was the weather. Within a couple of days of beating Oulton we were at training, as usual, and Dave Christie called us together and said bluntly: "Right, we've all enjoyed the celebrations, but we're here to play cricket. We've had luck on our side so far, with home advantage, but we can't keep relying on that. Let's make sure our Village Cup campaign doesn't end in Freuchie." That struck exactly the right note.'

At 48, Christie had long since graduated from the stage of being a star-struck teenager. So had his son. Both men would have critical roles to perform in the days ahead.

CHAPTER 7

THE ADMIRABLE CRICHTON

By any normal standards, 18 August 1985 remains an auspicious day in the annals of Scottish sport. On the golf circuit, the recently-crowned Open champion, Sandy Lyle, shot a terrific eight-under-par 64 to win the Benson & Hedges International tournament at Fulford; emerging athlete, Tom McKean, sprinted to victory in the 800m to boost Great Britain's European Cup challenge in Moscow; and, most romantically, Freuchie, previously unsung and unheralded, booked their passage into the National Village Cup final at Lord's with a riveting, roller-coaster triumph against Billesdon, which often seemed to be slipping out of their grasp, and where their normally unflappable skipper, Dave Christie, revealed later he feared he would be lynched by his own brethren.

As should already have been demonstrated in these pages, Freuchie's trenchant ensemble was as far removed from the bool-in-the-mooth brigade as it would be possible to countenance in an activity where many of the starched-collar panjandrums possess wonkier vision than Mr Magoo. Not for the Fifers the stuffy image perpetuated in Sir Henry Newbolt's verses, epitomised by 'There's a breathless hush in the close tonight, Ten to make and the match to win.' Instead, while Christie's efforts to proselytise the game echoed the dedication of the masters from the pages of *Goodbye Mr Chips* and *To Serve Them All My Days*, his personnel revelled in their working-class origins and were no more suited to top hat, white tie and tails than Ford Kiernan or Tam Cowan. Speaking to a collection of the 1985 team in the Lomond Hills Hotel earlier this year, their hospitality was suffocating, their consumption of the myriad glasses which arrived in our direction a formidable reminder that these players held no truck with the modern maxim which insists that sports stars should stick to Highland Spring or Britvic Orange. Within an hour, I was being invited to regale them with a Frank Sinatra song, and despite declining politely, the rounds subsequently stacked up with the inevitability of a PGA Tour season, and suddenly I was embroiled in a raucous karaoke version of that well-known Old Blue Eyes standard: 'Twelve For My Baby (And None For The Road)'.

All of which explains why the 1985 campaign was not for the faint-hearted or those without sturdy constitutions. Billesdon, a Leicestershire-based team who had travelled up to Scotland on a 400-mile hike on Saturday, stopping at Newcastle for lunch, were invited by their hosts to partake of a modest tincture, or five, and, rather than be dragged into an excess of carousing, opted for early retirement. Within the next 24 hours, they discovered the folly of that policy as their Fife opponents, and their supporters, made merry with the malt, blithely ignoring the probability that their livers might eventually come out with their hands up. Indeed, one only has to attend these Freuchie festivities to appreciate the absurdity of the conclusion reached by right-wing satirist, P.J. O'Rourke, in his analysis of the Scots' alleged racial characteristics: 'Sour, stingy, depressing beggars who parade around in schoolgirls' skirts with nothing on underneath. Their fumbled attempt at speaking the English language has been a source of amusement for five centuries and their idiot music has been dreaded by those not blessed by deafness.'

This is rich, coming from a devotee of George W. Bush, a man whose battle with his mother tongue has resulted in serial matricide, who derives inspiration from the music of slack-jawed Texan Country and Western acts, and whose own refusal to spend money on health care or social security has transformed his country into a divided land, half of whom believe they were abducted by aliens or visited by guardian angels (or both), and who preach the gospel according to Ned and Maud Flanders. Freuchie, by comparison, partied as if sobriety were a mortal sin, worked for each other in the spirit of collectivism and concentrated as much on their colleagues as themselves. 'There were no egos in the team, and it didn't matter a jot whether you were Dave Cowan and going off to represent Scotland, or Niven McNaughton, a good, honest club player, all that concerned me was that the lads knew their jobs, practised hard and maintained their discipline to be as fit as they could be to do their best for Freuchie,' says Dave Christie. 'That much was obvious from the previous rounds of the Village Cup. Yes, Davie had been important for us, both with bat and ball, but so on different occasions had Andy Crichton, Alan Duncan, Terry Trewartha, Stewart Irvine, myself, my son, Niven, the whole bloody lot of us. Basically, we would never have achieved what we did with everything revolving around a couple of prima donnas and eight or nine journeymen, and Freuchie's strength has always been based on everybody contributing something, whether it's a catch, a run-out, a smart bit of fielding, a stubborn few overs of resistance or a wicket at a crucial time. Sure, the boys enjoyed their Saturday night out, but they wouldn't play to form if they didn't.'

The contrasting approach of the teams masked their mutual recognition that the losers would forever be consigned to vain reveries of how frustratingly close they had advanced to a Lord's assignation, only to falter at the final hurdle. In this competition, with its climatic vagaries, quirks of fate, and sheer number of entrants, there was scant prospect of organisations such as Billesdon and Freuchie being able to envisage regular visits to the home of cricket, hence the tangible tension in the air as the beginning of the match beckoned. The Englishmen had even flown home their wicket-keeper-batsman, Ian James, from a holiday in the United States, so that he could participate in the contest and, bolstered by a fine opening bowler in John Ford, who had gorged himself on victims like a latter-day cannibal in the village competition, and marshalled by a cerebral captain, Graham Butler, who had exhibited the same unstinting commitment throughout the campaign as his counterpart, Christie, the stage was poised for an enthralling battle of wills. All that was left was for the heavens to open, and soon it was raining cats and dogs so prodigiously that the attendant throng had to avoid stepping into poodles.

Undaunted, the rival skippers convened and decided that, whatever else transpired, they would reach a gentleman's agreement whereby, regardless of how dismal the weather became, they would stay on the field and prevent the dreaded bowl-out if it was remotely feasible. It was a gallant gesture, although the pact would provoke furious debate later in the proceedings, but when Christie lost the toss and his men were asked to bat there were ample reasons for the 1000-plus crowd to be apprehensive as soon as Ford strode into action, adroitly orchestrating the action and twisting the plot, akin to his directorial namesake. Alan Duncan was the first to suffer the paceman's wrath on a treacherous surface, dismissed for 0, and, as a congregation of fretful Fifers watched with trepidation through half-shut fingers, a dire clatter of wickets threatened to leave the Scots in tatters. Andy Crichton was the second batsman to be undone by the rampaging Ford on four, as the collapse intensified and Mark Wilkie's 38-minute vigil ended in the same manner when he was comprehensively bowled for a tentative 7. George Wilson, meanwhile, was undone by John Stimpson at the other end, his stumps shattered for 2, and in the space of a desperate three-quarters of an hour for the hosts, they had been reduced to 19 for 4 in the first 10 overs and their hopes of progressing to London were in freefall.

From the safety of the boundary, George Crichton surveyed the wreckage with the jaundiced view of a fellow accustomed to strife and discomfort and padded up in preparation for marching to the crease at the fall of the next wicket. 'I'd been sitting in my van watching the procession and I kept thinking to myself: "Ach no, here we fucking go again, making things difficult for ourselves. Fair enough, it was a wet pitch, and the lad Ford was nippy, but we all knew in advance that it would be a hellish sickener if we lost the semi-final, and here we were in the process of folding like a Jiffy bag", says the grit blaster, who frequently injected some of that commodity from his day job into his batting. 'We didn't make a decent start in any round of the tournament that year, and although we seemed capable of retrieving matters, Billesdon were a seriously decent side and I knew straightaway that if we were all out for 80 or 90, we would be beaten, simple as that. It was one of those situations where you have to forget about the weather or the pitch, and play every ball on its merits. That may sound simplistic, but when you looked at the faces of the spectators, packed into the ground, it was clear that they feared a rout and, given what Freuchie meant to me, that was enough incentive to do my Barnacle Bill act. I had nothing against the English, but the bottom line was that only one of us was going to Lord's and I was determined to work my arse off to ensure that it wasn't them.'

This chap is Mr Sangfroid, with a sense of humour as dry as a Nevadan desert, and his captain, Christie, lauds him with the kind of glowing report card which used to guarantee punishment for puny swots at the hands of the smokers' fraternity behind the bicycle shed. 'He never threw away his wicket, he was exactly the kind of nerveless customer you needed in a crisis, and his commitment to Freuchie was exemplary, even though he and Andy were rarely in the spotlight,' says Christie. 'It pretty much summed up Geordie that even when some of us were starting to fear the worst against Billesdon – and that genuinely was the only occasion in the summer when I felt pessimistic about the out-come – he went round, pepping us up and constantly reminding us of the prize at stake, and although his language wasn't designed for maiden aunts, it had the desired effect.'

These words testify to Crichton's infinite capacity for unstint-ing industry and they-shall-not-pass stubbornness. Although he and his Freuchie comrades were amateurs in status, they didn't know the meaning of 'taking it easy' and possessed a formidable mental toughness, sharpened by years of playing together as a unit. In the prelude to their Billesdon showdown significant sections of the media had started focusing on the Fife community and indulging in the normal hyperbolic twaddle which has preceded so many Scottish fiascos, dating back to the South Sea Bubble; but George Crichton was neither distracted nor hoodwinked by some of their dafter comments, which seemed to suggest that Freuchie merely had to turn up to book their London passage. On the contrary, as he recollects, he neglected to look at the sports pages in the tabloids and clung resolutely to his belief that losing a semi-final is the worst possible stage to be eliminated.

'I was never one for spouting grand statements or indulging in stupid forecasts. Cricket matches are won on the field, not in the bar or the pages of newspapers, and let's give credit to Billesdon, they had been forced into making a long journey up to Scotland, it was pouring with rain on the Sunday morning, and the elements didn't relent as the game advanced, but they were as keen as mustard to proceed, and they hit the ground running and found their rhythm straightaway,' says Crichton. 'With four of our boys already back in the hutch, we were on the ropes and I had a chat with Dave Christie and we both reached the same conclusion: that we had to scratch and scramble to a target which was defensible, and that would only happen with lashings of application and commonsense. Their bowlers held the aces, nonetheless. The Ford brothers, John and Dave, and John Stimpson had us in a stranglehold and the question was whether we could claw back some of the initiative from them after a start they must have dreamed about. My biggest fear was that we would crumble completely and the afternoon would unfold into a ghastly anti-climax, in front of all our friends and neighbours. But if Freuchie were blessed with one quality, not just in 1985 but for as long as I have been involved, it was guts.'

With the Animals now in the middle, there was certainly no shortage of pugnacious intent, and a couple of sweetly-struck boundaries and a resplendent six from Cowan, the sole Scot to strike a boundary all day, relieved a fraction of the tension. Yet, to their credit, Billesdon maintained their discipline, and although the partnership reached 47, Bill Armstrong's catch from Stimpson's bowling removed Irvine for nine and, shortly afterwards, with the score on 76, Cowan also departed, the first of four wickets for Armstrong, a reliable medium-pace bowler, whose accurate spell induced mounting panic in the Freuchie ranks. 'I was growing increasingly excited at this stage, because the boys had a real grip on the match, and you could sense the agitation and anxiety amongst the Scottish crowd,' recalls Paul Miles, the current Billesdon chairman, who travelled with the side on their epic trek north 20 years ago. 'Given what had happened in the previous rounds of the competition that season, we felt that we had plenty of reasons to be optimistic. One of our all-rounders, Phil Greasley, had scored 53 and taken 5 wickets in our 6th-round victory against Bramhall, from Staffordshire; another, John Elliott, was our star performer in the summer of 1985; and the youngest member of our team, Andy Townley, subsequently developed into one of the finest amateur cricketers in the history of Leicestershire cricket, with over 100 centuries to his name as well as amassing the highest-ever individual score [212 not out] in the annals of the Leicestershire Premier League. We had known from the moment that Graham Butler received the news, in the New Greyhound Inn, that we would be facing Freuchie following our win over Welsh team Northop Hall in the quarter-finals, that it would be a tough challenge and that their main strengths were their bowling and fielding, but at 76 for 5 we had to be delighted with the penetration of our own attack and we were definitely in the box seat.'

The next phase settled down into a protracted cat-and-mouse confrontation between Crichton and his tail-enders, and the English second-string bowlers, with the latter continuing to dominate. Terry Trewartha fell victim to the wily Armstrong for a duck, and Dave Christie walked to the middle with his side in serious grief, and plenty of overs remaining to be negotiated. His partner, meanwhile, was stoically pushing the odd single, whilst defiantly refusing to be intimidated by the unnatural hush which had descended over the Freuchie ground and, oblivious to Butler's astute switching of his attack, Crichton was hell-bent on

making a fist of things, hiding behind a carapace of cool and
drumming home the mantra: 'Nothing stupid, Geordie, nothing
daft, we haven't come this far to throw it away.' He clung on
tenaciously for 66 minutes, intent on blocking rather than
bludgeoning, and the statisticians logged a hailstorm of dot balls
in their books, but as chairman of the self-preservation society he
was acting to perfection.

As events unfolded, this was one of several factors which
ultimately proved crucial. Firstly, although Billesdon's line-up
smelt victory, they were neither as nimble nor as efficient in the
field as their opponents, and eventually conceded 21 extras –
Freuchie conceded just 4 by comparison – which proved a vital
consideration at the dénouement. Secondly, although Crichton's
innings was a triumph of fastidious precision over free-flowing
panache, he attained his ambition of pushing the tally beyond
100, then onwards to 117, which, although hardly earth-shattering, at least afforded Cowan, Christie and their confederates a
glimmer of hope for the second half. 'If I'm being honest, it was
damage limitation and sheer bloody-mindedness which kept me
going, because we had already bowled out plenty of sides for
under 100 in the Village Cup, and getting to the century mark
was some kind of psychological victory, especially after the
problems we had encountered at the beginning,' says Crichton,
whose obduracy steered him to 28, before he was bowled by
Elliott, striving for acceleration in the 38th over, while the
miserly Armstrong polished off the Christie duo, leaving Niven
McNaughton unbeaten.

'At the interval, none of us harboured any illusions – we had to
make quick inroads when the action resumed and prevent any of
their batsmen from getting into their stride, otherwise we were
done for. All it would take was for one of their lads to hit 40 or 50
and we were snookered and, understandably, we weren't exactly
cracking jokes throughout the tea-break. Our spectators were
similarly concerned, and you have to take your hats off to
Billesdon: they must have brought about 100 fans, whilst we
had over 1000, squeezed into every section of the park, but the

visitors handled the occasion brilliantly and I actually think they were the best team that we faced that summer – and I'm including the finalists, Rowledge, in that assessment. Perhaps it was appropriate that it all went down to the wire, but, believe me, some of us were shitting ourselves by the end.'

The frisson in the rival camps reflected the battle between fear and expectation which lurked in the bosoms of these players. For Paul Miles, absolutely nothing was being taken for granted. 'There had been several thrilling matches leading up to the semi-final and Graham, who turned out for Billesdon from 1958 to 1988, had made it clear his biggest desire was for us to do well in the Village Cup, and the fact that the team reached the last 16 in 1984 before being eliminated by the eventual winners only increased his ambition,' says Miles, whose club was distraught when the hail-fellow-well-met Butler succumbed to cancer on Christmas Day in 2001. 'Rather like Dave Christie, he was one of those individuals whose life revolved around cricket, and he wasn't just a player and a captain, but he also maintained the ground and square at Billesdon, he was elected to the general committee in 1961, and sport was in his veins, whether in cricket or with Houghton Rangers Football Club. He kept telling us that he was pleased with our bowling at Freuchie, but that the job was just 50 per cent done and that we could anticipate a backlash. He knew that the Scots would come out all guns blazing, and maybe he suspected that Billesdon should have restricted them to 20 or 30 runs fewer. We did spill several catches and the contrast between us and Freuchie in that department was noticeable.'

Uncharacteristically, Dave Christie was a gloomy figure at that stage. Within the dressing room, he had no option but to exude bullishness and a Micawberish mien, but privately, his mood was as dark at the clouds that hovered over Freuchie. 'I genuinely thought there was no way we would win at the midway point, because they had been thoroughly professional in their approach, we had batted poorly, the weather was terrible, and it seemed as if everything was conspiring against us,' says Christie. 'I had chatted to Graham the night before, and he was clearly steeped in cricket, and was a lot more articulate than I was, and although I had faith in my lads, and realised they would fight every inch of the way, 117 shouldn't have been enough and, in normal circumstances, it probably wouldn't have been. We returned to the fray facing the greatest test of our mettle in the biggest game in the club's history, and all we could do was fling everything at them and do our best to grab every chance going, because anything can happen in the sphere of village cricket. The Lord's odyssey was still in the lap of the gods, but personally, I would much have preferred to be in their position with my cup of tea.'

As sheets of rain enveloped the village Billesdon's openers, Butler and Ian James, the latter fresh from his American vacation, and only involved in the contest after a frantic dash by train and car to Fife on the morning of the semi-final, marched out in the knowledge that all they required was patience, not pyrotechnics: a run rate of less than three an over meant that Freuchie, for all their jack-in-the-box heroics around the covers, were unlikely to stem the tide unless they inflicted early damage to their rivals' top order. Yet, precisely when it was needed, Cowan was stinginess incarnate and although Niven McNaughton's opening three deliveries proved a mixed bag, featuring a wide, a 6 and the wicket of Butler, dextrously caught by Mark Wilkie, one or two of the airy flourishes from the visiting batsmen offered the Scots renewed salvation. The same bowler and fielder combined to remove Rob Nourish as Billesdon slumped to 12 for 2, and while opener James and the dangerous John Elliott threatened to guide the contest out of Freuchie's reach, the ensuing fraught battle brought howls of approbation from the spectators, most of whom had grown accustomed to wearing galoshes, Mackintoshes and all the other accoutrements devised by Man to cope with the Scottish climate. The competition regulations dictated that Billesdon had to bat a minimum of 20 overs before a result was possible, and gradually their task became more difficult, with the ball sticking in the glaur and the boundary starting to

(20p) **LORD'S** (M) **GROUND** (20p)

The National Village Cricket Championship
ORGANISED BY THE CRICKETER
FINAL 1985
FREUCHIE v. ROWLEDGE
SUNDAY, SEPTEMBER 1st, 1985

ROWLEDGE	Innings	
1 R. E. C. Simpson	c Crichton b Cowan	6
2 A. P. Hook	b McNaughton	28
3 N. S. Dunbar	run out	33
4 C. Yates	b D. Christie	10
*5 P. Offord	run out	0
6 R. J. Dunbar	c Irvine b Trewartha	12
†7 A. J. Prior	b Trewartha	6
8 P. R. Cooper	b Cowan	12
9 B. A. Silver	c Wilkie b Trewartha	0
10 A. D. Field	not out	10
11 J. Reffold	l b w b Trewartha	0
	B , l-b 9, w 7, n-b 1,	17
	Total	134

FALL OF THE WICKETS

1—15 2—56 3—73 4—74 5—94 6—108 7—117 8—117 9—133 10—134

ANALYSIS OF BOWLING

Name	O.	M.	R.	W.	Wd.	N-b.
Cowan	9	1	25	2	...	...
McNaughton	9	0	31	1	2	...
B. Christie	9	0	28	0	1	...
D. Christie	5	0	17	1	1	1
Trewartha	7.3	0	24	4	3	...

FREUCHIE	Innings	
1 M. Wilkie	b Field	10
*2 A. S. Duncan	c Yates b Silver	16
3 A. N. Crichton	l b w b Field	0
4 G. Wilson	c Offord b Yates	14
5 D. Cowan	b Silver	10
6 S. Irvine	c and b Prior	24
7 G. Crichton	not out	24
8 T. Trewartha	b Reffold	1
†9 D. Y. F. Christie	run out	11
10 B. Christie	not out	0
11 N. McNaughton		
	B 6, l-b 8, w 2, n-b 2,	18
	Total	134

FALL OF THE WICKETS

1—23 2—25 3—42 4—52 5—85 6—91 7—101 8—133 9— 10—

ANALYSIS OF BOWLING

Name	O.	M.	R.	W.	Wd.	N-b.
Field	9	1	15	2	1	2
Reffold	6	1	25	1	...	...
Prior	9	0	31	1	...	...
Yates	9	0	31	1	...	...
Silver	7	0	18	2	1	...

Umpires—R. Axworthy & R. H. Duckett   Scorers—L. Horne, Miss S. Moss & E. Solomon

† Captain   * Wicket-keeper

Play begins at 1.30   Tea Interval between innings

Total runs scored at end of each over:—

Freuchie	1	2	3	4	5	6	7	8	9	10	11	12	13	14
	15	16	17	18	19	20	21	22	23	24	25	26	27	28
	29	30	31	32	33	34	35	36	37	38	39	40		
Rowledge	1	2	3	4	5	6	7	8	9	10	11	12	13	14
	15	16	17	18	19	20	21	22	23	24	25	26	27	28
	29	30	31	32	33	34	35	36	37	38	39	40		

Rowledge won the toss

Freuchie won having lost fewer wickets

The scorecard reveals just how closely fought the battle was for Village Cup supremacy at Lord's, but Freuchie lost fewer wickets than Rowledge, so won, despite the scores being tied.

Dave Christie, the inspirational Freuchie captain, lines up his men for an impromptu practice session at the Public Park in the Fife village.

Never before had so much Tartan been witnessed at Lord's as during the 1985 final.

Freuchie's cricketers pose for the cameras at Lord's, the game's spiritual home.

The Scottish players were granted the rare privilege of being allowed to use the net facilities at Lord's in the build-up to the final.

One Freuchie fan exhibits the pawky humour and refusal to be cowed by the patrician atmosphere at Lord's.

Above. Yes it's true, Freuchie are playing on the grand stage at Lord's. Niven McNaughton comes in to bowl, whilst Alan Duncan, Terry Trewartha and Stewart Irvine await any mistakes from the batsman.

Right. Dave Christie was nearly 50 by the time of the final. But he had the energy and industry of a player half that age.

Far right. A pensive group of Freuchie players gaze out from the Lord's balcony as their openers set off in pursuit of Rowledge's 134.

Captain Christie departs, to a hero's reception, run out for 11, with the Fifers so close to their target on 133 for 7.

Dave's son, Brian, holds his bat aloft, after ensuring that the Village Cup would be heading to Scotland for the first time.

Mission accomplished: Dave Christie proudly clasps on to the Haig National Village Cup.

The team, adorned in kilts and sporrans, show off the trophy in front of their adoring supporters.

Brian Christie, Dave Cowan, Dave Christie and man-of-the-match, Stewart "Jasper" Irvine, bask in the adulation of going where no Scots had gone before.

Right. In the awful summer of 1985, it was perhaps appropriate that rain greeted the Freuchie team's return to Fife, yet nothing could dampen the celebrations.

Below. Dave Christie shares a few hours with Ian Botham, who has clearly been enjoying the product of the Village Cup sponsor (Haig whisky).

Above. Dave Christie and Dave Cowan receive their prizes at the 1985 Scottish Sports awards.

Left. Freuchie have forged an alliance with Ian Botham and duly took to the roads when the England all-rounder arrived in Fife during one of his charity walks.

Dave Christie may now be in his 70s, but age has not diminished his passion for cricket, nor his work on behalf of the Freuchie club he loves. *David Cruickshanks*

Another generation, another addict. Graeme Christie is Dave's grand-son, but remains equally in thrall to the summer game. *David Cruickshanks*

Three Amigos – Dave Christie has been the heart and soul of Freuchie CC for the last 50 years. Here, he is joined by his son, Brian, and grand-son, Graeme, both of whom have also experienced the thrill of the National Village cup competition. *David Cruickshanks*

resemble some distant mirage, forever out of reach of the beleaguered Englishmen, save for the occasional belligerent riposte from Elliott, who looked eminently capable of producing a match-winning innings.

By now, any pretence at sangfroid from the participants had vanished completely. They were slugging it out in classic Las Vegas heavyweight style for a Lord's appointment and the civilities could go hang! Elliott crashed one Trewartha delivery into the car park, but perished in attempting to repeat the feat for 27, with Wilkie snapping up his third catch as if groomed by Izaak Walton, whereupon the resilient James slipped in the mud and was run out for 15 to reduce the English team to 62 for 4. Yet whilst the prodigy, Andy Townley, was soon back in the hutch, another victim for McNaughton, the Ford brothers batted sensibly, sprinting singles regularly and rotating the strike, and their partnership mounted steadily as the climax loomed into view with the weather deteriorating and tempers fraying amongst several of the combatants.

George Crichton, for instance, was incandescent at the notion of being defeated in the midst of a deluge and beseeched Dave Christie to accept the umpires' offer of abandonment. 'It was crazy, the clouds were doing their worst, we were soaked to the skin, and we would have won on run rate, but Dave kept harping on about gentleman's fucking agreements. Sod that!' recalls Crichton. 'I told him as much and we shared what I think is described in diplomatic circles as "a frank exchange of views", and although I might have been reacting in the heat of the moment, I stand by my argument that we had already gone an extra mile to get the match finished and that there comes an instant where you have to put your hands up and cry: "Enough is enough". Looking back, I suppose I have total respect for Dave's behaviour and it was nothing more than you would have expected from the man. But at the time, I could happily have shot him!'

For a few brief minutes, Dad's Army was imperilled by the risk of mutiny and Christie confesses that he feared he had wandered into a minefield of etiquette grappling with expediency. 'One or two of the lads wandered up to me and said: "Dave, come on, let's walk off, we're winning, they've had enough overs to increase the run rate and they haven't managed it", and I was trapped between a rock and a hard place. Basically, I had given Graham Butler my word that we would stay out there, come what may – short of a tornado or an electrical storm hitting Freuchie – and I had no choice except to stick to my promise. Don't get me wrong, I was as worried as I've ever been on a cricket field, and the thought kept flashing through my mind: "Jesus, if this backfires on me, I'll never be allowed to walk into the clubhouse again and there will be a lynch mob waiting for me if Billesdon beat us and we're denied the trip to Lord's because of me striving to be fair." Geordie Crichton gave me a look that would have curdled milk and insisted that our first priority was observing the rules, not being hindered by them. Well, the ball was wet and the outfield was treacherous, so I guess we were being penalised by the conditions. But equally, they had travelled all that distance, they had kept up their end of the bargain and I reckon that it would have been pretty shoddy if the result had boiled down to us scraping home by a narrow percentage on run rate when they were so close.'

Crichton, as Sherlockians may have rapidly deduced, was no shrinking violet with an MA from the Nigel Bruce school of bumbledom. Hilariously, the *Express* reported Freuchie's exploits as if dwelling under the impression that the Fifers should have sought alternative employment in the original cast of *Trainspotting*. Hence their blathering summation: 'English opponents ought to be warned that the hardest man in the team is a batsman called George Clayton [sic], as hairy a Scotsman as ever terrorised a village green. A shot-blaster by trade, Mr Clayton, it is said, can grow a beard at a wedding.'

Certainly, Crichton deserved his reputation as a formidable adversary. Yet, as Billesdon continued to disregard the elements, he and his fellow-grumblers accepted that Christie was deadly serious in his stance and that they had better proceed as instructed

– the recriminations could wait. More courageously still, with the mercury shooting upwards in the temperature gauge, the Freuchie captain re-entered the attack, collected his thoughts, and steeled himself for what promised to be a critical spell in the encounter.

Initially it appeared that Crichton's misgivings might be justified, at least while the visitors, spearheaded by the safety-first Ford siblings, were progressing cautiously to 88 for 5, just 30 runs short, with 48 deliveries remaining. But if the contest had briefly tilted in their favour, suddenly, in the space of three minutes fizzingly crammed with pulsating melodrama, between 7.15 and 7.18, both these redoubtable characters had been removed and Paul Miles and his compatriots groaned in disbelief. Perhaps inevitably, Dave Christie was a pivotal performer in the tussle's closing scenes when he dismissed his namesake, Dave Ford, easily caught by Trewartha for 17, and John quickly followed him to the pavilion, pouched by Alan Duncan off McNaughton for 16, and the pendulum had swung decisively as gloom encircled the square, but not the boundary edge, if these words mean anything to anybody with an IQ inferior to Professor Stephen Hawking.

Billesdon's tail-enders were now confronted with the task of staging a finale straight out of a Spielberg fantasy, and unsurprisingly they froze in the headlights, with Stimpson and Armstrong mustering minuscule contributions before falling prey to the onliest Christie, who wrapped up victory with an analysis of 3 for 11. 'Yeeeessssss!', 'Yaa Beeaaauuutttyyy!' No wonder that the Public Park resounded to the din of an entire village spontaneously going potty. Freuchie breathlessly, frenetically, energetically had completed their triumph by 12 runs, which was a dozen more than had seemed probable amidst their bickering, and they had secured their passage to St John's Wood.

'I remember just crumpling in a heap for a few seconds at the finish and I was knackered. Mentally, physically, emotionally, the lot. It had been a titanic struggle and there was a huge outpouring of joy from all of us when we grabbed the final wicket and victory was ours, but it was definitely tinged with a massive feeling of relief,' says Christie. 'I received the Man of the Match award, and gained a Duncan Fearnley cricket bat in the process, but without being disrespectful to the sponsors, that was fairly irrelevant in the grand scheme of things and I truly felt very sorry for Graham Butler, because both sides had suffered blips and disappointments and endured highs and lows, and when it went to the wire, either of us might have prevailed. It was funny. We had dreamt about going to Lord's for so long, but there was a wee period at the end when things were a bit quiet. I am not over-dramatising it, but I am convinced that reflected the fact that we had been put through the wringer by Billesdon and tested to the very limit of our abilities and what can you say? Yes, we passed the exam, but phew, it was a hellishly tough ordeal.'

Sport's contrasting fortunes were never more evident for the rest of the evening. On their previous Village Cup assignations that summer, Billesdon's members, Martin Mortimer and Adrian Tudor, accompanied by pianist Ivan Raybould, had led the post-match celebrations at the New Greyhound hostelry, and the club had basked in unprecedented adulation. 'Numerous companies and individuals provided sponsorship to help towards the cost of taking the players north for the match, with one coach leaving Leicester early on the Saturday and another on Sunday morning, packed with fans, and there was this incredible excitement and anticipation on the eve of what might have been our crowning moment,' says Paul Miles. 'But, as you can understand, the boys were extremely low at 8 p.m. on Sunday and, as we traipsed back to the Lomond Hills Hotel, we could only ponder on what might have been. Some of the players had delayed their holidays and risked falling out with their better halves to focus on the tournament, and Ian James had partaken in a frantic Stateside dash to Fife, so it was incredibly frustrating to get so near and yet so far. In the end, though, what sunk us was the ferocity of the Scots with the ball and in the field. Graham Butler told the *Leicester Mercury* at the time that Freuchie were the best bowling combination he had tackled all season and he was spot on.

Ultimately, we weren't familiar with the abilities of the Mean Machine beforehand, but you can be sure that we knew all about them by the time we were heading home.'

So, as it transpired, did the rest of Britain. But, in trademark fashion, Dave Christie and his regiment were less bothered about ingratiating themselves with strangers than in cementing the bond with their community, who had tolerated the vicissitudes and vile weather of these matches with an ingrained pride in their confrères. One by one, as the Christies, the Crichtons, Terry Trewartha, Niven McNaughton, David Cowan and their colleagues walked into the clubhouse, showered and refreshed, at shortly after 8 p.m., they were cheered to the rafters by the huddled hordes who hung around for the post-match presentations, flooded into the bar en masse and launched into a party which, for many in their ranks, lasted over a fortnight. It might have been remarked, at various times, about Kenny Dalglish, Alex Ferguson, Graeme Souness or Jim Telfer, that you would never catch them in a pub during a Happy Hour – on the basis that these individuals are at their cheeriest when casting others into fits of Stygian despondency – but no such strictures applied to the cricketers of Freuchie, and emphatically not to such larger-than-life customers as Cowan, blessed with a permanently Panglossian philosophy.

'When we got to the quarter-final, we sat down and had a chat with Dad, and we basically decided that, whatever happened, we were going to enjoy the experience and play hard, but try to remember that it was a game, not a matter of life or death, and we could still enjoy a laugh and a joke. By the time of the Billesdon fixture, we recognised that was the crunch and that if we were beaten, especially on our own patch, it might be the first and last opportunity to advance to Lord's so, in many respects, that *was* the final, and thereafter, I was confident the adrenaline would take over once it had sunk in that we were poised for the adventure of our lives,' says Cowan. 'There is a lot of talk about pressure in these situations, but I always thought that in tight spots, such as in the climax against Billesdon, the match was there to be seized by the collar, and that, if you relaxed and focused on doing your best, you were far more likely to succeed than by worrying yourself to death and walking around with the weight of the world on your shoulders. Maybe this is just me, but if you have a smile on your face and your opponent thinks you are enjoying yourself, it is more likely to intimidate him. So there was no need to be scared of those afternoons in Freuchie, with the rafts of home supporters screaming their support, armed with their brollies and their anoraks and flasks of coffee. In essence, they were like an extra man to us, and that counted. Some people think the rain helped Freuchie, but personally, I believe our fans were more significant in roaring us on through the difficult periods and helping us on the road to London.'

This is a familiar refrain from these Scots. Namely, that it is doing them a grave disservice to intimate that, had Michael Fish discerned a few more 'Highs' on the horizon during the summer of 1985, Freuchie would have posed less of a challenge on the Village Cup trail. Granted, Tony Huskinson, the managing director of the *Cricketer*, who was amongst the audience at the Billesdon tussle, waxed eloquent about the talents of the Fifers' attack – in fact it was he who christened them the Mean Machine – but the likes of Christie and Allan Wilkie were correct to nip this misnomer in the bud and accentuate the merits of the Freuchie crop of 1985.

'It is downright ridiculous when first-class players walk off the field when it's spitting a little rain. Sure, it rained all summer in Fife, but you shouldn't forget that it rained on both teams. The bowlers can't bowl so fast, because they have to worry about their run-ups, but then the batsmen can't count on the ball running along the ground to the boundary. But the key factor is that it affects everybody equally, and let's not forget that Freuchie had beaten English sides in the competition in dry weather before 1985 and they did it plenty of times after 1985,' says Wilkie. 'Why can't people simply accept that in the matches against Cleator and Billesdon, both clubs fought 100 per cent and that these were two fantastic sporting encounters in which

Freuchie happened to be the winners on both occasions? Is that really so hard to swallow?' Not to any fair-minded observer it isn't. But, there again, even 20 years later, there remain commentators for whom the pairing of Scotland and cricket go together like Robert Mugabe and Peter Tatchell.

Mulishly undaunted by sneers, sniggers or sardonic critiques, Freuchie's players and officials toasted their Billesdon achievement on a long night's journey into bleary-eyed Monday, and a return to reality. Behind the scenes Christie had checked on the outcome of the other semi-final between Rowledge and Kilve of Somerset and discovered that the latter had suffered the kind of merciless pummelling traditionally reserved for British women at Wimbledon. Batting first, the Surrey personnel accumulated an impressive 242 for 6, with Tony Hook scoring 72, and then peremptorily routed their opponents for 77, to continue an outstanding sequence of results in the competition. 'When we learned the details we knew straightaway that they would be installed as favourites, and that was exactly how it panned out. In fact, I suspect that whatever English team had reached the final, we would probably have been regarded as rank outsiders because the prevailing wisdom was that we might have shown courage and guts in front of our own supporters, but that it would be a different script when we had to leave Scotland and head down south,' says Christie, throaty chuckle to the fore. 'In most folk's eyes, we would be the hicks from the sticks, the country bumpkins merely content to reach Lord's and not be so presumptuous as to actually believe that we could go out and win . . .'

Which, of course, was precisely what Christie desired.

CHAPTER 8

LIGHTS, CAMERA, ACTION . . .

The mood around Freuchie on the morning of Monday, August 19, was understandably subdued. The previous night's celebrations had stretched long beyond the normal Sabbath tincture for the villagers, and many inhabitants awoke with sore heads, dry mouths and a hankering for Irn-Bru, Resolve, Andrew's Liver Salts or any of the other numerous hangover cures which flood the market without solving the problem for those poor souls who have supped half-a-dozen over the eight. For Dave Christie and his team there was consolation to be derived in the exultant banner headlines commemorating the triumph against Billesdon, which stared out at them from the newspapers in the village shop, but the next few days gradually developed into a media circus, with the Fifers besieged by requests from film crews on both sides of the Border as Freuchie's players and officials discovered how quickly the media's interest can turn to intrusion.

Thankfully, even though some TV executives sought to treat the Fifers like performing seals or dancing bears, Allan Wilkie, a feisty, flinty individual with a determination that his club would not be messed around, emerged from his usual role as secretary of Freuchie to mastermind the build-up to the final at Lord's. Predictably, his job wasn't all sweetness and light, particularly in dealing with a string of English observers who regarded the idea of a group of Scots in a cricket final as if it was the weirdest, wackiest story they had ever heard, but Wilkie was no starry-eyed ingénue, ill at ease with PR stunts and press inquiries. On the contrary, he differentiated astutely between those who wanted to acclaim Dad's Army and those who wished to take advantage of them.

Mind you, it was often a fine balance. 'We knew there would

be a lot of attention on the team in the aftermath of the semi-final victory, but I was committed to ensuring that our lads weren't mucked around or forced into embarrassing situations because, first and foremost, they were ordinary blokes who had worked hard to reach the final and the last thing they deserved was anybody devaluing their achievement, or leaping on a passing bandwagon, exploiting them, and making a fast buck at their expense,' says Wilkie, a peripatetic businessman with a pragmatic philosophy, capable of detecting bullshit at 50 paces and intuitively suspicious of flannel merchants. 'Within 24 hours of the news hitting the English papers I was contacted by a film company who had followed Sunderland's footballers in the week leading up to the FA Cup final, and they were seeking full access to Freuchie's build-up; they wanted to shoot the programme like a fly-on-the-wall documentary, and if we had agreed to the proposal we wouldn't have had a moment's peace or privacy. Worse still, in the circumstances, they were asking for everything on their terms, and yet wanted us to do it for nothing, so I nipped that notion in the bud. They seemed both baffled and astonished when I turned them down flat, but as I let them know at the time, I didn't have a television in my house, I simply walked along to the clubhouse if there was something worth watching, so I wasn't in thrall to the box, and I certainly wasn't impressed by Englishmen speaking in hoity-toity voices trying to convince me that I should be grateful for their attentions. Aye, right.

'The same thing happened when this lad from London Weekend Television phoned me up and said breathlessly: "We want to fly your team down on Friday morning, to be on our flagship evening programme, which is presented by Michael Aspel." He sounded as if I should be jumping for joy, and that irritated me, so I just cut to the chase and said it was a non-starter. He couldn't believe it, he was spluttering: "But, but, aren't you going to ask the players?" And I responded: "No, because they have livelihoods to worry about, they can't afford to give up their Fridays, and we are actually attempting to focus on cricket, which is our No. 1 priority." Eventually, I talked to Scottish Television and discussed the possibility of them doing a documentary and, by the by, I asked them for £1000. They stumped up the cash straightaway and we had a deal. Funny that, eh: but no, I was absolutely hell-bent on ensuring that nobody made fools out of Freuchie.'

There was never likely to be a similar problem in their homeland. Indeed, on the Wednesday evening after the Billesdon success Wilkie and Dave Christie attended a bicentenary dinner commemorating 200 years of cricket in Scotland and, while enjoying their cock-a-leekie soup, Tay Salmon Hollandaise, Roast Quarter of Lamb and Pêches Grand Marnier, the couple were fêted by many of the guests, who included the former England captain, Mike Denness. Casting an eye over the toast list, the cynic would be entitled to conclude that this function was hardly representative of the Caledonian game: the occasion included speeches and presentations by F.G. Mann, CBE, DSO, MC, President of the MCC, Maj. Gen. the Earl of Cathcart, CB, DSO, MC, and Lt Col W.B. Swan, CBE, TD, the Honorary Vice-President of the SCU. But, undaunted by the pomp and circumstance on display, the Freuchie men renewed acquaintances with several old friends and adversaries and were reminded of the emotive passions which the sport can provoke in Scotland. 'One of the first people we met was the captain of the Dunlop side we had knocked out of the Village Cup, and he rushed over to congratulate us on reaching the final, but that wasn't all,' recalls Wilkie. 'Next minute, he was declaring: "Aye, but we could have beaten you on the day if one or two small things had gone in our favour." Given that we had skittled them out for 69 and won extremely comfortably, I couldn't quite follow his logic, but he was emphatic on that point, and it summed up the competitiveness of these organisations. It was also a reminder that people in Scotland were expecting us to handle the pressure and put up a good show against Rowledge, and in some respects it was a welcome return to reality. I think there were a lot of folk in Freuchie dwelling under the impression that we had done the hard part and that we could all go

merrily down to London for the mother of all parties, irrespec
tive of the result. But we had to knock that belief on the head
and prepare as we would for any other big game. It wasn't easy,
what with flashbulbs popping everywhere and a posse of journalists arriving at the Lomond Hills Hotel from the length and
breadth of Britain, but Dave Christie was tremendous in keeping
the players' feet on the ground. We needed his experience and
savvy to calm the boys down.'

Around the village itself, the inhabitants found themselves
caught up in the frenzy, and even those heretics who were not
passionately devoted to cricket were scarcely dilatory in rallying
to the cause. 'The response to the club's success has been nothing
short of phenomenal, and I have had phone calls from all over the
country asking about our community and how to get here,' said
the Freuchie postmistress, Mina Sanderson. 'Already, the number
of visitors has increased noticeably and we could even be on the
verge of a tourist boom. Cricket is all that the villagers are talking
about at the moment, and just about everybody here is making
plans to travel to London for the final.'

Along the Main Street, Irene Veitch, the proprietor of John
Bryce General Drapers, was equally abrim with ebullience. 'I
never used to be a regular watcher but I have become hooked on
the sport and the atmosphere was incredible during the semi-
final. I will certainly be aiming to go to Lord's and cheering them
on,' said Veitch. 'The whole place is steeped in celebrations and,
to be honest, I don't think the parties will stop until long after the
team return from London with the trophy safely in their grasp.'

Obviously, this close-knit camaraderie was gratifying to Dave
Christie and his compatriots: after 77 years at the heart of affairs in
Freuchie, the level of support from the residents was evidence of
the profound impression which the cricketers had etched on the
consciousness of their neighbours and friends. But on the debit
side, as Wilkie relates, there was a rising tide of misguided opinion
that the Fifers had achieved their goal simply by sealing their
appointment with Rowledge. This notion had to be eradicated,
amidst the ordering of kilts, composition of anthems, impromptu

holiday bookings anywhere near St John's Wood and general outpouring of triumphalist fervour. 'For sure, the attention was overwhelming and it was impossible not to be spellbound at the thought of what lay in store – many people in the village rarely left Fife, so the prospect of a mass exodus Down South was lip-smacking – but there was a danger that the team would begin to think the job was finished and that they could moonlight in the spotlight at Lord's, which is why we held a meeting at the club on the Wednesday, in which several of the more experienced, long-standing committee members talked to the players and rammed home the point that the Village Cup wasn't merely about reaching the final, but getting the job completed. One by one, they forcibly observed to the lads: "Listen, there were 639 clubs in this tournament at the start: now, there are just two, and you have a golden opportunity to cement your place in the archives." It was a timely message, because one or two of the local newspapers had printed stuff, effectively saying that win or lose, we could be satisfied with our campaign. Well, as you might anticipate, that wasn't the kind of stuff which sat too comfortably with some club members. Scotland already has a history of glorious defeats, and we didn't want to add to the list.'

This was a mere seven years after the tragically hilarious ineptitude of Ally's Tartan Army on the march at the World Cup, where the squad departed Glasgow with aspirations of lifting the trophy fuelled by the grandiose hyperbole of their coach, Ally MacLeod, and predictably they crashed to earth like Icarus, undone by Peruvians, who the SFA's finest hadn't even bothered investigating and Iran, with whom they could only draw. Of course, Scots being masters of the futile gesture, they subsequently defeated Holland, assisted by the spontaneous hooraymanship of Archie Gemmill, whose fabulous foray through the opposition defence briefly reawakened the possibility that his side might beat the Dutch by the requisite three goals, only for the candle to be snuffed out with inexorable inevitability. A year later the chance for devolution was spurned, and Margaret Thatcher arrived in Downing Street with an attitude towards Scotland which suggested she regarded the citizenry as guinea pigs for her more exotic experiments in dismantling society. Little wonder that by 1985, in the aftermath of the miners' strike, the closure of the British Leyland car plant at Bathgate and a crippling rise in unemployment, many Scots were low on self-esteem and high on self-parody.

In this climate, Dad's Army clearly had to avoid repeating the pitfalls of their soccer brethren, and the practice sessions in the days prior to their sojourn south resonated with a burning intensity. Christie, casting his gaze over their previous Village Cup encounters, reinforced his conviction that the fielding would be one of the major priorities, given that neither of the finalists was accustomed to participating on such a large ground. 'It was pretty simple really: we had to grab any catch which came our way and chase down every single run, and restrict them to as few boundaries as possible. There were guys in the team on whom we could rely 100 per cent not to drop any chances – I don't recall Mark Wilkie or Stewart Irvine, for instance, spilling anything. If the ball came to them, it stuck – and basically, I wasn't asking them to change their approach to the game. It would have been understandable if the boys had allowed themselves to get a bit carried away, but that never happened, and we were a team on a mission, who refused to be sidetracked.

Elsewhere, tracks of another variety were being recorded as the clock ticked down to the London foray. One composition, 'Freuchie Go To Lord's', written and performed by Dave Slater, actually came close to winding up on *Top of the Pops*, which, in the 1980s meant selling rather more than the 37 copies which nowadays seem to merit a chart hit. 'Originally, the song was laid down onto small cassettes by Dave, working in his own bedroom. He could only produce one at a time and it quickly became evident that he would be recording all night, every night, to keep up with demand, so we contacted an agency in Edinburgh, who mass-produced the tapes for us,' says Allan Wilkie. ' "Freuchie's March to Lord's", with which Pipe Major Alistair Pirnie led the "boys" down St John's Wood and through the Grace Gates, was specially recorded for the other side of the cassette, with the studio in my front room, which was being decorated at the time. The musicians featured were John Crawford, from Freuchie, who composed the tune, on accordion; my wife, Stella, on the fiddle; her friend Maureen Copeland on keyboard; and Tom Clark, my father-in-law, on second accordion. The harmony was written by Maureen, a music teacher in Dundee, only minutes before the recording, but they were all very experienced musicians and you can tell that they all enjoyed playing together. I'm not surprised the cassettes sold in huge numbers.'

By Thursday, 29 August, there was no longer any doubt that Freuchie, en masse, was decamping to the capital of Britain. Initially it seemed that British Rail would lay on a service for the flock, after Wilkie approached the organisation and enterprising Scotrail executives presented him with a schedule for the 'Freuchie Flier', leaving Ladybank station for King's Cross with team, officials, press and fans, at a cost of only £20 return each. However, just when the plan was poised to materialise the train operators came back with the news that they couldn't find seven spare carriages in Scotland; they would have to borrow them from Midlands Region, and the Fifers would be forced to shell out extra cash. Which was the end of *that* discussion. Consequently, coach operators Moffat & Williamson were asked to lay on ten buses, which would carry passengers, door-to-door, from the village and surrounding communities in Fife to north-west London for a return fare of £14.50 each, and they acceded to that request. Yet with every passing day the number of wannabe spectators kept increasing and, as George Crichton recollects, the company had to charter vehicles from other firms, such was the clamour for tickets in the prelude to the Fifers' shot at glory. 'It was a wee bit intimidating to notice the fashion in which everybody went mad in the space of a few days and I remember phoning up my brother-in-law at Moffat & Williamson and saying: "How many more buses can you get your hands on?" It wasn't merely folk from Freuchie who were searching for seats, they were coming from all over the Kingdom and from other parts of the country, and I guess that is the moment when it struck me that this really was a big deal and, sure as hell, we had better not screw up with thousands of Scots advancing behind us to Lord's,' says Crichton. 'A week before the final we had secured 14 buses, all supplied with toilets and air conditioning, but by the Wednesday, the figure had gone up again to 17 and my mate was growing pretty worried. He eventually had to phone his colleagues in other towns and the price was more expensive for the latecomers – it rose to around £17.50, I think – but there was nothing we could do about it. The situation was in danger of spiralling out of control, but somehow we managed to keep a grip on it.

'Indeed, with hindsight, I reckon that mushrooming demand for tickets was one of the reasons which stiffened my resolve, and the other lads would tell you the same story. In these circumstances, with your pals and your relatives and the wider world of Scottish cricket joining forces to support a wee team from Division Two of the East of Scotland League, you couldn't help but be inspired by their pride in you and I am a fairly tough character, but when you saw how much it meant to them, you would have needed a heart of stone not to feel a lump in your throat. Honestly, it sent chills down my spine, and while I was telling myself inwardly: "Christ, we can't afford to let all these folk down, or it will be the mother of all anticlimaxes", I clung to the belief that we had more than enough talent and commitment to guarantee we weren't going to get a gubbing.'

Crichton's quiet confidence was as warranted as his trademark resilience was infectious. In the hours leading up to the final, the Good Luck telegrams had been flooding into the village, including one from Queen's Park FC at Hampden, passing on best wishes from the first Scottish club ever to play an English team to the maiden Scottish cricket side to compete at Lord's. There was also a tele-message from Sir George Sharp, the head of the Glenrothes Development Corporation, which simply read: 'Remember to lord it at Lord's!' and the Fifers' fame had reached a crescendo. On the eve of their departure, Freuchie's squad members were guests of honour at a sponsors' night at the

ground, where the players took the opportunity to thank their
backers and benefactors for the assistance they had received.
Once again, with almost heroic self-sacrifice of the body, they
imbibed their toasts, refilled their glasses and basked in the party
atmosphere, although as Dave Cowan recollects, one or two of
these hardy cricketers were itching to dispense with the frivolities
and cut to the chase. It might be true that cricket boasts many
noble virtues – and as the éminence grise, Alistair Cooke, once
wrote: 'It's not the winning that matters, is it? Or is it? It's
the amenities that count: the smell of the dandelions, the puff
of the pipe, the click of the bat, the rain on the neck, the slow
exquisite coming-on of sunset and dinner and rheumatism' – but
Freuchie's stalwarts were growing tired of the flummery, the
expectation and the bloody hanging around. Some of them were
also risking cirrhosis of the liver, and as Dave Christie remarked,
if he had supped every pint and savoured every whisky which he
had been offered by a village worthy, the only way he would
have gone to London was in a wooden box.

Eventually, however, the waiting concluded. Friday, 30 August
was, perhaps predictably, drizzly and depressing, but the battalion
of coaches was ready for the assignment, and thus it was that the
team, their bus overflowing with bonhomie and pent-up energy
(and a copious amount of alcohol) set off at 8 p.m. on their epic
mission. Despite the rain, hundreds of well-wishers thronged the
Main Street to salute their laddies and the initial leg of their
journey steered them west, through Falkland, Strathmiglo and
Gateside to the M90 motorway. At the Forth Road Bridge,
Scottish Television's cameras captured the captain and his confrères singing with the collective heartiness which had characterised their efforts in the competition and the pictures from that
evening trip provide a revealing psychological insight into their
mental state. Flick along the passengers, and the different temperaments of these personnel are manifest: Christie Snr looks
relaxed, resilient, the glint in his eye betraying the steel behind the
genial countenance; his son, meanwhile, is chatting eagerly to
Dave Cowan, whose giant grin and joie de vivre mark him out as a

natural-born roaring boy; a few rows further down, Niven McNaughton is his usual mass of tics and restless nervousness, holding onto a cigarette as if it were Harry Potter's Philosopher's Stone and surpassing Alex Higgins in his facial intensity; while up and down the aisles Allan Wilkie and the rest of the passengers are belting out Scottish songs accompanied by Stella Wilkie, whose gifts with a bow in her hand suggested that the joyful spirit of Stephane Grappelli was alive and thriving as the hours elapsed and night turned into morning. Whilst some players slept fitfully, dreaming of hitting the winning six into the Mound Stand, others flicked the pages of the latest Peter Benchley, Robert Ludlum or Stephen King novel, and one or two cracked open the cans and tested their constitutions to breaking point.

In actuality, their trek had barely commenced before they were heading back swiftly in the direction of Fife, across the Forth Bridge, much to the bemusement of the non-television specialists in the party. 'We earned some funny looks from the guys at the toll barrier, but the first time we made the crossing, STV didn't get the pictures they required – they told us there was something wrong with their camera angle, so we agreed to do a Take Two . . . as long as they agreed to pay the toll charge,' recalls Alan Duncan. 'Even at that stage, there were a few mellow souls on the bus, and we could probably have shot the scene 20 times for all they would have noticed. But we moved on, and attempted to make some kind of dent on the drink, even though we must have been supplied with more alcoholic beverages than there were on the shelves of the Albert Tavern.'

Perhaps it was hardly surprising that sniffier sections of Scotland's Calvinist population have chosen to depict the Fifers as men on a collective mission to recreate Ray Milland's voyage of discovery in *The Lost Weekend*. Certainly, nobody could quibble with the declaration that Freuchie's cavaliers excelled in the art of tippling. But, as their skipper relates, they were professional when it was necessary and, throbbing heads or not, nobody ever feigned excuses to miss training after nights on the tiles. 'We had only three ambitions in our heads on the road down, and they were that, come what may, we would enjoy ourselves, we would aim to do ourselves justice and we would make the whole experience something to cherish for the travelling contingent,' says Dave Christie. 'We had discovered snippets of information about Rowledge, and we appreciated that we were the underdogs, especially after digesting the facts that one of their batsmen, Chris Yates, had already attained three centuries in the Village Cup that summer, that they had been champions of their league for the last five years, and had appeared at The Oval in Surrey competitions twice in recent seasons, so they were no strangers to the big stage. Of course, there were all manner of questions and different emotions filtering and swirling through our minds: What would Lord's be like? What would the English think of the kilts? How would it feel to step onto the hallowed turf? How would the anthem sound on the morning? And would we perform to our potential, given all the fuss which had been sparked by the media? But I can't say I was anything other than optimistic that we would offer a good account of ourselves. We had been together as a group long enough and I knew my boys well enough not to be overly concerned about how they would respond. They loved every minute of it. They didn't need a nursemaid or a nanny.'

Naturally, there were plenty of gags, reminiscences and chestnuts rolled out as the hours drifted by. Every team contains a couple of resident wits and Dave Cowan's vault of anecdotes has induced belly-laughs from the most saturnine listener. On one occasion, he told me of a sweltering afternoon on East League duty, where the pitch was a bowler's nightmare and taking wickets was harder than titanium. Eventually, summoning every ounce of strength in his body, he induced his opponent into a snick, straight to the keeper, only for the umpire to turn down his appeal. Infuriated by this, he sped in even faster and trapped the batsman directly in front of his stumps, plumb lbw. Again, his anguished cry of 'Howzat' was received with disdain. Eventually, with steam surging out of his ears by this stage, Cowan sent down a superb yorker which shattered his foe's stumps. Whereupon, he turned to the umpire and said quietly: 'Must have been close, eh!'

Niven McNaughton, too, was a bulging receptacle of tales from the school of coarse cricket, and regaled me with assorted accounts of nefarious officialdom and/or decisions which had gone against him over the years, with a deadpan delivery which left one questioning whether we were dealing with apocrypha. 'There was one match, where the umpire genuinely replied to my lbw shout: "Sorry, but I couldn't see the wickets for his legs." And another, where we had eight or nine men around the bat, their last man was at the crease, and he popped up an easy catch. We began to walk off the pitch, when the umpire announced: "Sorry, I signalled a no ball." A couple of minutes later, the batter was lbw, as plain as the nose on your face, but the cry "No ball" went up once more. At the end of the over, I went to square leg and the batsman immediately hit the ball in my direction, but as I moved to pouch it, the umpire crashed into me and we both fell to the ground. "Dead ball!" he cried out. It was impossible, we were never going to remove this guy. Until the final over of the game when we went up, half-heartedly for a dubious lbw appeal, and suddenly, to our amazement, the umpire put his finger up in our favour and said, quite sincerely: "It's nice to keep these matches exciting to the end, isn't it!"

The banter continued relentlessly on the London road: here were customers with more sauce than HP, and an insatiable Bunteresque appetite for mischief. But nonetheless, it was a bleary-eyed group who checked into the Westmoreland Hotel at eight the next morning, as the prelude to these resilient characters gaining a second and, in several cases, third wind, which allowed them to participate in TV broadcasts, practice sessions, embark on another protracted bus tour and yet retain sufficient vigour to attend the *Cricketer* reception on Saturday evening. By this stage, the little-leaguers' arrival in the big city had attracted the interest of such diverse programmes as ITN's *News at Ten*, *Saint and Greavesie* and *Test Match Special*, where Brian Johnston's efforts at pronouncing Freuchie proved on a par with Archie Macpherson's strangulated efforts to master various Croatian, Czech and Russian surnames on the European soccer beat.

Typically, the aforementioned Jimmy Greaves, a man perfectly equipped to portray the views of the archetypal London cab driver – 'String 'em up, guv'nor. It's the only language they understand' – indulged in some ritual Jock-baiting, whilst his sparring partner, Ian St John, defended the right of Scots to play cricket as if it were a treasonable act north of the Border. For those unacquainted with this duo, they were the Ally McCoist and Terry Venables of their day, a pair of populist pundits with saloon-bar platitudes in abundance, and a non-PC approach ideally suited to an antediluvian world polluted by real-life Ron Managers, before women started entering the boardroom, demanded admission to football writers' dinners (quite why they would wish to attend these horror shows is another matter) and began churning out talented players in the vein of Mia Hamm and Julie Fleeting, who became household names in their countries.

Yet if anybody imagined they could garner some cheap laughs from Freuchie, they were soon disabused of that notion by Allan Wilkie, whose behind-the-scenes industry was unstinting. ITN were informed, in no uncertain terms, that while they were welcome to film the kilted procession into Lord's for that night's news programme, they would not be permitted onto the team bus en route to the ground. Similarly, a member from the *On The Ball* production crew was soundly harangued for failing to persuade Greaves to respond to Freuchie's challenge to have a net with the Scots. Even 'Jonners', the epitome of civility and British Empire-derived etiquette, received a short, sharp lesson from the Wilkie manual, observing that the Fifers weren't called Freetchy, Frootchy or Frookie and that there never had existed a creature called the Lock Ness Monster.

'As the Saturday rolled on, I was contacted by all manner of media outlets, and I knew that lots of Scottish supporters were walking around London, seeing the sights – Buckingham Palace, the Tower of London, the usual suspects – and I guessed that while this was an entirely different situation from Scottish football's invasion of Wembley in 1977, some of the English papers would looking for pictures of tartan-clad hooligans, and that, if any trouble did erupt, it would be a fresh chance to bash the Scots,' says Wilkie, who coped heroically with the communication and logistical glitches, which were commonplace in the pre-mobile phone era. 'The *Daily Express* managed to find a bunch of fans at Trafalgar Square and took photographs of them with their flags and kilts – and if you wanted a snap of an invading horde, that would be ideal – but my worries were eased when I learned that my old grandmother was in the middle of the crowd scene and she was 73, so she was hardly the type of person to get involved in serious bother with the police. It might sound paranoid at this distance, but I was determined that nothing, absolutely nothing, was going to spoil Freuchie's weekend and that the focus revolved around the cricketers, because they were the reason we were there in droves.'

Once Christie's corps has breakfasted and showered they climbed back, a tad gingerly, onto another coach, in search of the Indian Gymkhana Club on the Great West Road, where they had arranged an eagerly-awaited work-out on a strip of grass in the direction of Heathrow, which will forever be a part of Asian culture in Britain. This organisation was founded in 1916 by the Maharajah of Patiala, who had toured England as Indian captain a decade previously, and decided to bestow a gift of £1000, specifically designed to provide students in the United Kingdom with a base for their cultural and sporting activities. Granted, the connection between a subcontinental relic of imperial India and the rough-and-ready burghers of Freuchie may appear as obscure as the gobbledygook which masquerades as prophecy in Dan Brown's ludicrous *The Da Vinci Code*, but at least there is a logical explanation where the cricket is concerned. Namely, that an Indian touring party had visited Scotland two years previously, and Dave Christie and Allan Wilkie had forged links with their hosts which they were determined to preserve.

'Honestly, the Gymkhana lads couldn't have been more supportive, we had enjoyed their company up in Fife, and we were overwhelmed with the scale of the hospitality at their club. They laid on a huge buffet for us, with all kinds of food [including garlic naan, layered parathas, malai kebabs, aloo tikki, and juicy paneer tikka] and a lot of the Indian members, not just their cricketers but folk from their football and hockey sections as well, trotted along and watched us practise and get ready for Lord's, and it was a really relaxed environment in which we could stretch our legs, sharpen up our bowling and get rid of any tension which had been building up on the journey down,' says Christie, whose admirable attitude to his beloved game is that cricket matters, not the colour of the man wielding the bat. 'The sole problem was that we couldn't find their ground, and we were driving around in circles for a couple of hours – perhaps a wee bit extra research would have helped – but although there was some grumbling from the players, the mood soon lightened and it was actually a relief to enjoy some cricket and exercise, because our normal routine had definitely been disrupted as the publicity machine cranked up.

'That is the principal reason why the Saturday session lasted so long: the boys were desperate for a thorough work-out and the facilities at the Gymkhana were first-class, which wasn't surprising, given that they were used to hosting international touring teams [as well as staging an annual fixture against an MPs select]. Originally, we had contemplated trying to buy tickets for the Test match at The Oval, but with the English in the process of wrapping up the Ashes that idea was shot to pieces, and although a few of the lads also discussed going to a football match if West Ham or Chelsea or Tottenham were playing at home, I thought the best option was to have a no-holds-barred practice and go flat-out for two or three hours. It worked a treat. I didn't have to motivate them, they just ran out and did their drills and were absolutely dripping with sweat by the finish. Then we tucked into that brilliant spread. The Indians couldn't have done any more and my only regret was that we couldn't accept their invitation to go back on the Sunday evening after the final. But alas, there are only so many hours in any day.'

As it was, Christie had one unenviable task to perform. Even though it can't have been a colossal surprise to Fraser Irvine and

Peter Hepplewhite, neither of whom had been involved in the semi-final victory, the captain was confronted with the job of telling them they wouldn't be required in Freuchie's starting XI. There is no easy way of relaying this kind of information: bad enough that Irvine should wind up as twelfth man, charged with the bat-replacing, drinks-carrying chores, but worse still that Hepplewhite was designated thirteenth man, which, under the *Cricketer* regulations, meant that he wasn't even eligible for an official medal at the climax of the Sabbath showdown.

Yet, true to form, Christie and his two surplus characters were able to conclude the formalities without rancour or bitterness. The opposite, in fact. 'Don't get me wrong, it wasn't exactly pleasant breaking the news, but you have to be honest and open in these circumstances and I wasn't going to leave them in suspense because we had to show faith with the lads who guided us to success against Oulton and Billesdon, and both Fraser and Peter quickly acknowledged that argument,' says Christie. 'They took it well, the two of them, and really put themselves out to help us in the next 48 hours and I suspect they realised, even whilst we were heading down to London, that they would only be required if one of the other boys contracted an injury or got hurt in an accident, and we were all too close for anybody to wish ill on another. So I did what I had to do.'

Hence the confirmation of the Freuchie line-up, which would lock horns with Rowledge the following day. Mark Wilkie: a safe pair of hands. Alan Duncan: a dogged wicket-keeper/batsman. The Crichton brothers, Andy and George: obdurate run-gatherers whose labours had already proved crucial in the Village Cup. George Wilson: a reticent pillar of solidity. The Animals, Dave Cowan and Stewart Irvine: characters who could be relied upon for a middle-order blitzkrieg. Terry Trewartha: coach, bowler and bit-part batsman. The Christies, Dave and Brian: their value beyond assessment. And at No. 11, Niven McNaughton: a big-hearted worker in the Stakhanovite tradition. No wonder that as his charges limbered up for their equivalent of the Oscars by supping a few ales and spirits whilst Rowledge were otherwise engaged elsewhere, the captain seemed content in his estimation that their unique band of brotherhood would do all right, regardless of the fact that Freuchie's footmen had never pretended to belong to a Benedictine order.

'It was a grand dinner and I think that both the *Cricketer* magazine and ourselves benefited from the publicity which was being doled out to the team, because the game in Scotland had never seen anything like this in its history before,' says Christie, who was as mystified at the non-appearance of his opponents as anybody in the audience. 'We found out from the tournament organisers that Rowledge had a population of around 2000 and they were very much in the commuter belt, 40 miles south-west of London, and their captain [Alan Prior] later told me that they were so close to being in Hampshire that a big hit for six would send the ball into a different county, so they weren't hugely different from us. Their community had two pubs, a post office, a village store and the cricket, and that was about it. But perhaps they were so near to Lord's that there wasn't the same thrill and sense of expectation that we felt after travelling 500 miles.

'Whatever the answer, we held no sway over what the other team did, we just had to concentrate on our own performance and let them worry about us. I remember glancing around me that night, with everybody enjoying themselves and the party in full swing and thinking: Well, Dave, this is what we have been aspiring to since we first heard about the Village Cup competition: gaining the opportunity to reach for the stars and go where legends have been. And, without being sentimental, I also appreciated that, at 48, I probably wasn't going to get this chance again, so I had better make it count, and particularly with all those Fife busloads already on their way down to join us.'

As the chimes of midnight reverberated around the corridors of the Westmoreland Hotel, the Scots gradually retreated to the sanctuary of their beds and the jack-the-lads dreamt of giant-slaying. Within 24 hours, these part-timers were to march intrepidly into the cricketing chronicles like none of their compatriots, before or after.

CHAPTER 9

A SWEET SEPTEMBER SONG

It may have resembled Gracie Fields arriving at Balmoral Castle for an impromptu spot of caber-tossing, but if there was one feature which characterised Freuchie's trip to Lord's, it lay in the team's absolute determination to enjoy the experience, absorb the memories and bask in the limelight. The stereotypical tabloid summations of their Village Cup final joust with Rowledge would have us believe that the event was a clash between a lager-swilling, string-vested group of working-class Gaels and a patrician bunch of affluent, toffee-nosed suburbanites – Rab C. Nesbit meets Kenneth Williams – but the reality was altogether more complex. Ultimately, this was an unprecedented opportunity for Freuchie's players and travelling faithful to take the home of cricket by storm and demonstrate that sporting obsession comes in myriad guises.

From the moment that Pipe Major Alistair Pirnie led Dave Christie and his colleagues through the Grace Gates to the accompaniment of the specially-composed 'Freuchie March To Lord's', the incongruity of the spectacle was only equalled by the depth of passion for the Fifers from the hordes who had swarmed down to London. 'It was quite humbling actually: there were many times in the build-up to the match when I had to rub my eyes and ask myself: Is this really happening?' says Christie. 'I had seen the pictures of Lord's on my television screen, and read about all the wonderful cricketers who had played there, and suddenly, here were 11 Scots lads striding into the same amphitheatre and gaining the chance to walk where legends had walked. It was breathtaking and although I was initially happy just to be involved in a game at Lord's, I soon changed my mind

when I looked out at the ground. I recall thinking to myself:
Stuff this, we are not here just to make up the numbers, let's win
the competition. You could scarcely believe otherwise when
you spotted all the Scots in the audience.'

The crowd, on an overcast but relatively tranquil afternoon,
was certainly partisan. One couldn't miss the woman with a yard-
high top hat, bearing the slogan 'Freuchie of Scotland'. Or the
bearded chap carrying a banner, 'Remember Bannockburn'
(some of us rather wish our compatriots would ignore that
tiresome message and disengage from incessant navel-gazing,
particularly after sitting through the execrable *Braveheart*, but
painting the past in a romantic hue is a strikingly Celtic trait).
Or the fellow whose T-shirt despatched the message to the
English observers in the members' stand: 'Mi Lords, it's Freuchie,
not Frookie!' Robert Smith, a 35-year-old glazier from Freuchie,
had even brought his own trophy, a haggis-shaped glass model of a
Scottish cricketer called Hamish, and there were a plethora of
references to 'The Flower of Scotland', that ancient ballad written,
oh, some time in the 1960s. Also at the party was nine-month-old
Callum Glasgow, from Glenrothes, who was escorted to Lord's
despite his father's protest. 'I banned the family from taking the
wee lad to the game, but my wife pointed out to me that she had
brought him along to every other match in the tournament, and
there was no way in the world that he was missing the final,' said
Tom Glasgow, the brother-in-law of Freuchie wicket-keeper,
Alan Duncan. These words neatly encapsulate the surreal, slightly
barmy spirit of Freuchie's date with destiny on a weekend when
PC Ian Gordon was left to oversee a near-abandoned Fife
community. In retrospect, what chance had Rowledge in their
joust, not simply with 11 men but an entire village?

Sifting through the newspaper reports from that September
Sabbath, there are references galore to bagpipers and kilted
warriors, to lucky white heather and distraught Lord's patrons
wondering whether their domain had been turned upside-down
forever, in the midst of an uncouth bunch of Scots invading their
private sanctuary. One finds myriad details of the prelude and the

frenzy which enveloped Fife in the build-up to this fantastic voyage: one also discovers glorious paeans of praise to Dave Christie and his troops, once they had completed their nerve-shredding triumph against Rowledge to cement their place in the archives. Yet, invariably, there is a gap at the heart of these accounts, like a novel with a beginning and an end, but no middle. It's almost as if the reason why Christie and his colleagues had devoted their sporting lives so obsessively to Freuchie – to playing cricket – had been forgotten, while pints were poured and the whole experience unfolded, as if directed by David Puttnam from a Colin Welland script, which, in some respects, is a shame. Fair enough if the final itself had developed into a tedious non-event, where only the result was important, but the reality could hardly have proved more different. This was a match which boasted everything: enough twists and turns to satisfy O. Henry, a classic contrast between the combatants, a pitch invasion as the confrontation reached a breathless dénouement, and palpitating tension from first to last delivery.

There had been controversy from the outset, when the rival captains, Dave Christie and Alan Prior, tossed an hour before the 1.30 start, the coin landed in the Englishman's favour, and he promptly marched off to lunch with his players before eventually plumping to bat, an option which he still defends even though it sparked surprise amongst sections of his companions. 'We were waiting to see what the weather might do, because there was low cloud cover and a possibility of rain, but it held off, I elected to bat first and there was nothing wrong with that call,' says Prior. 'Hindsight is a wonderful thing, and I realise that some of our spectators believed that we should have used the opportunity to field first as a means of becoming acclimatised to the conditions, but let's be honest here. That might be okay for players who are competing every day and are accustomed to appearing in major finals. But when you are working five or six days a week, as we were, pressure does strange things to you and basically, I always preferred to get the runs on the board and then attempt to keep the opposition at bay.'

For his part, Christie was delighted at earning the chance to bowl first, with his imposing attack primed to strike. That morning, he and his personnel had already completed their pre-match discussions, limbered up for the biggest afternoon of their lives, and there was no need for Churchillian grandiloquence as they prepared to march onto the Lord's turf. They had been ushered to their dressing room, complete with their own attendant, and served up a hearty meal around noon, which was enjoyed by everybody except Terry Trewartha, though his disquiet had naught to do with the quality of the haute cuisine. 'I was sitting, waiting for my roast beef, when the waitress asked me if I fancied some gravy,' he recalls. 'I answered in the affirmative and then the poor lassie lost her sense of direction and missed my plate, but landed the stuff all over my clothes, and I was covered in brown stuff. I was aghast, because I didn't have a spare shirt, but what do you know, the Lord's staff rushed to the emergency as it were an everyday occurrence, and within half-an-hour my whites had been washed, dried and ironed, and I was the smartest-dressed lad in the team. The roast beef was a wee bit dry, mind you . . .'

Out in the middle, as the congregation of banner-waving Scots raised the decibel level from the stands, Christie and his confrères luxuriated in the opportunity to stroll around cricket's cathedral and soak in the atmosphere, the ambience and the redolent immortality of the ghosts from summers past, whose heroics had reverberated around the globe. Grace, Bradman, Compton, Hammond, the Nawab of Pataudi, Walcott, Weekes and Worrell . . . all sharing a platform with The Animals and the Mean Machine! No wonder that the normally-measured Freuchie captain is positively lyrical in his reminiscing.

'The whole experience felt similar to a dream, a beautiful dream. The adrenaline was coursing through our veins, and although there were a few butterflies in our stomachs – it would have been worrying if there hadn't been – we realised that the pressure was heaped on Rowledge, they were the favourites, and one or two of their lads had gone on record as declaring that the match would be over in 90 minutes, which wasn't the cleverest manoeuvre,' says Christie. 'I stressed to the boys that we had to make them work for every run, and we had to remember all the lessons we had absorbed in practice about getting our fielding right and how significant that factor was to our hopes, but really, the notion that I would have to motivate or fire up my players was absurd. We were at Lord's, for heaven's sake, we could hear hundreds of our ain folk yelling their support outside, and we had been gearing ourselves up for this moment for years. There was nothing to be frightened of, except fear itself, and we were a team who could look each other in the eye and know instinctively that we were all in the fight together 100 per cent. Personally, the game couldn't start too early and it was music to our ears when they elected to bat, especially considering how long it took them to decide.'

Hence the spring in the step, the infinite enthusiasm and tightly-marshalled tactics of his charges when, amidst a bedlam of commotion and skirling of pipes from a crowd featuring as many as 3000 Scots (some have estimated that figure at 5000, but since admission was free and the entrance was left open, it's difficult to judge precisely) – compared with a small sprinkling of those with allegiance to Rowledge – the latter's openers, Bob Simpson and Tony Hook, strode along the hallowed Long Room, down the pavilion steps and steeled themselves for a challenge, which wasn't long in arriving. Indeed, from David Cowan's opening delivery, which landed precisely where he had directed it, the tone had been established by Freuchie's bowlers, and with Niven McNaughton finding his rhythm at the Nursery End, runs were hard to come by in the early exchanges and it was no surprise when Cowan quickly tempted Simpson into attempting an intemperate hook, the ensuing catch was pouched by Andy Crichton at square leg as if he were back on the Public Park, and the chanting intensified.

That made it 15 for 1, with Simpson gone for 6, and whilst Rowledge managed to consolidate in the next half-hour, their style veered closer to Trevor Bailey than Shahid Afridi, singles sprinted here and there, the intermittent boundary failing to silence the Scots in the crowd or disrupt the pattern of the Freuchie attack. Not until McNaughton was pummelled for 10 runs in the 10th over did Hook and Neil Dunbar hint at breaking the stranglehold and it gradually grew apparent that any trace of pre-match condescension by the Englishmen had been replaced with a recognition that their rivals were no eccentric men of Hamlet with the philosophy: Two beers or not two beers.

Hook, by this stage, had produced a couple of memorable straight drives and seemed capable of lifting the tempo, as the Surreysiders attained their 50 in the 17th over, with a fine shot to the long-on boundary, but just when he looked on the point of launching a necessary injection of acceleration, Niven McNaughton uprooted his off stump in his last over, and the match swung dramatically towards Freuchie as they collectively maintained their line and length, which, allied to characteristically tigerish fielding from their whole ensemble, induced a mounting sense of panic amongst their adversaries.

The score was 56 for 2 when Hook exited and the arrival of Chris Yates, Rowledge's star performer throughout a summer when he amassed a string of aggressive hundreds, proved a non-event. It was significant that Dave Christie, a wily interpreter of every situation, introduced himself to the fray in time to force Yates into dragging the ball onto his stumps while attempting to cut, and the English club's key individual had mustered only 10. The Fifers' jubilation testified to their capture of the prize scalp, and before Rowledge could recover their composure, they slumped into further disarray when Andy Crichton, a ubiquitous Jack-in-the-box in the covers, ran out Paul Offord for 0 with a superb stop and throw in one movement, to reduce them to 74 for 4. Already, there had been sufficient illustration of Freuchie's fleetness of foot around the Lord's environs, to suggest that anybody seeking sharp singles was asking for trouble, but the message appeared lost on Dunbar, who was clinically run out by Crichton for 33, with his team on 94, as an air of gloom and despondency enveloped their followers.

'We never allowed them to settle, we backed each other up and pursued everything like a cat on hot bricks,' recalls Cowan, whose early precision had been the catalyst for Rowledge's middle-order self-destruction. 'Dave Christie and Terry Trewartha had spent months or, more accurately, years, reminding us that whilst we might not be the greatest batsmen or bowlers in the world, we could be a match for anybody in the fielding stakes and it proved crucial during the final. We heard later that Rowledge were accustomed to posting scores in excess of 200 on a regular basis, but I would wager they didn't meet too many teams who snapped at their heels and persevered the way we did.'

That same restlessly energetic, livewire streak was obvious as Prior's brigade strove – and struggled – to generate any sustained momentum, especially with the introduction of Trewartha, whose stint ensured that Freuchie would not be chasing shadows later in the afternoon. First, he had John Dunbar magnificently caught at mid-wicket by Stewart Irvine, then Prior was bowled middle stump as he tried to hit the ball into the Thames, and Brian Silver holed out to Mark Wilkie in the same over, to reduce Rowledge to 117 for 8, with their ambitions of setting an imposing target fast diminishing. Thereafter, despite some frantic scrambling at the death from 'Nobby' Cooper and Tony Field, Cowan disposed of the latter and Trewartha recorded an excellent analysis of 4 for 24 by trapping Jim Reffold lbw in the last over as Rowledge only mustered 134.

'We were pleased at the halfway stage, but we knew there was likely to be a ferocious response from their bowlers, and the atmosphere in the dressing room was one of relief that we had done ourselves justice, but combined with an awareness that our batsmen hadn't always set the heather on fire,' recollects McNaughton. 'From my perspective, it was good to have shown we deserved to be in the final because, although most of the Rowledge lads were friendly enough, a couple of them had been mouthing off about how the Jocks shouldn't waste their time travelling to London, and that they were going to give us a right old stuffing. We didn't waste breath in responding, or at least not

until we were on the pitch. You would have thought they might
have appreciated that any side which qualifies for a final, from
639 entrants, have to have something going for them. But hey, if
they were complacent, nobody could ever accuse us of not being
hungry.'

At that juncture, Prior, an engaging character with a self-
deprecating air and an obvious passion for his cherished
Rowledge, admits that he feared the worst. 'It hadn't been
one of our better performances with the bat, but let's give credit
to Freuchie, they worked like Trojans, they never allowed us to
settle or grab the initiative, and whilst I was aiming at around 200
when we started out, we realised at the break that we had to
make early inroads and hope they would collapse,' he recalls.
'Perhaps we had all been a little awe-struck by arriving at Lord's
so early – we were there before the Freuchie lads – and it's hard
to take it in, when you're used to being on the village green
and then suddenly you're in this grand arena, surrounded by
generations of history and tradition. I'm not offering excuses for
how we batted, because Freuchie had clearly done their homework, and their run-outs and catching must have been as
tremendous for them as they were vexing for us. But, no doubt
about it, the advantage was with them at half-time.'

Privately, the Scots concurred, yet there was always the
nagging suspicion that grand theatricals would impinge on the
contest, given Freuchie's tendency to perform as if inspired by
Roderick Usher. Once the refreshments had been consumed,
Tony Field and Reffold were the men charged with the task of
making inroads into the Scots' top order, but although they
began accurately, Mark Wilkie and Alan Duncan survived the
onslaught, assisted by a reprieve for the former when he was
dropped by Yates at mid-off with the score on 8. The opener's
reply was unequivocal, hitting Reffold square to the short
boundary and then handing Neil Dunbar a lengthy chase towards the Warner Stand to prevent another 4. At 23 for 0 in the
9th over, the pair appeared to have weathered the storm but
suddenly, in a twinkling, Rowledge were celebrating, the Tartan

contingent on the sidelines were shaking their heads and the tussle had been transformed.

Field was the initial architect of his team's rally, bowling Wilkie for 10 and, almost before Andy Crichton had taken guard, he was trudging off, snared lbw by the seamer. At 25 for 2, with Prior and Field operating in tandem, the runs dried up for a protracted period, and worse was to befall the Scots when Duncan, vainly attempting to lift the tempo, was caught by Yates for 16, off the left-arm spin of Silver, with the tally on 42. This marked the entrance of Dave Cowan with his usual belligerent approach to digging himself out of scrapes, but the all-rounder almost perished first ball, when his lofted shot dropped perilously close to John Dunbar at long-on, neatly emphasising the wafer-thin margins which frequently decide these encounters. Yet, understandably, Rowledge's confidence had been bolstered by this flurry of activity and they were convinced they had perpetrated Cowan's stumping immediately afterwards, only for their mass appeal to be rejected. 'Offord had the bails off so quickly that the fielders could not believe the batsman was allowed to remain at the crease,' relates journalist Graham Collyer, who covered the match from the Rowledge perspective. 'Alan Prior said later that he had been flabbergasted with the verdict, but had been told that Offord's lightning-fast reactions removed the bails before Cowan's back foot actually lifted. It was very tight.'

Maybe unsurprisingly, this isn't exactly the Scot's memory. 'The game had become really tense, and there was a lot of excitement and gesturing when the incident happened,' says Cowan. 'But I was unfazed by the noise and the clamour. Sometimes, the best way of dealing with these flare-ups is to pretend that you are completely unmoved, and I just stood there impassively until tempers had cooled down. Inwardly, I was churning – don't forget that I was still pretty young and inexperienced in these powder-keg situations – but I wasn't going to show that to the English guys.'

Instead, after George Wilson had been caught behind by

Offord for 14, and with Freuchie perilously perched at 52 for 4, The Animals served up notice that, whether the setting was Largo or Lord's, their efficacious brand of aggression could discompose any attack. In just over 4 overs, Cowan and Stewart Irvine added 33 runs and the Englishmen, rattled by the counter-offensive, were, as Prior recalls 'a little ragged for the first time in their whole Village Cup campaign'. Irvine, the stolid quarryman, struck the Rowledge skipper for successive 4s, Cowan capitalised on some short-pitched deliveries from Yates, and it seemed that the pair who had made escapology their speciality as much as Harry Houdini, would steer their side to victory with a Botham-esque joie de vivre.

'We had to marvel at how Jasper approached the task. Here we were, involved in the biggest, most significant game of our lives, and he was laughing and joking and relishing every moment of it,' says McNaughton. 'It was as if he had been trotting out for a knock-about at Lord's every week, and maybe it sums up his temperament that he was in his element. Some of us on the balcony were chain-smoking and watching through the cracks of our fingers and our hearts were pumping. But Jasper and Davie were pretty cool customers. The rest of us started to think that our services wouldn't be required.'

Unfortunately, this being Freuchie, that Micawberish conviction was quickly quashed as the final swerved down another cul-de-sac of unpredictability. Prior reintroduced Silver in the 25th over and the ploy paid instant dividends, with the little spinner bowling Cowan around his legs. Irvine then provided the perfect riposte, by blasting Prior for a towering 6 over the top of the Mound stand – he later learned that he was one of only two people to have achieved that feat; the other was some chap called Garfield Sobers – but that was his last contribution, before the English captain had him caught and bowled for 24, and at 91 for 6, the tension and nerve-jangling had returned with an almighty vengeance.

By now, every run was greeted with howls of approbation from the Saltire-clad supporters, while a host of locals, drawn to the ground late in the afternoon by the sound of bagpipes and 'The Flower of Scotland', were captivated by the unfolding drama. The canny Prior juggled his bowlers astutely and, apart from Offord conceding four byes, the scoring had almost completely dried up. Trewartha managed to bring up the 100 in the 30th over, but was swiftly bowled by Reffold and the sprinkling of Rowledge devotees grew vocal, with the occasional reference to Culloden flung into the mix.

It was time for somebody to grasp the battle by the scruff of the neck, and throttle the breath out of the opposition. Maybe we should have guessed that Dave Christie would be that individual. Striding out to the middle, in poor light, the 48-year-old stalwart had a chat with his partner, George Crichton, and while he didn't relay the message, 'We'll get them in singles', he had noticed that Rowledge's fielding wasn't in the same league as his own players', hence his decision to scamper runs and dare his rivals to run him out. They almost managed it when Crichton scurried in, inches ahead of Simpson's throw, but mistakes proliferated as the dénouement beckoned. Offord let the ball go through his legs for two byes, and there were a number of fumbles to encourage Christie, but even so Freuchie had only advanced to 118 after 36 overs and they realised that McNaughton batted at No. 11 purely because the rules forbade him from being No. 12.

'We had another wee talk and agreed we would run for anything feasible and test their mettle, because we had spotted the errors creeping into the fielding,' says Christie, whose sangfroid under fire exemplified the mental toughness of most of the Scots. 'I recall that we only added 3 runs in the 37th over, but that we both dashed through for 2 singles in the next over and then left one of their lads flat-footed at mid-wicket and we had moved to 127 with a couple of overs left. It was still not cut and dried, but the balance of power had shifted to us and we knew that one boundary anywhere would seal it. Credit to Rowledge, they never ceased pestering and pounding us, but we had the scent of victory in our nostrils and that climax is etched in

my mind. First up, George hit the left-armer through the covers
for two, then rushed home for a quick single. I pushed the next
delivery into the covers and got a single and George took us to
133 with a shot, backward of square. But just when it looked as if
it might be all over, I was run out by [Neil] Dunbar's throw from
the gully and I was gutted. I trudged off, barely able to think
straight, but my son, Brian, was next in, and I pulled myself
together, looked him in the eye, and said simply: "Be sensible.
Whatever you do, don't get out, because we can't have Nivvy
coming in, because he's shaking like a leaf and hiding in the
toilets." '

In fact, if Christie was seething, he kept his emotions wonder-
fully in check. 'He walked back to the pavilion with a proud look
on his face and he was entitled to feel proud, because he could
hardly have come to the wicket in more difficult circumstances
and he got the tactics spot-on,' declares Prior, whose admiration
for his counterpart has since been reciprocated by a liquid-fuelled
liaison between the pair in the Freuchie clubhouse. 'When he
was out there was a moment where time seemed to stand still,
but the crowd, including the Rowledge fans, applauded Dave all
the way back and he turned to thank them before climbing up
the steps. It typified the whole occasion for me.'

By the time of his departure, Freuchie required two runs for an
outright win or a single, provided they lost only one more
wicket, under the Village Cup competition rules. As Prior
prepared to bowl the last over, the public address system appealed
for calm and for spectators to keep off the pitch until the players
were safely back in the pavilion. But frankly, they may as well
have asked every Scot in attendance to raise a glass to Jimmy Hill
and invest a fiver in Margaret Thatcher's retirement fund. With
the very next delivery, Crichton levelled the scores, eagerly
helping himself to a single which slipped through Simpson's
hands, and Lord's was engulfed in a sea of tartan and raucous
nationalism. Two balls later Brian Christie, surrounded by
fielders, ran for a leg bye, and as he recollects: 'Hundreds of
our singing, dancing, drinking followers invaded the ground

from in front of the Tavern.' Joy was unconfined, and there was hugging, mass back-slapping, paeans of praise to the victors. And then, in the midst of the melee and mayhem, the umpire at the bowler's end, a brave/foolhardy/pedantic fellow (please tick your preference) ruled the run was void because Christie had not attempted a shot.

'It was crazy and I had no idea what on earth was happening,' says Prior, who had received a litany of commiserations before order was eventually restored. 'We had to wait for a bit of calm to resurface, and that was nail-biting in the extreme, but I guess I had subconsciously accepted that we weren't going to win. For us to do so, I had to take 2 wickets with the remaining 3 balls, because we would then have scored our runs off fewer deliveries, but it was a big ask, and especially with all the racket.'

Upstairs, meanwhile, Niven McNaughton had stopped viewing the action. 'He had gone through around 30 fags in the space of half an hour, and he couldn't stand the tension any longer, so he went off to hide in the gents,' says Dave Cowan. 'You could forgive him, mind, because we had endured every imaginable emotion in the previous hour: elation, despair, renewed hope, anxiety, delight for Dad, and disappointment that he wouldn't be there to guide us to the trophy, which would have been the most fitting conclusion.'

In the event, it was left to Christie Jnr to guarantee Freuchie's triumph. Not with a sparkling boundary to surpass Rowledge's target, but by patiently, methodically, blocking the remainder of Prior's over. In the confusion, the Englishman actually bowled four more deliveries (it should have been three), but all to no avail. Christie defended stoutly, his team finished on 134 for 8 and the Village Cup was in Scottish hands.

Almost unnoticed amid the bedlam, George Crichton had, just as in the Billesdon encounter, proved himself the epitome of obduracy and tenacity in guiding his compatriots to their Holy Grail. There was nothing fancy in his repertoire, but every team needs an unvaunted hero or two, and the elder Crichton brother had once more negotiated treacherous waters with serenity under fire. 'I had spoken to a couple of my mates on the Saturday, and they told me about all the buses which had been booked to travel down to London that evening and I think I was absolutely terrified of letting all these people down, but I wasn't the sort of person to let my opponents know I was churning inside,' he says. 'The bottom line was that if I had been interested in personal glory, I could have attempted to smash a boundary to seal the victory, but what if I had failed? That would have meant Niven having to come to the wicket and he was shitting himself at the prospect and one or two of the others were bloody close to joining him in the toilets by the end, so I stuck to being sensible, and it was the correct strategy. No doubt there will be some purists ready to quibble at the fact that both teams scored the same number of runs. I couldn't care less. Only one of the finalists lifted the trophy and it was us.'

As that realisation started to sink in, Dave Christie confesses that he passed through shock, then delight, followed by the creeping sense that he had to thank Freuchie's travelling acolytes for the warmth and dedication of their support. 'I gazed down from the balcony and there was this canvas of Scotsmen and Scotswomen going completely bonkers, united in joy,' he says, eternally infused with a glow of satisfaction. 'During the pitch invasion, I had spotted my two sisters-in-law, with their high heels on, charging across Lord's and I thought: "Oh my God, what red necks." But of course there wasn't any malice involved, it was simply pure, unconstrained exhilaration at what was happening. Within the next few moments, I was presented with the Village Cup trophy by Ben Brocklehurst, the managing director of the *Cricketer* magazine, and Stewart Irvine collected the "Man of the Match" award – a cricket bat – and there were tears streaming down Jasper's cheeks. If anybody ever doubts whether Scotland can't be passionate about cricket, they should have been there during that ceremony, because some of the lads were crying, others were dashing around like dervishes, and it all felt like the end of a Hollywood movie. We discovered later that Rowledge had brought some champagne to their dressing room, for uncorking on the balcony if they won, but we hadn't dared to be so presumptuous. So Coca-Cola being sprayed onto the fans below had to suffice. I don't think anybody noticed, given all the singing and partying which had erupted at the climax, but most of us made up for it later that night.'

In retrospect, Christie's vagueness over the precise sequence of events is entirely understandable. On one hand he was being besieged by autograph-hunters and camera-carrying fellow-Freuchie citizens, on the other, he was trying to retain his dignity and composure in the midst of pandemonium, frenzy and Hallelujah choruses. One can only conjecture what the Lord's panjandrums made of the tableau but, had they allowed the stiff upper lip to crack for a moment or two, they must surely have appreciated that the Fifers had reinvigorated the competition and were worthy winners. Christie, however, was also searching for his parents, David and Margaret, who were amongst the throng, and when he eventually hooked up with them he finally permitted himself to unwind.

'It was a magic moment, and we just all looked at one another and then embraced and they were saying "Well done" and "We're proud of you" and I was utterly lost for words, let alone speeches,' he acknowledges. 'One or two of the journalists were doing their best to persuade me to analyse the match, but at that point all that mattered was the fact we had won, that we had done ourselves and our country proud and, to be honest, the small details seemed almost irrelevant in the grand scheme of things. Twenty years on, I have run through the match time and time again, and my conclusion is that I had envisaged Rowledge would be much better than they actually were and that they probably underestimated us. Their bowling attack wasn't up to much – which was just as well for our batsmen – but it was their whole attitude to the occasion, which was a bit strange. The night before, at the official reception, we were all present and correct, whereas they only had Alan Prior, Chris Yates and his wife, and all the talk centred around Freuchie this, and Scotland that, and it was a huge shot in the arm for us to seize the initiative before we had even tucked ourselves into bed on Saturday. Perhaps Rowledge naively imagined that we would drink to excess and that it would affect our performance on the Sunday. But if that was the case, then they clearly hadn't done their homework properly.'

Alan Duncan was involved in a family reunion as well, though this differed starkly from the jubilant embraces shared by the Christies. Half an hour after the dénouement, a Lord's steward approached him and said: 'Sir, there's a gentleman here to see you.'

'Well, I wondered who it was, but popped round the corner and there was my father, Alexander, standing with an exasperated expression. You might have thought we were poised for a scene out of *Field of Dreams*, but not a word of it,' says Duncan. 'Instead, he looked me up and down and declared: "You know, I drove all the way down from Fife this morning to watch you and you didn't even hit a six." Then he walked off and headed straight back to Scotland without another word. I was a wee bit gutted, because it would have taken me two shots to hit a six on a ground that size, but that episode has stuck in my mind ever since. I suppose you could say they breed them tough in Freuchie.'

Back home, the telephone lines were buzzing as cricket aficionados sought news of the outcome. The mass epidemic of Freuchie fever had prompted British Telecom to lay on a phone-in results service for the final – at the Kirkcaldy number 0592-262600 – but although the idea was sound in principle, the company had grievously underestimated the level of interest in the service. 'I did get through on two occasions as the match progressed, but to do so, I literally had to dial hundreds of times,' said Duncan Scott, one of the many callers, who was exasperated by the incessant delays (prompted, according to Dave Christie, by a selfish ninny staying on the line for an hour at the death). 'The last time I tried, I started dialling at 7.13 p.m. – and after 88 successive attempts, I eventually got through and discovered the Scots had won, even though my ears were buzzing.'

Nowadays, in the age of the internet and ball-by-ball updates on the BBC and Cricinfo, allied to Ceefax, Teletext and interactive options for satellite viewers, this primitive technology will sound quaint. But, by one means or another, the tidings of Freuchie's victory quickly spread. The triumphant captain had no sooner stepped into the Lord's Tavern for some liquid refreshment than he heard the barman shouting: 'Is there a Dave Christie at the bar?' and when he responded in the affirmative, he discovered that a few regulars from Freuchie's Albert Tavern were on the telephone, passing on their congratulations and searching for further details of the famous win. Outside the ground, meanwhile, a cacophony of Scottish chants testified to the outcome, and the Fifers chose to put all their kit on the bus and stay overnight in London, with their gear locked inside Lord's. 'Scottish Television had been in touch with us and asked us not to travel back until the Monday morning, so they could have time to set up their cameras and prepare for the home-coming,' says Christie. 'We didn't mind whatsoever, because we wanted to celebrate properly and savour every moment of our success. Besides, I had been awarded a gallon's worth of whisky by the sponsors, and there was no way in the world that it wasn't going to be finished by the end of the evening. Come to think of it, I think Ian Botham drank most of the stuff, but we'll come back to that later.'

For the other, younger personnel in Freuchie colours, these next few hours provided a kaleidoscope of imperishable images. Having returned to the Westmoreland Hotel, and changed into their kilts, the players were rapidly joined by the wives and girlfriends, and collectively decided to venture into Soho for a meal. Some requested an Aberdeen Angus Steakhouse, others fancied Indian cuisine, whilst Niven McNaughton, a hyperactive coiled spring of restless energy, wondered if he could lay his hands on a fish supper in London on a Sabbath evening. Eventually, to the disgust of several stalwarts whose notion of exotic fare stretched as far as adding a picked onion to their chip butty, the casting vote fell for Chinese food and Dave Christie, for the first and last time in the evening, was a picture of discontent. 'We booked a fleet of taxis, there were 26 of us, and it just wasn't my scene at all. I scanned the menu for something European, but I wasn't hungry in the first place, so I just stuck to whisky and left the rest of them to stuff their faces,' he says, showing a growly disinclination to let spare ribs, Peking duck or any other perceived foreign muck interfere with the taste of his national drink. 'It was a weird beginning to the night, because suddenly everybody seemed to know who we were, and although we were used to Freuchie people walking up and talking to us in the streets, it was a little different when complete strangers were asking us what had happened.

'I guess the kilts were a slight give-away that we were Scottish, and as soon as we mentioned that we had won a cricket final at Lord's, the expression on people's faces was priceless. We might as well have claimed to be aliens from outer space. One or two of them looked at us as if they believed we were kidding them on, and you have to bear in mind that, in 1985, there was still a huge amount of ignorance Down South as to the fact that Scots actually played cricket to any reasonable standard. So perhaps the baffled faces were justified. They made me laugh at any rate. Frankly, it was nice to have the equivalent of 15 minutes of fame in a different country, but we certainly didn't go looking for it and I don't know how the superstars, the Ally McCoists, David Beckhams, Ian Bothams and Andrew Flintoffs tolerate all the public attention and media intrusion, even if they are being well paid for their efforts. Money doesn't come into it when the alternative is being able to enjoy a wee bit of privacy.'

The Chinese Way was anathema to David Cowan and Niven McNaughton, both of whom agreed they couldn't squander the opportunity to enjoy the dubious delights of Soho, hence their impromptu peregrination through London as the night dragged on. At this stage, the details veer in dangerous proximity to an episode from *Minder*, the definitive 1980s series in which various Scottish actors, including Billy Connolly, James Cosmo and Brian Cox, locked horns with George Cole's Arthur Daley, usually with unpleasant consequences for Dennis Waterman's hapless Terry McCann. 'We were dressed in jackets and kilts and got a few strange glances, but what the hell, we were two Scots boys from Fife and how often were we going to be in the Big Smoke at the weekend?' says Cowan, with Spock-like logic. 'All we wanted was a chance to chew the fat and take the air, and it was a bit of a shock when this police car suddenly pulled up onto the pavement and this officer was staring hard at us. "Hey, are you Niven and Davie?" he asked.

'We looked puzzled, but we hadn't done anything wrong. "Aye we are", we replied.

'Well, c'mon, jump in the back of the vehicle then, because your Dad is looking for you and he's keen for the pair of you to get back to your hotel as quickly as possible.'

The 'Dad' in question was, of course, Dave Christie. 'I had flagged down a squad car, and informed the officer: "We've lost two of our party, and it would be great if you could track them down. They're wearing kilts, so you can't really miss them,"' he recalls. 'Well, it wasn't that I was particularly worried about Niven and Davie, because these lads knew how to enjoy themselves without going over the score, but I wanted us all to get to the Westmorland in one piece. We were leaving for Scotland early the next morning and the last thing I needed was a couple of our boys missing the bus.'

Back at the Westmoreland, Stewart Irvine was grappling with a different problem, stuck in a broken lift, trying to remain composed when every sinew in his body was straining to be with his colleagues. A reticent fellow, as laconic off the field as he was loquacious with a bat in his hand, Irvine admits that he was as surprised as anybody else to receive the Man of the Match plaudit – Terry Trewartha and George Crichton also had valid claims to the accolade – yet one suspects this remains the defining incident in Jasper's entire life. Disbelief, incredulity and all-pervading pride were etched on his face as his innings and fielding were honoured and the beatific expression on the balcony speaks volumes. Yes, within a week, he would have resumed his duties at the quarry, but for now, for a precious few days, he was king of the hill, top of the heap . . . and stranded in a bloody lift, twiddling his thumbs while the tankards were being drained downstairs.

'It was a mechanical fault and the hotel staff had to call the Fire Brigade to rescue me, and I was banged up in there for over 45 minutes, which feels like an eternity when you're halfway between floors, and there's no real information on what's going on,' says Irvine. 'I suppose I should maybe have been more worried, but after everything that had happened, I just wanted to be involved in the festivities and there have been one or two exaggerations as to the length of time I was stuck there. One report mentioned that I had spent two and a half hours in the lift, but if that had truly been the case, I reckon I would have been genuinely stir crazy. No, it was around three-quarters of an hour, and that was long enough, but it didn't spoil anything. I mean, how could it? Here I was, a 19-year-old boy at Lord's, with his mates, being presented with the individual award, whilst Freuchie were making history. Nothing ever since has eclipsed it. It was pure magic.'

Predictably, there were few early-bedders amongst the crick- eters as Sunday morphed into Monday, with the whisky flowing like the Tweed on a sodden January. Freuchie's personnel had already learned that they were sharing their hotel with the England team, which was in the process of wrapping up another Ashes series, and they were joined in conviviality by the onliest Botham, whose relish for inducing Australian petted lips was equalled by a capacity for Bacchanalian revelry in the wee sma' hours, which proved sufficient to solicit gasps of admiration from even the most hardened Freuchie soul.

'Some other guests in the hotel were coming up to Ian and asking for his autograph, but he ushered them towards us and declared: "No, no, forget about me, get these Scotsmen's autographs, because they have achieved something very special today,"' says Dave Christie. 'It was typical of our dealings with Ian that he didn't want to gatecrash the party, he was delighted to talk to us, and share in our joy, and I don't care what anybody else might say about Ian Botham – I know he hasn't always been flavour of the month with the establishment – but he has been a smashing bloke to us down the years.

'Mind you, he must have the constitution of an ox, because the big man had the lion's share of my gallon of whisky, and then caught a couple of screamers in the slips to sink the Aussies the next morning when the majority of the Freuchie lads were happy just to hold on to a paper and a cup of tea. But seriously, since that evening, Ian has been to our clubhouse, we have joined him on a couple of his charity walks – and we completed the 25 miles between Dundee and Freuchie – and he stopped for a night here in the village and, the following morning, he chatted away to the kids and carried out an unscheduled coaching session with some of the youngsters. He's welcome here any time.'

When the Fifers awoke on 2 September, they had attained nationwide publicity for their exploits, and any recourse to Alka-Seltzer or Resolve had to be postponed indefinitely whilst the players gathered their possessions, their snapshots and vignettes, and embarked on the homeward journey safe in the knowledge that whatever the snootier English commentators might pronounce on the previous day's events, Freuchie's name was carved in the chronicles, forever. Now it was time to peruse the verdicts. 'Lord's regulations are legendary, and kilted hordes bluffing their way into the pavilion was too good a prospect to miss,' wrote Mike Selvey in the *Guardian*. 'No denims surely can't mean no trousers at all, but emergency late-night discussions have deemed national dress permissible – providing nobody peeks up the stairwells. Hence the arrival of wee Freuchie, in the National Village Cup, and I guarantee that the noise they generated will not be surpassed at next week's NatWest final. The most striking feature of cricket at this level is that it has little to do with technique. That is as might be expected: the bowlers frequently bowl straight and the batsmen often bat less so. The Freuchie wicket-keeper [Alan Duncan] perched as a frog might on a lily pad and bombarded the stumps from four yards in vain stumping

attempts, while one Rowledge batsman was too good to be true
– painter's trousers and mum's cableknit sweater covering a nifty
line in beer gut.'

Yet, Selvey was replete with praise for the athleticism of
Freuchie in the field, an observation shared by Simon Barnes in
The Times. 'While the serious cricket was being played at the
Oval, even more serious cricket was being played across the river
at Lord's,' wrote the sporting scribe and part-time ornithologist.
'The Scots of Freuchie fielded with maniacal enthusiasm,
stopped everything, bagged a couple of run outs, charged about
all over the place, and only slowed down when they had to face
the bowling of Rowledge. The match developed into a desperate struggle of crawling nerves and creeping scoreboard, with
ones cheered and hits for two hailed in ecstasy as the Scots held
on, levelled the score in the final over, and won by virtue of
having lost fewer wickets. But all is made up in the pub afterwards and the point is that weekend cricket is for fun and nobody
takes the game too seriously – unless, of course, they win.'

The Scottish *Daily Record*, in contrast, splashed the story on
their front page and covered the triumph with a garish, centre-
spread exultation, headlined 'A Freuchie Freak-Out', as the
prelude to the stereotypes being trotted out with ritual abandon.
'This is the place where all those flaxen-haired young Saxons
used to dash off a century before going off to conquer India. But
the Scottish fans draped their banners over the railings outside the
famous Lord's Tavern and, every time the Freuchie boys did
anything, they set up a cheer that would have done credit to
Hampden Park,' wrote Colin Dunne, who, in his defence,
penned around 750 words before the inevitable soccer reference.
'Even by boys' comic standard, it was a nail-biting finish but the
Fifers were the winners.

'Who were the other team? Oh, they were from Surrey, or
somewhere like that. What would they know about cricket?'

One or two purists may bridle at this jocular treatment. But, in
retrospect, if it boils down to a choice between zero column
inches or an infestation of *Brigadoon*-style comments, the latter

seems preferable, especially when one remembers that this was 14 years before Scotland made their maiden appearance in cricket's World Cup and 18 summers prior to the introduction of Craig Wright and his Saltires to the NCL. In any case, there are occasions where only lachrymose sentimentality will suffice, and as Dave Christie's side crossed the Border on Monday afternoon, their fellow-villagers were hauling out the bunting, flags and fireworks, and fine-tuning the band for the mother of all hootenannys, overseen by a posse of photographers, TV crews and thirsty former players.

'The reception was unbelievable. There were hundreds of messages of congratulations from every corner of Scotland and from expatriates all over Britain and further afield,' says the skipper. 'International goodwill messages arrived from as far away as Australia, the USA, New Zealand, the United Arab Emirates, wherever you might find Scots who are devoted to their country and are keen to see us being successful. When we got back to Freuchie and were greeted by thousands of well-wishers, it took the breath away, because we had no idea, on the bus home, of the scale of the celebrations. The motif on our ties had been changed from 'Lord's Finalists' to 'Lord's Winners' and I can still envisage the scenes in my head when we neared Freuchie and the emotions welled up.'

Few, if any, of the residents missed the chance to toast the conquering heroes, the last leg of whose journey was delayed by the Fife police to give the Tullis Russell Mills Band, many of whose members had not heard of the hastily-arranged engagement until they returned from work, time to get there. Cue an explosion of tears and triumphant pageantry at 7.15, allied to signs of the pawky humour for which this part of the world is renowned. As a large crowd assembled at the western approach to the village, with foul weather pouring on their parade – well, why should the heavens miss out on the beanfeast! – one of the band members tuned up with 'Singin' in the Rain' and a drenched supporter shouted in response: 'That's great, just keep playing that yin!'

At which juncture, the local scribes stepped into the breach. 'Eventually the team bus drew into sight and David Christie, politely declining the offer of an umbrella, emerged clutching the Village Cup trophy to a terrific response from the throng,' reported the venerable *Fife Free Press*:

> Led by the band and Alistair Pirnie, the piper who had played at Lord's, the Freuchie side made their way up Main Street, with the odd member of their party breaking ranks as they spotted family or friends in the crowd.
>
> As they approached the clubhouse, a fireworks display began, and several hundred supporters crammed into the function room to hear Christie give his thanks to the villagers for their backing. The team then made their way onto the roof to salute those who could not find space inside, and after the speeches Freuchie set about, for the second night in succession, celebrating the most momentous day in its history.

Sitting in the Lomond Hills Hotel 20 years on, Dave Christie's remembrance of detail is exemplary. Ultimately, he accepts that luck played a role in his side's achievement, and a constant schedule of home fixtures and lousy weather ensured that Freuchie enjoyed the benefit of knowing the conditions and how the pitch would react to any circumstances. But that isn't to underestimate the camaraderie, the tireless energy and inherent cricket passion which combined as the catalysts for the graduation into the history books.

'If this had been one solitary season, where every fluke went in our favour, where every umpiring decision was unfair to our opponents, and if we had vanished off the map and never been heard of again, then I suppose you might have been entitled to describe us as being in the right place at the right time. But it didn't work out that way at all,' concludes Christie. 'On the contrary, when there are 639 clubs in the competition at the outset, anybody needs a damned sight more qualities than luck to reach the gates of Lord's. We might have lost to Meigle, but we battled and fought and prevailed in the end. We were toiling against Cleator, who were a quality side, and scraped through by the skin of out teeth. It was pretty much the same with Billesdon in the semi-final, yet once more we found players in the mould of George Crichton, who didn't shoot their mouths off, but knuckled down to getting us out of trouble, and flourished. En route to London, one bookmaker was offering odds of 6–1 against us, which is pretty incredible in a two-horse race. But if we demonstrated anything during the whole campaign, it was that we had guts, we cared deeply about cricket, and we were proud of our village. Personal glory just didn't enter the equation – none of us went on to fame or fortune, and we were happy to stay working at the quarry or with the council or in the painting trade. I will never leave Freuchie, my heart is here, and if you check on the rest of the team you will discover that most of their telephone numbers have the same 01337 prefix as mine.'

Whatever else happens in Scottish cricket lore, nothing can dent the Fifers' record. And, for those of us with an atheistic streak, it surely merits attention that the Christies, Crichtons and their comrades soared to glory without any divine intervention. Not for the local minister, the Reverend Iain Wright, any cheap tilts at bandwagon-jumping. 'Our Sunday service [on the day of the final] passed without a prayer being offered up for the team's success,' he said. 'I did think about the idea, but there were only several members of the local team amongst the congregation. Most of the rest were in London.'

It didn't matter. As events transpired, it was Rowledge who didn't have a prayer.

CHAPTER 10

THE HIGH LIVERS

If the triumphal scenes at Lord's testified to the fashion in which Freuchie's players, officials and spectators had managed to leave an indelible mark on St John's Wood, the delirium which surrounded their arrival back at base was merely the prelude to an outbreak of Bacchanalian indulgence which continued for most of the ensuing month. From the moment the team bus crawled into the village, allowing Scottish Television to justify the expense of hiring a crane to capture a panoramic shot of the reunion, the conquering heroes were toasted, whiskied and fêted almost to death. There was free beer in the clubhouse and an equal generosity of spirit, from the massed hordes of Freuchie folk, ready to party in honour of the greatest achievement in their hamlet's history.

Predictably, as chaos enveloped a group of individuals more accustomed to anonymity and tranquil afternoons playing their craft in front of a couple of hundred aficionados, the lumps in their throat were the size of Arnold Schwarzenegger's pectorals. 'It was incredibly humbling as the bus continued on its journey and we passed amongst friends and neighbours, young and old, male and female, and every single one of them was going utterly crazy,' recalls Terry Trewartha, who discovered in the process that we can't all be heroes, because others have to stand on the kerb and clap as the icons pass by. 'Everything about the trip to Lord's was spontaneous and it passed in a blur of frenzied activity, so while we were obviously thrilled to bits, it was all adrenaline and raw emotion during the time that we spent in London. But the fact that virtually the entire Freuchie population – and hundreds of other people from the whole Fife region – could still be so captivated and passionate 24 hours later sent a shiver up your spine. When you glanced around the bus, you could notice this strange expression in the players' faces. It was as if they were gradually realising that nothing would ever be quite the same again.'

In the next few days, odes were written, songs composed and newspaper headlines concocted in tribute to Dad's Army. They were 'Fabulous Freuchie', 'Fantastic Freuchie', 'Freak-out Freuchie', 'The Pride of Lords' or 'Scotland's Cricket Cavaliers', depending on which journal you digested, and unsurprisingly, Dave Christie found himself invited to more dinners than Mr Creosote could have tolerated. 'I wouldn't be here today if I had accepted all the hospitality offers which suddenly flooded in my direction. RAF Leuchars said they wanted to play against us and told us they would be putting on a free bar for the day, so we thought about sending three teams – one for the match and the other two for the bevvy,' declares Christie. 'There were numerous invitations to open fêtes, and make after-dinner speeches, and the mailbag was awash with congratulatory letters and cards and requests for autographs, which was incredible for a wee Scottish cricket team. I was even contacted by an Australian radio show in Adelaide and they said they wanted to fix up a live chat. It transpired that part of the reason for their interest was that the interviewer was also called Dave Christie and he pronounced Freuchie an awful lot better than the English commentators. We were on the phone for several minutes and he rounded it off by saying: "We're just like you, Dave. We like to get one up on the Poms and you lads have done that with a vengeance."

'I suppose, with hindsight, that some of the coverage sprang from a sense of surprise that Scots even played cricket, let alone with sufficient ability to succeed in a national event at Lord's. But in September 1985 and thereafter on to Christmas that year, I hardly had a spare moment to devote to my livelihood. We were too busy painting the town red for me to get the brushes out, and although it was excellent that Freuchie was in the spotlight, I occasionally look back and chortle to myself that I was nearly killed by kindness.'

Sadly, amid the revelries and deification of the high rollers, there was a reminder that the criminal fraternity never sleeps. Early on Tuesday morning, whilst the villagers were in the Land of Nod following the previous night's Happy Half-A-Dozen Hours, thieves broke into the clubhouse, smashed doors and locks, stole money and generally offered the proof that every community has a few miscreants for whom nothing is out of bounds. 'It was really sickening that it should happen, and an awful lot of people were feeling very down in the morning, which couldn't have been a greater contrast from the universal delight and joy which had been etched on their faces at the party on Monday evening,' recalls Dave Christie, who was awoken at 4.00 a.m. by the police with news of the break-in. 'Fortunately, though, whilst there was a terrible mess on our premises, the Village Cup, which was in the club, remained safely secured and wasn't interfered with, which was a massive relief to everybody connected with Freuchie CC. I mean, can you imagine the embarrassment if we had been forced to go to the organisers and inform them that, within 12 hours of the trophy coming to Scotland, it had been stolen? It doesn't bear thinking about and that is why we immediately made sure it would be placed in safe hands – locked up in the local police station. The positive aspect of what was a despicable act was that the community rallied round, a number of tradesmen helped us clear things up, and though the incident was very disappointing, we couldn't permit a few idiots to spoil it for everybody else. It was business as usual and, if anything, we were even more determined to spread the message that Freuchie wouldn't be deterred from celebrating.'

Christie doesn't exaggerate. In the following couple of months his confrères became Scottish Television's 'Team of the Year', they were invited to participate in a charity game against Glendarroch (the village in *Take The High Road*), and there were civic receptions and commemorative plaques from Fife Regional Council and North East Fife Regional Council, whilst Freuchie's citizenry saw no reason to curtail the festivities as the Yuletide beckoned. The Bowling Club hosted a function for the players, wives and girlfriends, as did Tullis Russell, Edinburgh Crystal, Dunfermline Rotary Club . . . and so the list goes on, relentlessly testing Christie's constitution as much as Rowledge had examined his captaincy skills. From Prestwick to Edinburgh, and Elgin to Edinburgh, he dutifully travelled the miles to be the centre of attention and accept their plaudits. It may not have come easy to this naturally modest individual, but he adopted the approach that the plaudits were for Freuchie, not himself, and duly made speech upon speech.

At the Dunblane Hydro, for example, Christie found himself in the company of former Hearts footballer and Scotland cricketer, Donald Ford, and the then-Clyde boss, Craig Brown, who would later guide the SFA's finest through what now appears a golden age of World Cup and European Championship qualification. Once the proceedings began, Ford, an accomplished orator with a memory in the mould of Leslie Welch, praised the never-say-die spirit exhibited by Christie's infantry and illuminated the occasion with some well-aimed barbs at the dear green place. 'I was once on my way to Glasgow for a ceilidh – you know, a distillery set to music. Well, they say that the city has the densest population in Scotland and I might just agree,' he declaimed, with the most posthumous of pans. 'I was on my way to the university and got lost en route, so I stopped at the side of the road and asked a worthy: "Hello mate, how do you get to the university?" He looked me up and down and replied: "Just stick in at your lessons, son." '

As the carousing continued relentlessly, Freuchie's part-timers grew accustomed to mixing in exalted company. During the Skol Scottish Sports awards at Glasgow's Hospitality Inn, Yvonne Murray, the bronze medal winner in the 1985 European Indoor Championships, engaged in passionate conversation with the Fifers whilst they collected their respective prizes. Sandy Lyle, that year's Open champion at Sandwich, and a member of the victorious European Ryder Cup team which had defeated the Americans for the first time since 1957, at the Belfry, was deservedly showered with accolades, but he was otherwise

engaged in the United States, so Christie and his personnel took
centre stage, and even if a few of Caledonia's cricketing sceptics
were starting to grumble that a little Rowledge is a dangerous
thing, the momentum didn't falter as 1985 progressed into 1986.
Indeed, they had advanced from being fringe performers to
seasoned television veterans when Archie MacPherson inter-
viewed Christie just minutes after they had been named as BBC
Sportscene Team Personalities, and there was a defiant message
from the heart of the Freuchie clubhouse. 'It was hard to win,
and it will be harder to win again. But that doesn't mean I am
writing off our chances. Far from it,' said the skipper, who had
become used to the glare of publicity. 'We will work hard in the
months ahead and I am actually looking forward to concentrat-
ing on cricket for a while. It has obviously been a tremendous
year for us and it will be very hard to surpass. But if this has given
a lift, not just to ourselves, but also loads of other Scottish clubs
with talent in their ranks and dreams in their hearts, it can only be
a positive stride forward.'

Nobody can possibly quibble with his assertion. As Dougie
Brown, an internationalist with both Scotland and England, and
a stalwart servant of Warwickshire, willingly testifies, Freuchie's
success was *the* vital spark which orchestrated a transformation in
the attitude of countless Britons to the vibrancy of the Caledonian game. 'I was only 14 at the time of their win at Lord's, but I
have no doubts whatsoever that Freuchie were the team who put
Scottish cricket on the map, not just because of the achievements
of the 11 players, but the manner in which they brought the
whole village down to London with them,' says Brown, whose
own career has already witnessed a handful of Lord's Cup final
appearances. 'Before Dave Christie's boys came along, cricket in
Scotland was pretty much regarded as a backwater pursuit, or
even unfairly dismissed as a joke by a lot of folk, but suddenly, at
a stroke, Freuchie's name was on everybody's lips and they took
the occasion by the scruff of the neck and demonstrated the
passion for cricket which exists throughout the whole country.
Every step of the road, from bringing the bagpipes and the kilted

supporters to Lord's, to joining Beefy [Ian Botham] on his charity walks was another brilliant piece of PR, and I wager that there will be many people in Scotland who, even if they know nothing else about the game, will be able to tell you that Freuchie went to London and beat the English.'

Mike Denness, the Bellshill-born former England captain, who learned his cricketing trade at Ayr's picturesque Cambusdoon ground, has shared opinions and swapped anecdotes with Christie on several instances and shares Brown's lofty regard for Freuchie's triumph. 'It doesn't matter where you end up as a player, you need somewhere to perform and gain encouragement as a youngster and there wouldn't be any top tier without the grassroots development, and Dave Christie has made an enormous contribution to raising the profile of Scottish cricket, not only in 1985, but during decades of passionate, selfless involvement with the sport,' says Denness. 'When I talked to him, it was evident that here was somebody who lived and breathed cricket, a man who was steeped in the lore of the game, and it's irrelevant what the competition is, you can only go out and beat the opposition, and for Freuchie to have emerged at the top of the pile from an entry of 639 clubs is one hell of an achievement, whichever way you look at it. I had been down in England, first at Kent and then at Essex, for over 20 years by the time that Freuchie came to Lord's, and while it's true that while there were one or two Scots, such as myself and Brian Hardie, who were competing on the county circuit, we were viewed by our English colleagues as very much being the exception rather than the rule. It just never entered their heads that cricket was played on such a widespread scale up in Scotland, but when the Freuchie team journeyed to Lord's and caused such a commotion it really made the English sit up and take notice. Personally, I thought it was a terrific shot in the arm, not only for Scotland, but the whole of village cricket. And that is a vital area of the game. Just look at where the Flintoffs, the Bothams and so many others first picked up a bat or ball, encouraged by the keen-as-mustard dedication of men like Dave Christie. I can't stress enough that we need these people to keep passing the torch down to the next generation for the game to stay healthy. Without that, we're in trouble.'

All these tributes were music to the ears of the Fife community. However, by the start of February 1986, Christie decided that the partying had to cease, and informed his squad that the stardust memories should be consigned to the chronicles. He initiated a series of training sessions which featured exhausting runs in the Lomond Hills and, come rain, hail, snow or ice, there were no excuses for absenteeism. Net practices also commenced at the local school, and whilst several of the team, sated on rich cuisine and a hundred thank-you tinctures, were understandably apprehensive about approaching the scales, the Back to Basics policy was an undeniable success. As the new season beckoned, the Fifers were rightly buoyant about their prospects of retaining their Village Cup title, but they accepted they would no longer be an unknown quantity and that the draw was unlikely to favour them with such a plethora of matches in front of their own supporters.

Yet, undaunted, the mood in the camp oozed with reinvigorated purpose. Their squad had remained largely intact; apart from an injury to Niven McNaughton, their captain Christie was back in harness, twinkling with self-belief in his fiftieth year, and his staunch personnel felt no trepidation about embarking on a fresh crusade. 'To be honest, it was a bit of a relief for the spring to arrive and for the media circus to disappear, because whilst most of us enjoyed being the focus of attention and rubbing shoulders with legendary figures from other sports, we all had our day jobs to worry about, and I have always believed that you should look to the future, not stick in the past,' recalls Dave Cowan, whose Scotland career was poised to blossom. 'Watching Dave being presented with the *Sportscene* trophy by Jim Aitken [the skipper of Scotland's 1984 Grand Slam rugby XV] emphasised the quality of the company which we were keeping, and I learned later that Aberdeen's European Cup-winning side had earned the inaugural award in 1983, so we were walking in the footsteps of giants and we had to make sure that we didn't come an almighty cropper in defence of our title. It has happened many times before, and especially in one-off cup competitions, that the reigning champions come horribly unstuck at the start of the following campaign, so we sweated buckets throughout March and April in a major effort to ensure that the same heroes-to-zeroes phenomenon didn't trip us up.'

Their exertions paid dividends: even as the Freuchie dwellers began congregating once more for their weekend fix, the team posted notice during their early displays in the newly-christened Norsk Hydro Fertilisers National Village Cup (a bit of a dung-twister, isn't it!) that their aspirations of achieving a double were credible. Glendelvine were brushed aside, with the minimum of discomfort in the opening match, and there was similarly sedate, professional progress throughout the rest of the journey to the Scottish final, which, as it had done the previous year, paired them with Meigle, but this time on the latter's strip. The contest soon developed into a coruscating battle of wills, with the hosts harbouring occasional hopes of beating their opponents, but ultimately Freuchie's fielding proved far superior, and their athletic scampering saved around 40 runs, whereas Meigle's masters of dropsy conceded that number in fumbles and spilled catches.

At the outset, with Willie Scott and Ralph Laing laying down a solid, albeit unspectacular platform of 45, before the latter was caught behind by Alan Duncan off Andy Crichton for 18, the Mean Machine was parsimonious without being especially penetrative, but they kept their opponents in check. Scott eventually reached an excellent 50, with a 6 and a quartet of 4s to his credit, but was removed immediately thereafter by Dave Christie and that dismissal established the tone for Meigle's afternoon, where they kept losing key wickets of well-set personnel at critical periods in their innings. Peter Drummond was smartly run out for 40, Mike Walton departed, bowled by Trewartha for 20, and despite their attempts at raising the momentum, the Perthshire men only mustered 151 for 6, even though none of the Freuchie attack took more than one wicket.

'We were a wee bit flat that day, as if the tension was affecting the players, and they were starting to appreciate that being champions brings pressures of its own. That is no disrespect to Meigle, and Willie, in particular, who batted beautifully, and made me feel worried for a while, but there were quite a few loose deliveries, and it was a different experience to go to other people's grounds and hear the din and appreciate that most of the crowd were desperate for us to lose,' relates Dave Christie. 'At the interval, we knew that chasing 150 should be a fairly straightforward task if we made any kind of decent start, but after the events of 1985, we had attuned ourselves to the simple fact that our bowling was far more reliable than the batting. I wouldn't actually say we were sitting there waiting for a collapse, but let's just say that nobody was surprised when it occurred and we just had to thank our lucky stars that they missed so many opportunities.'

Alan Duncan and Fraser Irvine launched the reply, and darted to and fro like startled rabbits, in a frenzied pursuit of quick singles. To an extent, the tactic worked: it wouldn't have done had Meigle's fielders been a trifle sharper and more accurate. Granted, Irvine was undone with the score on 26, run out from a terrific throw by Michael Anderson, but the Fifers rode their luck for the remainder of the tussle. In the 14th over, George Wilson survived an extremely confident appeal for catch behind, and he was dropped in the next over, before being trapped lbw by Scott for a less than convincing 8.

Fortunately for his side, Duncan was in prime nick, capitalising on anything loose, dominating his opponents and resolutely daring them to win the psychological battle. They signally failed. By the climax of the 25th over, the keeper–batsman reached his 50, from 69 balls, and Meigle were guilty of overthrows, misfields and continued sloppiness, which allowed Duncan a life, at the expense of Jeff Colville, from a skied full toss.

It had developed into a frenetic, error-strewn affair, and although Michael Anderson had Crichton caught at cover by Colville for 15, another chance went a-begging in Terry Trewartha's favour, at which point the result was no longer in doubt. Even despite the subsequent removal of Dave Cowan without scoring, Duncan marched on in imperious fashion and struck 2 successive 4s in the penultimate over to finish undefeated on 90 as Freuchie triumphed and their rivals sighed in the knowledge that matters could have been significantly tighter for the visitors if they had grasped their opportunities.

In some respects, this afternoon bore resemblances to the heady heroics of the Lord's trail. There was a niggardly group of bowlers, assisted by a ferociously competitive fielding unit and, on the debit side, the abiding sense that the wheels could fall off the Fifers' juggernaut at any minute. It certainly made for a compelling spectacle for audiences across Britain, but although Dave Christie still insists that his men genuinely believed they could reproduce their previous exploits, one suspects they were deluding themselves, not least because the Village Cup isn't some piddling tournament where the same three or four teams are vying for supremacy every year, but rather an ascent of Himalayan proportions. And how many people have scaled Everest twice?

'There definitely wasn't the same feeling of elation after the second victory over Meigle as there had been in 1985, and perhaps that was simply down to the fact we had won at Lord's; we had achieved something which had never been done before by a Scottish club, so how on earth could there possibly be a similar level of intensity next time around?' says Trewartha, who was already starting to argue that Freuchie should seek to recruit a professional in search of success in the East of Scotland League. 'Naturally, the villagers didn't view matters in this light and I'm not claiming there is any right or wrong in this debate. But, increasingly, all our focus began to revolve around the Village Cup and, personally, I think it gradually became an obsession for some people. Maybe we should have been prioritising on taking on the Granges and Heriots instead of putting all our eggs in the one basket, but it was probably understandable, following the win at Lord's, that the club wanted another trip there. From my perspective, I had been there, loved it, stored everything in my memory bank, and now it was time to move on. But, of course, in 1986, we wanted to defend our crown and that was fair enough. Later, hmm . . .'

These concerns would increasingly be aired by several of Christie's lieutenants, but, as June passed into July and the Fifers defeated Spofforth in Tyke country to reach the last 16 of the nationwide event, one detected a rising crescendo of anticipation amongst the patrons of the Lomond Hills Hotel and Albert Tavern, even if they were receiving little chance to watch the team on home soil. Frustratingly, in what developed into a sun-drenched, dragonfly summer of resplendent vistas across Fife, the scenery replete with evening matches which stretched on until 9.00 and 9.30, Freuchie were drawn away again to Carlton, another team from Yorkshire and, just to complicate matters, they had a Derby meeting with Falkland on the Saturday prior to their excursion southwards.

It seemed a poisoned chalice of a double date, but there was no hint of the travails in store when Dave Christie asked his fellow-Fifers to bat on a firm, fast surface. Regular openers Brian Watson and Rab Nellies survived an early onslaught and appeared in prime shape to profit on their half-century stand, with Cowan and Trewartha unable to make the breakthrough, but the rest of the innings stank like Madonna on a film set, as the Christie duo were the catalysts for a dramatic disintegration. Junior was the principal architect of Falkland's ruin during a spell of 12 overs, which yielded 7 maidens and the same number of wickets, for a meagre 8 runs, and suddenly, from a promising beginning, the visitors were routed for 84 at 4.34 p.m., prompting a frantic run chase from Freuchie which saw them sprint to their modest target, Alan Duncan crashing Bill Suttie's first over for 3 bound-aries as the prelude to similar swashbuckling from Fraser Irvine and George Wilson, who shouldn't have been unbeaten at the death. Having top-edged a catch off Gus Speake, he had already started meandering back to the pavilion when the Falkland

keeper, Stuart Lindsay, sparked one of those awful 'Swallow me
up, now, please God' moments by allowing the ball to slip
through his gloves. Sadly, that neatly epitomised his side's
performance and, a world removed from the normal edge
and sledge which typified these encounters, this was all quiet
on the western front.

Glancing at the scorebook, one could easily be forgiven for
lampooning the quality of the Falkland batsmen, who capitulated
from 62 for 2 to 84 in less than an hour, mesmerised by Christie's
spell much as a cobra captivated by a mongoose. But I write this
having watched Zimbabwe – allegedly a Test-ranked country –
plummet to 54 all out against South Africa, with a wretched series
of wild swipes, lapses of judgment and meekness of spirit which
proves how quickly a cricket team, *any* team, can be ripped apart
once the initial trembles have developed into a full-scale earth-
quake. In any case, Brian Christie had shown on plenty of other
occasions that he possessed a talent for wreaking mayhem in the
right circumstances and this was one of those days.

The trouble was that although Freuchie embarked on the road
to Carlton quicker than they could have envisaged, their fragility
was still evident. They had recorded a magnificent sequence of
15 consecutive wins in the Village Cup, but sooner or later the
sequence had to be terminated. 'We weren't overly worried on
the bus going down, but we recognised that somebody, somewhere, was going to set us a total which we would struggle to
chase, because we couldn't keep relying on our bowlers, particularly on away missions,' recalls Dave Christie. 'It's one thing to
be playing at your own ground and be walking to the club as
your fans are tooting their car horns, giving you the thumbs up
and almost serving as an extra man, and quite another scenario to
be heading somewhere you have never been before in conditions
which are alien to you. We had been blessed with the luck of the
draw in 1985, but I think it evened out the following year.'

Carlton, from West Yorkshire, were a well-balanced side,
accustomed to amassing large scores, and they didn't suffer from
depending on two or three individuals. On the contrary,

although Cowan took an early wicket, their line-up chipped in with valuable contributions, with 20s from the twin Kens, Taylor and Barrett, while David Fairburn produced an excellent knock of 50, and the tail-enders kept the board ticking until the end of their innings. It wasn't a bad display by the Fifers, but although Cowan finished with 2 for 23 and Trewartha 3 for 50, they required 181 and their hopes were hanging by a thread. Clearly, they would require a decent platform, but equally, couldn't afford to loiter in their response. They needed a dash of derring-do and a peck of patience.

Sadly for the 150 supporters who had accompanied their compatriots to the small community near Leeds, what they got was an awful clatter of wickets as Freuchie's top-order crumpled in a heap, undone by an excellent spell from David Warren. Fraser Irvine perished for a duck, as did Mark Wilkie, and with Alan Duncan, Bruce Munro and Andy Crichton failing to reach double figures, the visitors' innings was in tatters. By that juncture, their opponents were justifiably jubilant, and other sides in such dire straits might have folded completely. Yet, befitting the qualities which had steered them to Village Cup triumph in the first place, George Wilson flung himself into an immensely courageous rearguard action, initially in tandem with Cowan, and while this duo were together there was still hope. It was a marvellously pugnacious riposte in adversity from Wilson, so often the cleaner-up of messes upon his arrival at the crease, and despite losing Cowan for 21, bowled by the impressive Fairburn, he and George Crichton orchestrated the hint of a Hollywood-style revival with a half-century stand, as the Fifers, against all odds, passed 150, then 160, with the most vocal of the home acolytes temporarily silenced. In the end, the resistance proved futile – Freuchie concluding on 167 for 7, only 13 short of their goal – and they had to shake their opponents' hands. But it was a measure of the inherent pride amongst the Scots in the crowd that they didn't slink off forlornly into the night, but rather hoisted George Wilson, who had moved to an unbeaten 81 by the close (Crichton was 24 not out), and carried him off the pitch and into the bar as the precursor to a lusty rendition of 'The Flower of Scotland'.

Later in the evening the post-mortems would commence, principally revolving around the deficiencies in the early stages of Freuchie's reply. But although there were frustration and disappointment in the air, there was also an acknowledgment that Carlton had been the better all-round team on the day and these Fifers were no dour grouches in defeat. 'It is a piece of cake to be magnanimous in victory, but it's a mark of any good side that you can still raise a glass when you have lost and toast your opponents, and we could have no complaints about the result, especially when we were 30-something for 5. At least we battled on, and our heads didn't go down, and George Wilson played superbly, but we were always toiling to get back into the game and it was purely down to him and Geordie Crichton that we got as near as we did,' recalls Dave Christie. 'Their fellow [David] Fairburn had put in a good shift; with a 50 and a couple of wickets he was worth his 'Man of the Match' prize and we wished Carlton all the best in the competition. And then we headed back to Freuchie and that was the return to reality. There was no shame in it, though. Quite the opposite. To have won 15 games in a row, including six against English opponents, was fantastic, and while a few of the boys were a bit low on the bus home, we had given it our best shot and we had gone out with our heads high.'

Back home, the recriminations were shortlived. In such an arduous environment as presented by the Village Cup, there will always be giddy summits and sloughs of despond, and although one challenge had been snuffed out, Freuchie have never wasted breath in pondering futilely on times past. Instead, with the positive influence of Christie, Dave Cowan and Alan Duncan to the fore, they have constantly picked themselves up, dusted themselves down, ordered the drinks and followed Robert Browning's words: 'The best is yet to be.' Indeed, what is most noticeable about their exploits since 1985 is how consistent the Fifers have been in oh-so-nearly knocking at the Lord's gates again. Away from their Sabbath assignments, more dissenting voices began to suggest that Freuchie would benefit from hiring an overseas professional and focusing their attention on raising the stakes in domestic competitions. 'I'm not saying that Dave Christie was wrong – he stuck defiantly to his principles and the village admired him for it. But the fact was that although we won the First Division of the East League in 1989 [admittedly with a little help from opponents having points deducted and rain on the last Saturday of the campaign], we had the choice of emulating our Scottish rivals and importing a professional, or continuing to regard the Village Cup as the be-all and end-all and I happened to believe we should go for the former option,' says Terry Trewartha, who eventually left to join Falkland and took his talented sons, Grant and Gary, with him, although they returned to the fold, briefly, in the mid-1990s. 'I know that Freuchie signed a pro, in the shape of Indian, Manu Nayar, and he did a good job. But once the Village Cup rules were tightened up to ensure that participants didn't have any paid players in their ranks – even if he didn't get involved in the Village tournament – we should have bitten the bullet and moved on to pastures new. The team was certainly good enough to be challenging for Scottish league and cup honours, but no matter how we fared in the 40-over competition, we were invariably struggling to match the city teams on Saturdays. I'm not disputing the positive influence that the Village Cup had on the wider community – and the home games were brilliant occasions for Freuchie – but I still think we got a bit carried away with it at the expense of other things.'

The Fifers certainly stumbled into one or two rows with the Scottish Cricket Union. In 1989, a fixture clash led to the club being banned from the Scottish Cup for failing to choose their strongest side, although this issue could and should have been resolved with a little more flexibility from the governing body. Then, in 1991, Freuchie were unable to enter the Village Cup because of Nayar's professional contract. Some of this smacks of petty bureaucracy, hinting perhaps at jealousy amongst other organisations at the unprecedented profile and publicity enjoyed by Dad's Army. But ultimately, Christie had to make a choice and, unsurprisingly, he elected to aim for another crack at Lord's.

'It just seemed the most sensible approach, because we were a village side, one of our great strengths was the close-knit sense of community in the ranks, and we couldn't risk jeopardising that by trying to poach players from the Glasgow and Edinburgh clubs and heading down the route where the club lost its soul,' says Christie, a steely glint in his eyes illustrating that he has no qualms about his stance. 'I respect Terry's argument, and we didn't fall out or anything. In fact, I would be absolutely delighted to have him back here as coach, although I recognise he has a lot on his plate at Madras College. But, in the final analysis, I concluded that the Village Cup had been terrifically good for us, and that should be where our future lay. Why not? In the year we weren't involved, I must have had a couple of hundred Freuchie dwellers asking me what was going on and it did feel strange, because it is our natural milieu and one of the reasons for our success has been the fashion in which the residents have backed us. So it was a pretty easy decision.'

It was also the correct one. Anybody who has ever trawled around Scottish club grounds on a Saturday – venues wherein half-a-dozen men and a dog usually constitute a good audience – will be aware that Shergar, Lord Lucan and Osama Bin Laden could be sitting together in the stands and nobody would lend them the slightest bit of notice. In that light, if the choice is between pursuing a place in the Scottish National Cricket League or maintaining the grand tradition of Village Cup action, it's a no-brainer. And I should know, having witnessed the tension, whirl of activity and relentless ebbs and flows which characterise Freuchie's forays against the best that England can muster.

Consider, for instance, the tussle with Bedale, from Yorkshire, in 1987, which epitomised the excitement and visceral belligerence of these matches. The visitors had been good enough to polish off the reigning champions, Forge Valley, in the previous round – but they simply lacked the firepower and fielding expertise to thwart the Fifers. From the sidelines, I recall a female supporter emitting a piercing scream: 'Come on Freuchie, shove it up these fucking English bastards!' It wasn't exactly what anybody would have termed lady-like language, but it had the desired effect as Bedale spilled six catches, lost their composure and were sent packing with their tails between their legs.

In their ranks was a teenager, Paul Grayson, who would shortly begin training at Headingley and go on to represent his home county, Essex, and England, but although he produced an impressive spell of 3 for 14, the visitors had earlier managed only 156, bolstered by a superb half-century from left-hander David Ellis. When Freuchie replied, the pressure was tangible, not merely among the players, but also the fans, and the result hinged on which side would retain their bottle as tension enveloped the ground. Bruce Munro and Alan Duncan had made a decent opening – by Freuchie's standards at any rate – with 16 and 27 respectively, but the dismissal of both Fraser and Stewart Irvine in rapid succession heightened the drama. The decisive moment probably arrived in the 30th over, with the outcome finely balanced, when George Wilson skied a top-edge over the wicket-keeper. The latter, Ian Gill, and another fielder, nicknamed 'Gillie', converged on the ball to be met with a call from another fielder 'It's Gillie's catch,' whereupon they both left it and the red oval landed in the middle of the duo. Thereafter, Wilson advanced to an unbeaten 45 and, with solid backing from Andy Crichton (16) and Dave Cowan (18), steered his side to a 4-wicket triumph which was more fraught than it possibly sounds. Freuchie duly progressed to the quarter-finals, only to be undone by Cleator, one of the adversaries they had conquered en route to their appointment at Lord's.

Year after year, they conjured up some implausible successes, and there was a genuine sense that they could book a return passage to St John's Wood. In 1992, they beat Meigle, then brushed aside Harome, as the prelude to gaining revenge on Carlton in a bowl-out. When they subsequently edged a tight last-8 match against Woodhouses, and secured a home semi-final meeting with Methley, the PR machine cranked into life again. And, on this occasion, the Scots actively believed they would cruise past their foes, explaining why I travelled to Freuchie on Saturday night, for the *Scotsman*.

Alas, it was nobody's finest hour. In the prelude to hostilities, a massive crowd had gathered and they buzzed with anticipation and throbbed with raucous bias, akin to the baying mobs in *Gladiator*. But not for long. As I wrote at the time:

> Harry Barclay shook his head sadly and the veteran official of Freuchie was hardly alone in his tristesse. Babies wept as if it was expected of them, tears welled in the eyes of the players' wives and even the dogs yelped mournfully in a discordant chorus of disappointment.
>
> In any other Scottish community, you might confront such an overwhelming outpouring of grief were we talking about the national football side making its now-accustomed fast exit from the World Cup. But Freuchie has always been a law unto itself, and these fans were mourning the loss of their cricketers in the Village Cup. The observers, who numbered around 1500, had arrived from all over Fife, and as far afield as the Lothians and Glasgow, but the incentive of a second trip to Lord's never threatened to materialise as the spectators gradually slumped into a resigned bout of gallows humour.
>
> A dreadful opening period saw the Fifers lurch along from 2 for 3 to 25 for 6, and when their innings eventually ground to a halt on 96 for 9, it was hardly surprising that the Englishmen smirked. In the score box, meanwhile, Barclay was inconsolable: 'It wouldn't have been so bad if we had performed to the best of our abilities and fallen short, but we didn't and that's what hurts so much,' he said with a lachrymose air after the visitors had knocked off the runs for the loss of three wickets. 'Fair play to Methley, they have come here today and established an immediate stranglehold and not too many sides have done that to us in this tournament. But that wasn't a true reflection of our talents and there will be some depressed lads in the dressing room at the moment. Ach well, never mind, we'll be back next year, you can rely on that.'

To the club's credit, they fulfilled their promise, reaching the same stage of the competition in 1993 (despite all their fixtures being away) before losing to Kington in a match marred by some disgraceful behaviour from the latter's acolytes, and Freuchie advanced to another semi in 1997, only to lose to the eventual champions, Caldy, by 34 runs. Yet, over the piece, they have proved as consistently difficult to master as any team in the history of the event, which justifies Christie's affirmation that, whether he has to wait until 2010 or 2015 or after he has gone to that grand pavilion in the sky, there is no valid reason why there can't be a second hoisting of their flag in London.

'The competition has changed down the years. Some teams have basically cheated to try and increase their chances, and have employed ringers or professionals to enhance their prospects, which has meant the organisers have been forced to check every application stringently,' says Christie. 'But in the final analysis, regardless of the less pleasurable experiences we have encountered on journeys to God-forsaken places, the National Village Cup remains a shining beacon and a wonderful challenge for amateur players such as ourselves. We have made friends, we have taken part in some thrilling white-knuckle rides across Britain, and we have been in the latter stages often enough that our record speaks for itself. Of course I am proud of Freuchie's exploits, but the more significant thing is that some of the original entrants might have vanished, but that this tournament promotes the very essence of cricket at the grassroots and that has to be worth promoting and cherishing. I know that I have gained many precious things from these matches, whether in the pouring rain on our own patch, or in glorious sunshine at Sessay or Feniton, Liverton Mines or Heslerton, Humshaugh or Lindal Moor.'

Even the names resonate with a poetic evocation and Christie's love of the romance and innocence which surrounds these magical mystery tours of British hamlets is contagious. Freuchie have served their country and the game of cricket well and only a fool would rule out their chances in the future.

CHAPTER 11

REELING IN THE YEARS

Anybody devoted to Scottish cricket might empathise with the man who walked into a Louisiana K–Mart store in 2004, laid a $20 bill on the counter, and asked for change. When the clerk opened the cash register, the customer pulled out a gun and demanded all the money that it contained. This was promptly handed over, as the prelude to the robber grabbing it and fleeing the store, leaving the $20 behind him. And the total amount of moolah which he extracted from the till? Ah yes, it amounted to $16.70.

As a microcosm of the process whereby cricketers in Caledonia have occasionally to take one step forward to move two steps back, that farcical episode is symptomatic of the problems which have befallen ambitious clubs, players and senior administrators who dream of the day when Scotland has earned one-day international status, boasts a fully-professional squad and is tackling the likes of Australia and England on a regular basis. Nobody is arguing that this process will happen overnight, nor that Ricky Ponting and Adam Gilchrist, or Andrew Flintoff and Michael Vaughan, will ever travel to Edinburgh, quaking in their boots at the possibility of being flayed to all corners of the Citylets Grange, but there is no logical reason why the burgeoning Scottish representative squads, at under-13, under-15 and under-17 level, cannot eventually become competitive on the global stage, if – and only if – they manage to secure the requisite funding to progress beyond operating as willing part-timers. 'We don't have access to a magic formula, but the Scots have to create a situation where their leading personnel are on full-time contracts, because they can't prepare for ODI competition on a shoestring,' says John Blain, the Penicuik-born Northants and Yorkshire paceman, who was a member of his country's maiden World Cup foray in 1999, where they performed creditably against Australia, were destroyed by Shoaib Akhtar, slumped to a pre-lunch defeat at the hands of West Indies, and should have beaten Bangladesh before allowing their rivals to escape with an unconvincing win. 'It was a little thing, perhaps, but, in retrospect, I reckon that summer was about the first time your average Joe realised that Scotland had a decent national cricket team, and began learning their names. Okay, perhaps they didn't linger in the memory for long, but the substantial crowds of kilt-wearing supporters at the matches demonstrated there is a lot of interest in cricket north of the Border, and the trick now is to graduate to the next stage. If the youngsters are hungry enough and dedicated to forcing their path into a Scottish side which convinces the ICC that it merits ODI status, we can definitely move forward. But that can't happen without money, and lots of it. Yes, representing your country is nice, but the hard fact is it doesn't pay the mortgage.'

Gradually, albeit tentatively, one or two blue-chip businesses have lent their financial backing to the Saltires, whilst the recently-renamed Cricket Scotland has sharpened up its act after a period when it seemed to be stuck in the 1950s, and although it would be folly to contemplate any premature fast-tracking up the ladder, which leaves Craig Wright's personnel staring at the same painful diet of humiliation and humblings endured by the Zimbabweans and Bangladeshis of late, one doesn't have to be a cock-eyed optimist to believe that the Scots can eventually reach similar levels to the Sri Lankans.

Certainly, at the grassroots, the likes of Freuchie have been instrumental in encouraging an ethos where children are growing up with a cricket bat for company, and anybody still inclined to be sceptical about the results should trot along to one of their practice nights, where upwards of 60 kids, aged between 8 and 15, will be trying their little hearts out to follow in the footsteps of the Village Cup victors or George Salmond's World Cup

debutants. Dale Cowan, the son of all-rounder Dave, is already a
member of his country's under-13s; Alan Duncan Jnr is on the
ground staff at Lord's; Brian Christie's son, Graeme, became part
of the Freuchie First XI in 2005; and Scott Gourlay, a former
Scotland internationalist, has been preaching the game to his
three nephews, to such effect that the trio have already exhibited
precious talent in the batting and leg-spin bowling department.
'Scottish cricket definitely has a bright future, if the evidence at
Freuchie is any pointer. We are currently running three junior
sides and I am going into the schools around the village,
including Ladybank, Kingskettle, Pitlessie and Markinch, and
doing my utmost to circulate the message that this is a hugely
exciting period to be involved with the sport,' says Dave
Christie, as eager and puckishly bright as ever at 68. 'In the last
couple of years, we have had a dozen boys picked as part of Fife
and Central regional selects, and the whole emphasis has to be on
encouraging our own players, not relying on the services of
foreigners with no long-term affinity to Scotland.

'It doesn't require a genius to notice how the mass influx of
overseas signings at Rangers and Celtic, and the majority of the
other clubs in the Premier league, has had a negative impact on
our national team and we should guard against a similar man-
ifestation in cricket, because if people aren't good enough to win
caps for their own country, whether they are from Australia,
New Zealand, South Africa or wherever, they shouldn't be able
to use the Saltire as a flag of convenience. I am really hard-nosed
about this issue, and if it were up to me I would introduce a
regulation whereby a minimum of nine players from every
SNCL club had to be eligible to represent Scotland. If we
encourage and nurture our own talent, we have nothing to
be frightened of, in terms of moving ahead of the other emerging
nations. But we have to avoid the situation, which I have
witnessed at some organisations, where the first three or four
in the batting order have foreign accents and they are basically
preventing local lads from gaining an opportunity. That is just
daft, especially at a time when there are so many promising

youngsters being groomed from every part of the country, who are desperate to be involved at international level.'

Refreshingly, the game's governors have also succeeded in wooing significant numbers of Scots-born Asians to their ranks and the benefits are self-evident. Kasim Farid, for instance, can't remember a time when he wasn't wielding a cricket bat and searching out patches of green space in Glasgow to indulge his passion. The same applies to his Scotland and Clydesdale team-mate, Zeeshan Bashir, a puckish sprite with the sobriquet 'Bambi' and the spontaneous banter between these two players is typical of the 'Hooray for Bowlywood' philosophy which is permeating the Scottish game.

Unlike football, where the influence of multiculturalism has not extended so far as to unearth a single Asian squad member in the current SPL ranks, cricket in Scotland is positively thriving from the labours of a group of youngsters in Kasim's mould: namely, Scots of Indian and Pakistani descent, with a similar penchant both for Irn-Bru and the Old Firm and for inswinging yorkers and off-breaks. At 19, Farid has become the first-ever player from an ethnic background to captain his country and, more remarkably, at least for those who would strive to depict Caledonia's cork-and-willow brethren as a bunch of minority Micawbers, no fewer than seven of the fourteen teenagers in the squad which trounced Durham University in the summer of 2004 hailed from an Asian background. In this light, the phenomenon can no longer be dismissed as a curiosity – instead, there is sound method and natural progression behind the development of Kasim, Zeeshan, Allauddin Farooq, Gautham Hariharan, Umair Mohammed, Navdeep Singh Poonia and Sean Weeraratna, whose potential is bolstered by the likes of Moneeb Iqbal, Scotland's youngest-ever internationalist (now at the Durham Academy), Qasim Sheikh, who has spent time on the ground staff at Lord's and Majid Haq, a fully-fledged Saltire. Other names to watch out for in the future include Edinburgh University student, Rajeev Routray of Ferguslie and west of Scotland's Jatinder Singh, who was singled out for acclaim by

Indian maestro Rahul Dravid at one of his master classes in 2003.

Indeed, the bare bones of this story provide a stirring antidote to those inclined to cling to the lapels of the wretched 'Tebbit Test'. None of which is to pretend that Kasim and his confrères haven't suffered abuse over the colour of their skin – they have – but merely to highlight that whilst other Scottish sports, from football and rugby through to squash and hockey (which one might have assumed would have attracted a healthy Asian following) are still largely white-only enclaves, cricket has recognised there is no sound argument against different races and religions being integrated, with the right attitude.

'Okay, we have endured some racism on the field – name-calling, disparaging references to our colour and the like – and it is never a pleasant experience, but we still think that the vast majority of Scots are decent people and we have learned to rise above the taunts of a few idiots and persevere with the one thing which really matters to all of us,' says Kasim, whose calmness and tactical acumen testify to the personality of this engaging individual, who visited Robben Island, the scene of Nelson Mandela's incarceration, during a West District tour of South Africa in 2002 and quickly discovered a proper perspective on life. 'I have climbed up the Scottish age-group teams at under-13, under-15 and beyond, and there is a genuine feeling amongst the boys that they have the opportunity to take centre stage at the most exciting period in the history of Scottish cricket. I mean, those of us who are 17, 18, 19 will be 19, 20, 21 at the next World Cup in the West Indies, and there couldn't be greater motivation. Surely that is more important than racial issues, and because I have grown up in a close-knit environment at Clydesdale, I know we're all in this adventure together, spurring each other on, but having a laugh as well.'

As he acknowledges, however, the process hasn't occurred by accident. On the contrary, there have been pivotal figures instrumental in chipping away at the cultural barriers, such as Colin Dawson, the junior convenor at Glasgow Academicals for the past 25 years; David Barr of Renfrew, a veritable Pied Piper of cricket who, even at 71, is cajoling scores of children into the game; and Mike Stanger, whose labours at Clydesdale are summed up by Kasim with the tribute: 'He just doesn't care about colour. He only cares about whether somebody is interested in cricket or not. If the answer is yes, then he will do whatever he possibly can to help them and that is his sole concern.'

As for Dave Christie, he harks back to the Indian Gymkhana's involvement in the 1985 triumph and speaks with robust, sturdy commonsense. 'Black, brown or white, there are good people and bad people, and it's plain stupid to judge anybody by the colour of their skin. I can honestly say that in 50 years I have talked about cricket to folk from every corner of the globe and we are all Jock Tamson's bairns, aren't we?' he says, scything through the cant and flummery which often pervades this subject. 'Back in '85 we had already forged links with the Indians down in London, and it seemed like the most logical thing in the world to renew acquaintances with them when we were down there. Life would be a lot simpler if we searched for the common strands which bind us together, wouldn't it, and when push comes to shove, if I find another human being who loves cricket I'm interested in what he or she has to say, not what colour they are.'

All of which rather begs the question: if this can happen in cricket, why not football, particularly when one considers the sizable number of Scots, of Indo-Pakistani heritage who are participating in the country's national sport? Yet sadly, in several cases, the Asian community has chosen to form their own leagues, which has established a new form of segregation. 'We have to be honest and accept that ending the discrimination in football circles is going to be a long-term project and, even now, I am hearing stereotypes being perpetuated by Scottish coaches and fans, to the effect that Asians will never be good footballers because of their diet, or their physique or some other nonsense,' says Prem Singh, a prominent member of the Scottish Asian Sports Association.

'It is absolutely brilliant that cricket has got its act together in Scotland and taken steps to encourage kids from across the racial spectrum. In fact, there are lessons here for other pursuits, because this country simply isn't good enough at football, rugby or whatever to ignore any part of the population. But, unfortunately, racial abuse has been so prevalent even amongst the Sunday morning soccer brigade, that a lot of people from the ethnic communities have decided it was better to have safety in numbers and play among themselves. Of course, it's not an ideal situation, but there again, you have incidents like the Ron Atkinson episode [the former manager had to resign as an ITV pundit after calling Chelsea's Marcel Desailly a 'lazy nigger' on air], which demonstrate the kind of attitudes which we are up against. I would love it if there were no need for an organisation such as SASA, and we could pack our bags and shut up shop . . . but although cricket is showing what can be done to bring races together, I'm afraid we are still a long way off from the day when we can contemplate a similar scenario in football.'

The Asian influence is an exemplary illustration of Scottish cricket's prescience, and the pool of talent extends further than was remotely the case a decade ago. As Mike Stanger, tireless proselytiser for his vocation, argues, there has never been a stronger collection of youthful protégés than in the current climate, where many of the teenage brigade can sense the ICC is poised to invite the Scots to the top table of international recognition. 'I am very excited by the calibre of emerging players such as Richard Berrington, who was born in South Africa, but his mother is Scottish and he has lived in Scotland for the last ten years. Then you have Gordon Goudie and Kyle Coetzer, who has already been snapped up by Durham, whilst there are plenty of bright prospects aged around 19 or 20,' says Stanger, who led some of these personnel on a ground-breaking, month-long tour of Australia earlier this year. 'Clydesdale's left-arm spinner, Ross Lyons, is improving all the time, so is Ian Young [who started a six-month contract with the MCC in March], then there is the Arbroath seamer, Chris Anderson, all 6ft 6in of him; and further down the representative ladder, Glasgow Academicals' Roddy Kelso has amassed a stack of runs, and Drumpellier paceboy, Calum MacLeod, is awesome for his age [16], 6ft 2in and still growing. So the buzz around Scottish cricket is undeniable. More and more of our youngsters are also flying the nest and wintering abroad in Australia or South Africa, so they are developing the mental toughness and growing used to performing day in, day out, in countries where cricket is part of the landscape. Obviously, we will have to wait to see how these individuals fare as they gain experience and become more streetwise, but whereas there was deep depression when Scotland failed to qualify for the 2003 World Cup, the situation has been transformed in recent times. Personally, as somebody who has been involved in cricket for over 40 years, I am genuinely optimistic for the future.'

It wouldn't do to pretend that the game is all sweetness and light. Violence does occasionally rear its head in Scottish cricket and even Freuchie have not been immune to the odd spat, with teddies flung out of prams and petted lips all round. Indeed, their acceptance, with insouciant pride, of the monikers 'the Mean Machine' and 'The Animals' hints at their reputation for being ferocious adversaries, and when they marched on London, with pipes skirling and kilts swirling, there was nobody in the city daft enough to suggest to them that winning was less important than taking part.

Instead, the Fifers derive an almost masochistic pleasure in disproving all the pat theories about Scottish cricket being a pastime for gentlemen with starched shirts and even stiffer lips. In its most innocent form, as I discovered during a typically rumbustious scrap with their Second XI, the phenomenon usually manifests itself in a vocal cacophony to rival any of those customers who used to hurl abuse in the direction of second-rate comedians at the old Glasgow Empire. Thus, in the process of trudging back to the pavilion after being caught on the boundary, I was accosted by an elderly home supporter who yelled in my ear: 'Dearie, dearie, dearie, son, what a bloody awful shot that was.'

Oh well, that's life, and you have to grin and bear it, especially when the insults are being delivered by a senior citizen. But in 2002 Freuchie were implicated in a more unsavoury saga, when Alan Duncan Jnr reputedly shoulder-charged the Hillhead professional, Tinus Enslin, after bowling him neck and crop, whereupon his father, it was claimed, dug his elbow into the ribs of the Glasgow side's overseas amateur, Drian Steyn. This, of course, was manna to the tabloids and the cry erupted that the Fifers were a belligerent bunch of hirsute Scots with too much testosterone in their veins. Even at this stage, Dave Christie looks distressed about the incident and wishes it had never happened. Yet, befitting a man with an ingrained loyalty to his troops, he strives to place it in perspective. 'I am not defending the conduct of our players at Hillhead, but the match was simmering with bitterness from the outset. For starters, the pitch was an absolute disgrace, one of the most atrocious surfaces I have ever witnessed, and then it was as if every umpiring decision went in their favour,' recalls Christie, a pained expression etched on his face. 'I mean, when the guy, Steyn, snicked the ball, you could hear it on the boundary, but what *really* inflamed the situation was the fact that he turned to the wicketkeeper and said: "Yeah, I nicked it, but I'm not walking unless the umpire gives me out." Well, that was blatant cheating, and there is something rotten about Scottish cricket if we allow that sort of behaviour to become the norm.

'The SCU investigated the matter and ultimately gave both clubs a slap on the wrists, and the press turned the business into more than it was, but I'm still sorry it occurred. Anybody who knows me will appreciate that Freuchie have always striven to play hard but fair, and I certainly don't condone loutishness, but it was as if we were suddenly being portrayed as a bunch of foul-mouthed yobs, which simply isn't true. In fact, while I was captain, I always did my best to defuse confrontations and I wasn't averse to telling my own lads to put a sock in it if I thought they were overstepping the mark.'

David W. Potter, one of the umpires who regularly covered

Freuchie fixtures, confirmed these words and, mercifully, acts of bampottery are scarce in the Scottish annals. Yet, as he relates, even if it hardly amounts to a cricketing equivalent of Hampden Babylon, trouble and strife have cropped up in the chronicles since as far back as the 1850s, when a match between Hurlford and Kilmarnock Portland was seriously disrupted because of the conduct of the home crowd, who 'acted in an anything but gentlemanly fashion'.

And there's more. 'In 1905, at the North Inch, Perthshire were playing Stirling County; the latter had never defeated their hosts before, and on this occasion only did so after a confident lbw shout was turned down by the umpire. The crowd, much fuelled by alcohol on a baking hot day, duly rioted. Some tried to attack the officials, but others were not as rational as that and picked a fight with anybody in sight. The constabulary made scores of arrests,' recalls Potter, the author of *The Encyclopaedia of Scottish Cricket*.

'Barrachnie Park, where Garrowhill used to play, was by no means the most salubrious of spots and on one occasion, when they played Weirs, a crowd of over 100 teenagers appeared. Sadly, this was not to watch the cricket, but rather to see a fight between two girls. Appeals by the players for the young Amazons to ply their trade elsewhere were refused in a torrent of unlady-like language and the game had to wait a while.

'On the field, a somewhat unsavoury incident hit the national press in 1996, following a match between Penicuik and Gala. The latter had reached 130 all out and, having suffered some not particularly good-natured sledging in their innings, decided to retaliate. David Simpson, Gala's New Zealand professional, ex-changed a few pleasantries with a Penicuik batsman, who eventually snapped and marched down the wicket to join in the conversation, as it were. What happened next is in some doubt, depending on who you listen to, but Simpson was quoted in the papers as saying: "It was a little head-butt, nothing major. He was waving his bat around a bit, so two of our side took it off him." At this point, the captains and umpires intervened and everybody agreed that the batsman should retire "hurt". He came back later, but could do little to save his side who were dismissed for 90. It was an unfortunate episode and reflected little credit on either club, both of whom have otherwise done a great deal for the cause of Scottish cricket.'

Praise be that these descents into anarchy are isolated aberrations and not part of a wider malaise. On the contrary, as Freuchie have discovered, whether in the adulation of their community, or in their meetings with such luminaries as Botham, David Gower and Tom Graveney that cricket has the ability to unite individuals from all manner of diverse backgrounds and bring them together in a common obsession. One only has to recall the afternoon in 1992 when Freuchie were beaten by Methley in the Village Cup semi-final to recollect Dave Christie's response to the disappointment: at the end of the contest, he was chatting amiably to the triumphant Englishmen, both retaining his dignity and demonstrating the innate sportsmanship which epitomises this stout character. Of course, he was inwardly deflated, but there was nary a hint of that in his demeanour.

Let me take you back, as the Beatles once sang, to an afternoon in 1985 when a distinctly moderate cricketer, with no great pretensions, was asked to open the batting for Atlas against Woodhall on a balmy (for once) Saturday afternoon in June. Hence the scenario in which I marched to the crease with Fred Robson for company and, prior to the commencement of hostilities, he marched down purposefully to the middle of the pitch and declared: 'Right, get yourself settled, there are runs up for grabs today.' Heeding his advice, I immediately launched into an ambitious cover drive from the opening delivery and the ball missed the stumps by the tiniest of margins. Barely had I thanked my lucky stars before Robson strode in my direction and said: 'Watch my lips. We've trusted you to do a job. And that doesn't involve doing a crossword or drinking Coke.'

After a few minutes, I pierced the field with a decent square cut, then scampered a few singles, and we began to forge a decent little partnership prior to my partner's departure, trapped lbw in dubious circumstances. (This, inevitably, proved the catalyst for a string of muttered imprecations from my colleague.) Harry Cockburn was next in, and progressed with his usual impersonation of a snail on Valium, until he too perished. By this stage, I was starting to feel increasingly confident, and had advanced to 20 when the third wicket fell, which prompted the arrival of my brother, Alastair. 'Okay, bruv, don't do anything stupid,' I beseeched him. 'I'm sure we can post a good total on this surface, so stick in.' In the event, I may as well have been talking to the trees, because he and Brian Hazzard had spotted an attractive-looking girl among the sprinkling of spectators and were focused on other priorities than cricket. In the space of four balls, he had amassed nine – including a magnificent, towering six which crashed into the bushes – as the prelude to proffering a desperate yahoo, which saw him comprehensively bowled, and amidst the celebrations of the Woodhall men, I was forced to watch as batsman after batsman discovered new means of getting themselves out on a featherbed pitch. Hamish McIntyre was stumped by yards, Hazzard hardly paused to take guard before rushing back to the pavilion in search of scoring elsewhere and Jim Notman enacted his usual whirling-dervish routine, cigar perched on ear, and was soon at liberty to resume humming the Hamlet tune. At 65 for 8, the situation was fairly desperate, but young Barry Montgomery displayed some of the application which had been lacking from his elders in front of him and we inched on cautiously, determined to complete our allocation.

Soon, I had reached 40 and took a liking to the hosts' spinner, a chap who grunted in a style reminiscent of Monica Seles after every delivery, clattering him for a brace of boundaries in a couple of minutes, and then sprinting a quick run to retain the strike. Here I was on 49, having never achieved a 50 in a competitive league match, and we had just 2 overs left with Robson having returned to the greensward in an umpiring capacity. Could I remain disciplined and maintain my concentration? Could I demonstrate to some of the lovesick, lustful chumps in our ranks that they should really carry on their courting elsewhere by staying focused and being a model of sangfroid?

Could I hell!

Instead, I determined that I would attain my half-century in the grand manner, and immediately spooned a gentle lob towards square leg. The Woodhall man placed there sauntered in to seal my misery, but suddenly, amidst an ecstasy of fumbling, dark curses and sprawling limbs, Robson had collided with him, both men were on the ground and I had escaped. When a semblance of normality was restored, Robson stood up and, cool as Antartica, his face a perfect picture of innocence and respectability, proclaimed: 'Dead ball.' At which juncture, the dishevelled fielder turned furiously to him and cried out in exasperation: 'You'll have fucking dead balls if you ever do that again.'

It might have been the spark which ignited a feud, but, to their credit, our opponents clapped magnanimously when I finally passed 50. They were even more generous when I carried my bat for an unbeaten 57, which at least ensured we reached 100. Strolling back for tea and cakes, every member of their side shook my hand, offered their collective congratulations, and I was infused with a warm glow which continued for the rest of the match, as Robson, McIntyre and Notman bowled Atlas to an against-the-odds victory with one stunning catch sticking in my hands, whilst my brother, his attention no longer diverted by comely wenches on the periphery (the damsel in question had departed to a nearby pub with her boyfriend) hung on to a screamer at cover point, as if temporarily possessed by the spirit of Jonty Rhodes. At the death, and oblivious to the frustration which he must have been nursing, their skipper strolled towards me and said: 'You were the difference today. Without you, we wouldn't have been chasing 50. Well done.'

None of this will be remotely surprising to the thousands of part-time, coarse cricketers who love the game in Scotland. On other days, in exactly the same circumstances, I was about as much use as Long John Silver at an arse-kicking party, but whether it is the 18-handicap golfer who achieves a hole-in-one, or the third-XV rugby winger who finds a sidestep he didn't know was in his repertoire and dives over for a clinching try, sport constantly serves up these kinds of miraculous occasions where the inept feel inspired, where anonymous journeymen are allowed a brief spell of basking in the limelight. Magical may be too strong a word for it, but that's what it felt like.

Speaking about this to Dave Christie, it was evident he shared the sensation and appreciated that, although Freuchie and Atlas may have been miles apart in terms of ambition and organisation, there was a mutual bond between the Fifers and their West Lothian counterparts. 'Ever since I was a youngster, cricket has gripped me, captivated me and held me in its spell, and it's true what you're saying: I've been involved in social matches and friendlies and seen sheer rapturous delight from a player who has struck a sweet boundary or held on to a terrific catch, and I have been almost as excited for them as they were themselves,' says Christie. 'Obviously, going to Lord's was something that very few players have the opportunity to do, but I have always stressed at Freuchie that there is a place for you if you enjoy the game and you want to play, and the main thing isn't winning at all costs, but deriving pleasure from what you're doing.

'That's one of the cherished aspects of village cricket, which we have to preserve: the notion that it is fun, that whether you're in the Firsts, or the Juniors, or the social team, your contribution is equally important to the *club*. Clearly, it's another matter altogether at county and Test level, where livelihoods are at stake, and there is a different emphasis and intensity. But ultimately, for those of us at a lower grade, it has to be enjoyable, doesn't it? Otherwise, where are the next generation of youngsters going to come from? And I felt the same as you when I scored my first 50. Terrific, no?'

As long as Christie and his cohorts are continuing this tradition, whilst Cricket Scotland pursues its inclusive strategies and the leading luminaries forage for new challenges, the future seems assured. Golden, even. And as long as there are little-league organisations there will be those minions inclined to echo the sentiments of the writer, R.C. Robertson-Glasgow: 'Can cricket be defined? You can see it, in perfect miniature, in the small, howling schoolboy, rushing from work some midsummer day, where an irritable master, who would fain perhaps himself be watching at Lord's, has been trying to supplant with Corn Laws or Equinoxes the crowded imagery of the cricket-stuffed mind – rushing from work to bat like Herbert Sutcliffe or bowl like Hedley Verity – noble imitation! Then to dream away the night in some fairy Test match, where he has been chosen to bat first, and is just taking guard, when the morning bell clangs out the close of play!'

CHAPTER 12

THE ARMY REUNION

It's late March in 2005 and a full-blown spate of nostalgia seems to be enveloping Britain. Peter Kay has resurrected Tony Christie's cheesy 'Is This the Way to Amarillo' and steered the song to the summit of the charts: *Dr Who* is back on our TV screens, with enhanced effects – not that they could have been any worse than the original – and the Daleks for company; whilst a Grand Slam for Wales has evoked a million dewy-eyed reminiscences from the Land of my Fathers, led by Phil Bennett and Gareth Edwards. The month has also witnessed the return of *The Two Ronnies*, Ian Pattinson is working on a new series of *Rab C. Nesbitt*, and the *Captain Scarlet* theme tune is ringing out on mobile phones across the nation. How long, perchance, before some perverse contemporary critic starts clamouring for a reassessment of the comic genius of Arthur Askey or a *Mojo* music writer asks us to reconsider the iconic status of the Brotherhood of Man?

In Freuchie, meanwhile, Dave Christie has invited the 1985 team to an impromptu reunion at the clubhouse, following their second practice session for the new season at Lochgelly. One or two of the Lord's cavaliers are unable to attend – Terry Trewartha has severed his connections with the club, whilst a couple of others are at work or on holiday – but within a few minutes of Rangers trouncing Motherwell 5–1 to collect the CIS Cup, a collection of us are sitting down and examining our wrinkles. 'God, it's scary, isn't it, when you look round and notice how old we all are,' exclaims Andy Crichton, who still retains a spry and wiry physique. 'Mind you, it can't be so bad for you, Dad. After all, you were old even by the stage we were travelling to London 20 years ago!'

Around him, on the walls of the function suite, hang an

impressive collection of accolades and plaudits, testifying to the
fashion in which this little village has stamped its imprint on
cricket for the past three decades. Yet, more significantly, the
verbal ping-pong which immediately breaks out between the
assembled personalities, allied to a machine-gun-style, rat-a-tat
recitation of anecdotes – some of them even repeatable –
highlights one of the reasons why this particular group of
individuals made history where other, more talented, Freuchie
collectives, failed in their objective. 'We're not being modest,
there have been sides since 1985 with more gifted players than us
in the ranks and they really should have marched to Lord's again
at least once,' says George Crichton, a diminutive coiled spring of
hyperactivity with a penchant for the F-word in all its Anglo-
Saxon finery. 'But, do you know something, what we lacked in
ability we made up for in this.' He points to his heart and several
of his confrères nod their heads spontaneously. Whatever else has
characterised this Freuchie vintage, they have never wanted for
lashings of courage or cussed obduracy, and manifestly revel in
the challenge of transforming adversity to advantage. Their hair
may be greyer, and (in a few cases) their guts more inflated, but
there remains a tangible sense of the lurking mischief within
these men's psyches. No wonder that the telephone at the
entrance to the club offers a roster of excuses/alibis to be used
in case of emergency, such as inquiries from anxious wives and
lovers. 'Sorry, but he's out in the middle at the moment', is on
the list. Ditto: 'He's in a committee meeting.' Quite how this
policy operates, when the club is situated in the middle of
Freuchie, within ten minutes' walking distance of any part of
the hamlet, is a mystery, but these Fifers have stuck together
through thick and thin, so presumably there is something to be
said for the philosophy of positive drinking.

   Sitting in the corner, behind the Crichtons, the Christies, Allan
Wilkie, Peter Hepplewhite and 'The Animals', David Cowan and
Stewart Irvine, Niven McNaughton's presence offers a reminder
of the swaying-on-the-edge mentality which is shared by several
of these brethren. A roaring boy with an insatiable appetite for

straying down perilous cul-de-sacs during years of living danger-
ously, McNaughton looks gaunt, and occasionally slurs into
incomprehension, but the remarkable thing is that he was able
to join the party at all. Less than two months earlier, in the
bleakness of January, he had been on a life-support machine, his
lungs knackered, his relatives pondering whether there was any
hope of recovery, and his doctors trudging around with all manner
of pessimistic prognoses. They had to insert a tube in his throat as
the prelude to striving to resuscitate him and bring him off a
ventilator. The process failed once. Then twice. But he is a
remarkable battler, this fellow McNaughton, and within a fortnight he was on his feet, with the help of a zimmer frame, and
continuing to shake his fist at the scythe man.

'I'm fine, perhaps better than I have any right to be, but whenever I return to the club I feel young again. There have been some
great days, and some rotten days, but I wouldn't have missed the
experience for the world. I was disconsolate when I started to lose
my breath and I had to retire from cricket, but we have packed a
helluva lot of adventure and incidents into our journey these past
25 years,' recalled McNaughton, whose penchant for scrapes and
close shaves leaves him resembling Oor Wullie in adult form.
'Down in London, at the Village Cup final, I was approached by
this lady of the night, who asked me if I wanted a good time. Purely
out of curiosity, you understand, I asked her much it would cost
me. She said, bold as brass: "£100". I was gobsmacked for a
moment. Then I responded: "Is that for me or the whole team?"
She looked annoyed, and thought it best to finish the conversation.
"Sorry love, but I would want to rent it, not buy it."

'There was another occasion when we ventured down to play
Panal, near Harrogate, in 1990, and we'd been in touch with the
B&B people and they'd fixed us up with a place in Morpeth.
Well, blow me if we didn't get there, late on the Saturday night,
and discovered that there was no bar. So, out we rushed, into the
town and we finished up in this tavern, and just as I went up to
order the drinks, the barman rang the bell and cried: 'Last orders'.
Fuck me, it was only around 10.20, but these were the licensing

laws at the time in England. Anyway, we caught his attention, and he noticed there were five or six of us, so he walked towards us and said: "Hello gents, what can I get you?"

' "Hello there, we'll have 30 pints of lager," I replied.

'He looked momentarily nonplussed, but to his credit, he called for assistance and for the next ten minutes he and his mate were delivering tray after tray to our table. Even as we started drinking, we noticed the pub being closed and the curtains drawn together, and it was obvious, from all the laughter and racket upstairs, that some kind of party was going on. Well, we soon twigged it was a lock-in, and we just stayed there and had a nice night, stretching into the next morning. By the end, the landlord was out on his feet. I remember asking for a whisky and he was fumbling around with the optic and the golden liquid was pouring onto the sleeve of his shirt, because he was in such a state. Eventually, we left the premises and drove on to Panal and gave them a good thumping on the Sunday afternoon. But we heard later that the owner had been done for drunk-driving the next morning. Ach, well, maybe he should have taken a bus, the same as the rest of us.'

Sometimes, those summer nights into oblivion inflicted their toll. On one instance, a Freuchie batsman lurched out to the crease, still the worse for wear from the previous evening's excess, used his bat as a crutch rather than a sporting implement, and while preparing to take guard, fell headlong onto the turf in a stupor. On another afternoon, en route to a dread destination at the back of beyond in Liverton Mines, the Fifers passed along row after row of dilapidated houses, where all the owners appeared to be replacing broken windows, and walked out to the field in a cacophony of hissing. 'Christ, we were shitting ourselves that day; the B&B had made Fawlty Towers seem like the Ritz Hotel by comparison, and all we wanted to do was finish the game and get out of the place in one piece,' recalls George Crichton, nobody's idea of a shrinking violet. 'We attained our aim, both of winning, and of emerging unscathed, but it was fucking scary and when we played Kington in the semi-final [this was in 1993], the atmosphere was even more hostile. It didn't help, either, that the attitude of a lot of competitors has changed, and not for the better and, as for the notion of Kington being a village, well ha, ha!'

This was a familiar theme amongst the reunion celebrants and emphasises why the tournament officials have gradually been forced to amend and toughen up on the regulations. Quite simply, many of the original communities which entered the event have mushroomed beyond recognition in the past 20 years, whilst the standard of league cricket in the south of England, bolstered by ex-county personnel and allegedly unpaid southern hemisphere imports, has improved to such an extent that Ben Brocklehurst's grand vision has required some major surgery. In 2005, for the first time in the history of the competition, a number of clubs were ruled out of participation for being too good, and although the Village Cup has embraced only those hamlets with a population of less than 3000 since its inception, that figure has now been increased to 4000.

'We accept that village cricket isn't what it used to be, and we need a system for keeping the competition at the game's grass roots. I believe an exclusion list of leagues is the fairest means of doing this, and while we acknowledge that things are changing, and that there has been a huge amount of housing development in greenbelt areas since the 1980s, I'm still confident that this event will enjoy a prosperous future, because it is a uniquely British institution, extending from the northernmost tip of Scotland to the southernmost area of Cornwall,' says Tim Brocklehurst, who inherited the mantle of competition organiser from his father. 'I'm glad that Freuchie have remained as keen as ever on retaining their involvement with us, because they are one of the sides who have brought a distinctive flavour to the Cup, and quite apart from the fantastic exposure which they gained for themselves and the sponsors when they triumphed at Lord's, they're a proper village, they believe that they should stand or fall on the efforts of their own community, and that is extremely refreshing. They have put themselves on the map forever and although there may be people living in the big cities who have no concept of the scale of the Village Cup being fought out on hundreds of pitches, we still have over 500 teams involved, and Freuchie have been one of the most influential sides in the pile.'

Sadly, or at least according to Andy Crichton, the die might already have been cast, in terms of preserving the initial rambunctious amateurism of the Village Cup template. Watching, for instance, STV's documentary on Freuchie's sojourn at Lord's feels akin to being transported back to the 1950s, not the 1980s, what with the accordion songs, the whole air of 'Let's Put the Show on Here', the parallels with the White Heather Club and the air of innocence which pervades these pictures from another time. Fast forward to the present and the tabloids would probably have sought to stitch up the Scots, or pay for some cricketing-style Rebecca Loos to arrange a text-message rendezvous with McNaughton or Davie Cowan. Whereupon, we could have anticipated a spate of bad puns and dodgy innuendos, with references to kilts a-flying, no balls and shots between the covers. Call me cynical if you like, but the culture has definitely changed in the intervening period, which probably explains why, for all their temporary starring roles in the spotlight, the Freuchie troops seem glad to have escaped with reputations intact.

'I don't know how the big-name sports stars keep their tempers when people are digging into their private lives, but one of our strengths lies in our attachment to the village and the fact that we're all proud of our roots and have never wanted to bring disrepute on the Freuchie name,' says Andy Crichton. 'That may sound obvious, but you have to bear in mind that the majority of the opponents we have faced in the Village Cup have never been remotely as close-knit as us. I remember when we came up against Methley in the semi-finals in 1992 [and lost] that one of their committee chaps asked me how many of our side actually came from Freuchie and when I told him that we had 11 players who had attended the same village primary school in our team that afternoon, his reaction was: "You are kidding me,

right? That is just fucking unbelievable." He then told me, rather
shame-facedly, that only one member of their ranks had been
born in Methley and the rest were outsiders and whilst it might
not have been the reason why they beat us, I still think it was
indicative of the way the competition is going.

'Basically, it's supposed to be the National *Village* Cup isn't it: a
celebration of cricket at the grassroots amongst teams who are
pretty much on a level playing field. But, at the end of the day,
the rules are open to exploitation and they will be abused,
because the prize of a place at Lord's is such a giant incentive. As
things stand, you don't have to live in the village, or hail from the
village, you merely have to have played X amount of matches for
the club, and not be a professional, and we have come up against
Australians and South Africans and Indians, on our journeys, and
you do sometimes wonder whether the event is not in peril of
being devalued. Yet somehow it endures, possibly as a consequence of the fact that once the nights start drawing out and it is
time to change the clocks in March, the adrenaline starts coursing
through the veins and you can hardly wait to be out there in the
middle with a cricket bat for another summer.'

Herein lies the spark behind Freuchie's success. These customers are the first to admit that they haven't always been
angels – 'A few punches have been thrown between Falkland
and Freuchie players when they have met in the right place at the
right time,' observes Allan Wilkie – and some of their weekend
excursions, fuelled by limitless reserves of pints and whiskies, owe
more to Ray Milland than Ray Lindwall. But, in the background, perpetually bringing restraint to the riotous activity,
Dave Christie's involvement, innate good humour and down-
to-earth decency have acted as a calming influence on the wilder
members of his territorial army. Other captains might have
reacted like Vesuvius to the decision of the Rowledge skipper,
Alan Prior, to keep the Scots waiting after the coin had been
tossed at Lord's. Not Christie, who reckoned that if the Surrey
team were so confident of having the tussle completed by 2.30,
they wouldn't have procrastinated over deciding what to do

next. Other leaders may have grown uppity amidst the cauldron of publicity which engulfed Freuchie for months afterwards, but not the sprightly sexagenarian, who has lived in the village, together with his wife, June, for over 50 years, and who is more concerned with the future than the past.

'It never occurred to us that we were special, and the worst thing that could have happened was if we had formed a clique and stopped the youngsters from rising into the first team, because they are the life-blood for Freuchie, and my main priority is in charting a path to prosperity for the club ten, twenty years from now, rather than wallowing in nostalgia, considering that the 1985 team have all had our ugly mugs plastered over the papers,' says Christie with the insouciance of a painter who has focused on a single canvas. 'We have an impressive group of under-13s coming through the ranks at the moment, and although there is a wee bit of a drop-off in the numbers between 18 and 21 – no matter the generation, the laddies always seem to find other interests at that age – we keep prodding away at them gently and reminding them that they don't have to be slaves to cricket, but that if they possess a talent, then it would be a pity to waste it. I suppose that it is the art of quiet persuasion and the notion that you can't force somebody to like a game, but that if you introduce them to it early enough, you can leave them to make up their own minds. Enough kids in Freuchie will keep coming back for more. I have no doubts about that, given the enthusiasm of the 12- and 13-year-olds on Fridays and when I see the sparkle in the eyes of the wee lad who bashes his first boundary or the jubilation from the young bowler who knocks down the batsman's stumps. You can try to analyse these things to death, but in the end, it boils down to the simple truth that cricket isn't brain surgery. If it was, I would never have got round to mastering it, would I?'

By this stage, the party is poised to disperse for a late supper, so it is time to ask one final question of this unit of Dad's Army. No frills, no flummery: what was your abiding memory of Freuchie CC during the year in which they stormed the Lord's citadels?

ALAN DUNCAN: 'It was the repeated fashion in which the lads came and saw me in hospital at the start of the 1985 campaign. They had plenty of other things to worry about, but they constantly cheered me up, even when the doctors were telling me that I wouldn't play cricket for the rest of that summer. I had already decided, come hell or high water, that I was going to Lord's if the boys made the final, even if I had to break out of the hospital, but their exhortations spurred me on a tremendous amount.'

ANDY CRICHTON: 'The night before the final was pretty special. We had gone down there, with the TV cameras filming our every step, but it still hadn't really sunk in that we were poised for the biggest match of our lives. Then Mike Denness turned up and we were chatting with a former England captain, and he told us just to go out and do Scotland proud the next day and he was confident we would be in with a shout. There was this mounting expectation that something special was in the air and when Rowledge only sent along a couple of representatives to the pre-match dinner, we thought to ourselves: "Okay, you might not rate us today, but wait until tomorrow . . ."'

NIVEN McNAUGHTON: 'The whole episode felt like a glorious dream, but it was when we went to Lord's on the Saturday and you immediately realised just why so many hundreds of village clubs fling their hats into the ring every year for the chance to reach this wonderful amphitheatre. I looked around me and the place was huge: there was history in every inch of the ground and the thought that we would have gone from playing at Freuchie Public Park to Lord's inside a week was mind-blowing. I can't recall too much about the climax, obviously, but I was fairly nervous. No, let's rephrase that: I was shitting myself and I am just glad the other boys finished the job.'

DAVIE COWAN: 'It's hard to pick one particular moment, but when Dave Christie led us along the streets of London, en route to Lord's, and you could spot the pride and the passion in his face, and the lump in his throat, I thought to myself: "They [Rowledge] might turn out to be technically better than us, but they won't surpass us for guts or spirit or commitment, and these are important qualities at Village Cup level. I was just a youngster and, obviously, I hadn't played in a match of that magnitude, but for a 21-year-old to be walking through the Grace Gates . . . what could possibly be better?" '

GEORGE CRICHTON: 'We had no doubt the English team believed they could just turn up and roll us over. But I saw them in the nets and thought to myself: "They don't look any fucking better than us. We have nothing to be frightened about." Clearly, we kept them to a manageable target, but we struggled ourselves, yet I was bloody sure that I wasn't going to throw away my wicket lightly and I've always been quick on my pins, so I was able to turn a few singles into twos and suddenly they lost their composure in their field and their captain started getting agitated. I remember smiling quietly to myself and saying: "They've lost this. As long as we maintain our composure, we'll be fine." Then Dave [Christie] was run out and it was tight again. But I was still 100 per cent confident. And when we did it, we had beaten the Englishmen in their own backyard.'

BRIAN CHRISTIE: 'It was being reassured by Dad as I walked in and noticing the look on his face. Sure, there was frustration that he wasn't there until the end, but also this quivering excitement at us being so close to history. I was nervous inside, of course I was, but all we required was common sense and if only I had managed to play a shot to the ball which sparked the pitch invasion, my Dad wouldn't have needed to go on the tannoy and ask the spectators to get off the pitch. But, in a way, it merely added to the drama and the spectacle and the climactic scenes were pure unadulterated magic.'

DAVE CHRISTIE: 'When we knew that we had won, I was almost in a trance, but suddenly there was this huge explosion of emotion and surge of patriotism and pride in what the boys had achieved. It was overwhelming. I mean, here I was at 48, and it had seemed as if we would never achieve our goal in the Village Cup. And then whoosh, hundreds of Scots were besieging us, whooping and hollering and singing songs about Freuchie, a wee village with 1476 residents. It was no wonder that some of us were speechless at that stage. Just try to imagine a local dramatic company actor winning an Oscar and you might have a tiny inkling of what was passing through our minds. Then I saw my parents in the crowd and that was when the dam totally burst.'

STEWART IRVINE: 'Hitting a huge six at Lord's was obviously a moment to treasure – especially when a gentleman in the Lord's enclosure told me that the only other batsman he had seen smiting a shot to that part of the ground was the great Garry Sobers – but the crowning moment for me was when I was announced as the "Man of the Match". I was a little surprised at the verdict, because I thought it might be Terry [Trewartha] or George [Crichton], but I was shaking as I went up to collect the prize and I couldn't restrain the tears. Looking back, I don't know why I was trying so hard not to cry. After all, let's face it, how many 21-year-olds are named man of the match at the home of cricket?'

PETER HEPPLEWHITE: 'Naturally, I had been a wee bit disappointed to miss out on playing and [as 13th man], I was forced to sit through the ebbs and flows and all the fluctuating fortunes which marked the final, without having the power to do anything about it. At 100 for 7 in our reply, I must admit I had a few doubts that we would win, but I had watched Dave Christie and marvelled at his sangfroid, and when he went out to bat, it was like a gladiator marching into the centre of the conflict and seizing it by the scruff of the neck, and although our hearts were in our mouths, there was this sense it was *our* day in the sun, our date with destiny, and we wouldn't be denied.'

ALLAN WILKIE: 'On the road back from Lord's to Freuchie, I had to keep up this pretence that I needed to check on affairs at my workplace when, in fact, I was arranging the homecoming with STV and with our village community, who were obviously planning the mother of all hoolies for our return. Every half-hour or so, I would ask the bus driver to stop at a garage with a pay phone – what wouldn't I have given for a mobile? – but the whole exercise was all worthwhile when we reached Hamilton and the players and the officials changed into their kilts and their ties, proclaiming them as Lord's Winners. Even now, I can recall the marvel etched on a lot of people's faces, as if they were having a wonderful dream, and although it was raining when we reached Freuchie, nothing, but nothing, was going to rain on our parade that evening. You can look back and perhaps reflect that we should have made a second trip to Lord's somewhere down the line. But I'm not selfish. Maybe we can work on that in the future.'

The mention of this prompts Dave Christie into an ironic laugh, but as we gaze out on his beloved ground, while a late-winter chill grips Freuchie in its embrace, it's plain that he hasn't surrendered hope of maintaining his team's splendid Village Cup tradition, even if one or two colleagues have subsequently defected elsewhere. Nor should he feel obliged to apologise for his stance. In the grand scheme of international cricket, Freuchie might merit a mere footnote, but their exploits have established a precedent for every child in Scotland who dabbles in reveries of sporting hooraymanship, without tantrums, hysterics or prima donnaism, but with a sheer refusal to accept second-best.

'I look out here, on to the pitch, and to all the houses around it, and I can reel off the names of virtually everybody who lives in them, because, come the summer, they will mill round the boundary and cheer on the Freuchie team in the Village Cup, which shows how the tournament has captured the imagination of the community. There is one little chap, over there [pointing west], who is as quiet as a church mouse the other six and a half days of the week, but come these Sunday afternoon fixtures, he's screaming and yelling out his backing for the boys and I am privileged to behold that kind of devotion,' says the redoubtable Christie. 'It seems an awfully long time since I was keeping the score book as a teenager, but whenever I switch on the video of 1985, the memories come flooding back in a tidal wave. I don't know whether Scotland will ever become a Test match country, or whether we can make our mark on the ODI circuit in the future, but listen to this: if we can encourage 11 Scottish boys to fling themselves into the challenge 100 per cent, there is no valid reason why we can't be competitive. And once that quality creeps into the equation, so will confidence and optimism, and the nation will support these lads, particularly if we start creating a bit of noise about cricket in our homeland.

'I know that we weren't world-beaters, and that the Village Cup isn't the ICC Trophy or the World Cup, but the underlying principle is pretty much the same, whatever the standard of the competition. Ian Botham told us, on the Sunday night at Lord's, that you can only beat the opposition who are pitted against you, and we achieved that objective 20 years ago. It has been the making of Freuchie, as I am the first to recognise. But equally, I think it has benefited the whole of Scottish cricket. Don't you agree?'

Who wouldn't? When the Fifers embarked on their crusade to Capital City, they delivered the perfect riposte to the pinched-lip brigade, who deplore inclusivity and innovation. They were noisy, aggressive, sociable, garrulous, massively enthusiastic ambassadors for their country and there were no arrests, no altercations with London casuals or unseemly destruction of hotel chambers. Allan Wilkie counted all his folk out and he counted them all back. It was a peaceful invasion with an auspicious outcome and there haven't been too many similar chapters in Scottish history at any level.

As for nine-month-old Callum Glasgow, the smallest spectator at Lord's for the final, he has eschewed the normal soccer route and developed a keen interest in equestrianism, while maintaining a passion for cricket. 'I have seen the photographs and watched the video and it is terrific that a group of Scots should have secured such a famous victory,' he told me, from his home in Kirkcaldy. 'I have been to watch them regularly, and although I got some ribbing at school because I was riding horses, not kicking a ball, I think you have to persevere and persist if you want to succeed at anything.'

Hmm. It sounds as if Master Glasgow has absorbed the Freuchie philosophy, even if he was too tiny to realise it.